No. 2705
$22.95

30 CUSTOMIZED MICROPROCESSOR PROJECTS

DELTON T. HORN

TAB BOOKS Inc.
Blue Ridge Summit, PA 17214

FIRST EDITION

FIRST PRINTING

Copyright © 1986 by TAB BOOKS Inc.

Printed in the United States of America

Library of Congress Cataloging in Publication Data

Horn, Delton T.
    30 customized microprocessor projects.

    Includes index.
    1. Microprocessors—Amateurs' manuals. I. Title.
II. Title: Thirty customized microprocessor projects.
TK9969.H67   1986   621.391'6   86-5855
ISBN 0-8306-0705-6
ISBN 0-8306-2705-7 (pbk.)

Contents

Introduction

E VERYONE KNOWS THAT COMPUTERS ARE POWERFUL DE-
vices that can be used for many tasks. Sometimes, however,
it is difficult to justify tying up a complete computer system to
perform two or three specific tasks. The solution is to build a special purpose computer around a CPU (Central Processing Unit) IC.

This book will help the intermediate to advanced electronics
experimenter design and build custom dedicated CPU projects. The
emphasis will be on customization for individual applications. The
reader is not limited to the circuitry the author considers useful.

The various projects in this book are designed for maximum
interchangeability to allow the experimenter to build almost any
customized system. The first half of the book discusses basic principles of circuit design and computer systems. The second half of
the book describes the projects.

List of Projects

Section I

The Basics

Chapter 1

The Basics of Circuit Design

T HIS CHAPTER IS NOT INTENDED TO TEACH THE NOVICE HOW to design electronic circuits. It is intended strictly as a convenient refresher for intermediate and advanced experimenters. If you do not have any prior experience in this area, I strongly recommend that you read a text or two on general circuit design before tackling the projects described in this volume. The principles of electronic design are covered in some detail in my earlier works, *Transistor Circuit Design—with Experiments* (TAB book 1875) and *Designing IC Circuits . . . with Experiments* (TAB book 1925).

SEMICONDUCTORS

All matter, as you should already know, is made of *atoms*. The primary components of an atom are *protrons* (positively charged particles), *electrons* (negatively charged particles), and *neutrons* (neutral particles). The protrons and the neutrons are clumped together in the nucleus. The electrons circle the nucleus like the planets around the sun.

Ordinarily, the number of electrons exactly equals the number of protrons. The negative charges cancel out the positive charges, and the atom as a whole is electrically neutral.

Some elements can accept extra electrons (gaining a negative charge), and/or give up a few of their own (gaining a positive charge). These materials allow electrical current to pass through them fairly easily. They are known as *conductors*. Most (but not all) conductors are metallic. Silver and copper are typical conductors.

In other materials, it is very difficult to change the number of electrons. These materials tend to block the flow of electrical current. They are called *insulators*. Typical insulators are rubber and glass.

Modern electronics depends heavily on a third class of materials, mid-way between conductors and insulators. These materials are called *semiconductors*, and usually are in crystalline form. The most commonly used semiconductors are germanium and silicon.

By itself a pure semiconductor material isn't good for very much. It can be used to make a fair resistor, and that's about it. But, if a small amount of an impurity (a second, related element) is added, the semiconductor begins to exhibit some special properties. The amount of impurity is very minute—often as small as one part in 10,000,000.

Let's consider what happens if a few arsenic atoms are added to a slab of germanium. The arsenic atoms will try to act like germanium and join in the crystalline structure. But arsenic has more electrons than germanium. Once the spaces in the crystal structure have been filled in, there are still a few electrons left over. Because these excess electrons are only loosely bond to the arsenic atoms, they will move about the entire crystal, "looking" for a place to settle. Since they can't find a convenient niche, they will continue to roam.

The loose electrons wandering around within our doped germanium crystal represent a small wandering local negative charge. But the overall charge of the crystal as a whole is neutral, because the number of electrons exactly equals the number of protons.

If an electrical voltage is placed across the crystal, the loose electrons will be drawn to the positive terminal, because there is nothing much to hold them in place within the crystal. So they leave the crystal altogether for the positive terminal of the voltage source.

Now, there are more protons in the crystal than electrons. The crystal, as a whole, has a positive charge. It will attract electrons from the negative terminal of the voltage source. This neutralizes the crystal's electrical charge, but the new electrons still can't find a place to "sit" so they are drawn out of the crystal by the positive side of the voltage source. This continues as long as the voltage source is applied to the crystal.

4

The semiconductor material is conducting electricity, but in a somewhat different manner than ordinary conductors. We will examine the significance of this shortly.

Using arsenic as an impurity adds extra electrons to the crystalline structure. Therefore, arsenic is called a *donor impurity*. Other donor impurities are antimony, bismuth, and phosphorous. The result of adding a donor impurity is an n-type semiconductor.

Alternatively, we could dope the crystal with an impurity that has too few electrons to fill the crystalline structure. In other words, there are several *holes* where electrons would fit if they were available. The surrounding electrons will keep trying to fill up these holes. They sort of play "musical chairs", but it doesn't accomplish much, since there are always more holes than electrons. In a real sense, the holes move around within the crystal, just as the loose electrons did in the earlier version. We now have loose holes. A minute localized positive charge drifts about within the crystal.

Once again, if a voltage source is applied to the semiconductor crystal, current will flow. Electrons will be pulled in from the negative terminal to fill the excess holes. This gives the crystal, as a whole, a negative electrical charge, which is tapped off by the positive terminal.

Impurities with too few electrons are called *acceptor impurities*. Typical elements used as acceptor impurities are aluminum, boron, and gallium. A semiconductor slab doped with an acceptor impurity is called a *p-type semiconductor*.

The Pn Junction

Neither n-type nor p-type semiconductors are particularly exciting or interesting by themselves. Their important properties show up when a junction is formed between the two different types of semiconductors.

It is important to remember that both n-type and p-type semiconductors have both electrons and holes flowing through them. The difference is in which type of carrier is in the majority. In an *n-type semiconductor*, electrons are the majority carriers and holes are the minority carriers. In a p-type semiconductor, this is reversed. When no voltage is applied to a pn junction, the carriers (electrons and holes) are more or less randomly distributed, as illustrated in Fig. 1-1.

In Fig. 1-2 we see the result of applying a voltage across the pn junction with the positive terminal connected to the n-type side,

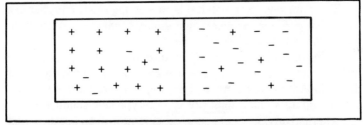

Fig. 1-1. Carriers are randomly distributed around a pn junction when no voltage is applied.

and the negative terminal connected to the p-type side. The excess electrons are drawn towards the positive terminal on the n-side of the junction. Similarly, the excess holes move towards the negative terminal on the p-side.

Virtually all the loose carriers are drawn to the ends of the semiconductor slab. There are almost no loose electrons or holes near the junction at the middle. Essentially, the junction is the same as if it had never been doped with any impurity. It acts as a fair insulator. The result is that almost no current will flow through the junction. It behaves almost like an open circuit. (There will be a very small amount of current flow due to the minority carriers but this is so small that we can reasonably ignore it here.)

Now, let's see what happens when the polarity is reversed, as shown in Fig. 1-3. The negative terminal is connected to the n-side and the positive terminal is connected to the p-side. Since like charges repel, the loose electrons in the n-type side are forced towards the junction. Similarly, the loose holes in the p-side are also driven towards the junction. The loose electrons and holes have

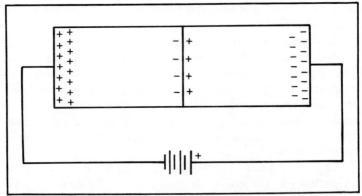

Fig. 1-2. Almost no carriers can cross the pn junction when it is reverse biased.

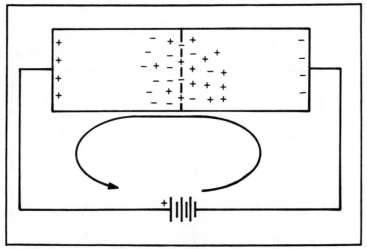

Fig. 1-3. Current flows through a pn junction when it is forward biased.

enough energy to jump across the junction and neutralize each other. The loose electrons fill the loose holes.

The p-type semiconductor has a negative charge because extra electrons from the n-side have filled its holes. Similarly, the n-type semiconductor has a positive charge because it has lost some if its electrons.

The positive charge on the n-side draws more electrons from the negative terminal of the power source, while the excess electrons flow from the negatively charged p-type material to the positive voltage terminal. This means the n-side again has loose electrons and the p-side again has loose holes. These are forced through the junction, and the process continues.

In other words, current can flow through a pn junction in only one direction. If current is applied in the opposite direction, it is blocked. A pn junction serves as a semiconductor diode.

The Bipolar Transistor

As useful as the diode is, we can do even more if we have a pair of back-to-back pn junctions, as shown in Fig. 1-4. In effect we have a semiconductor sandwich. This device is called a transistor. There are many different types of transistors. The simplest (which is shown here) is the *bipolar transistor*.

There are two possible combinations for a bipolar transistor. There could be two slabs of n-type material on either side of a thinner slab of p-type material, as shown in Fig. 1-4A. This is called

7

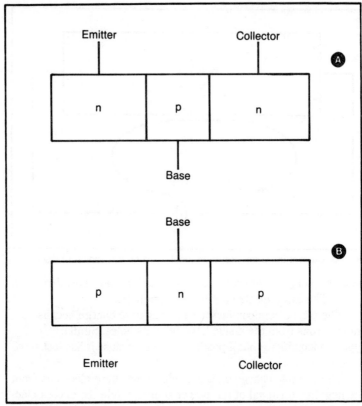

Fig. 1-4. A transistor is basically a pair of back-to-back pn junctions. (A—npn, B—pnp.)

a npn transistor. Alternatively, we could have a central n-type slab surrounding by p-type slabs, as illustrated in Fig. 1-4B. This is called a pnp transistor. The schematic symbols for these two devices are shown in Fig. 1-5. The three leads have special names—the *emitter*, the *base*, and the *collector*.

In the following discussion, we will discuss just the npn transistor. The principles are the same except for the electrons and holes, and all circuit polarities are reversed. The transistor permits signal amplification because the collector current is dependent on the base to emitter current.

Alpha

The correct relative polarities (biasing) for an npn transistor are illustrated in Fig. 1-6. When biased in this manner, more emit-

8

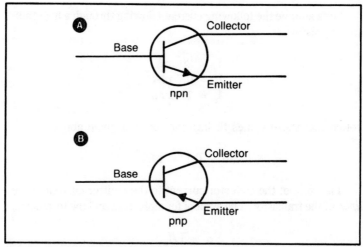

Fig. 1-5. The three leads of a transistor are easy to identify in the schematic symbol. (A—npn, B—pnp.)

ter current (I_e) will flow through the transistor than either base current (I_b) or collector current (I_c). In fact, ignoring a few minor losses, the emitter current is essentially equal to the sum of the other two currents. That is:

$$I_e = I_b + I_c$$

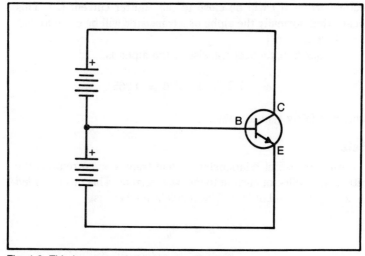

Fig. 1-6. This is a correctly biased npn transistor.

9

Let's assume the following currents flowing through a hypothetical transistor:

$$I_e = 20 \text{ mA}$$
$$I_b = 0.7 \text{ mA}$$
$$I_c = 19.3 \text{ mA}$$

Notice that these values fit into the formula given above:

$$20 = 0.7 + 19.3$$

The ratio of the collector current to the emitter current is the *alpha* of the transistor. The symbol for alpha is α, and the formula is:

$$\alpha = I_c/I_e$$

The alpha is a constant for any given transistor. If the emitter current changes for any reason, the collector current will change accordingly. The alpha will always be less than 1. This is because the collector current must, by definition, must be smaller than the emitter current:

$$I_c = I_e - I_b$$

Ordinarily, the base current (I_b) will be very small, so the collector current (I_c) will be close to the emitter current (I_e). This means that normally the alpha of a transistor will be close to, but slightly less than 1.

For our hypothetical transistor, the alpha is:

$$\alpha = I_c/I_e = 19.3/20 = 0.965$$

This is a fairly typical value.

Beta

Another useful relationship among transistor currents is the ratio of the collector current to the base current. This ratio is called beta, and its symbol is β. The formula for beta is:

$$\beta = I_c/I_b$$

Because the base current is always very small, as compared

to the collector and emitter currents, beta will normally have a fairly high value. Typical beta values for silicon transistors range from about 10 to about 1000.

The value of beta for our hypothetical transistor works out to:

$$\beta = I_c/I_b = 19.3/0.7 = 27.57$$

The value of beta can be derived from the value of alpha, by using this formula:

$$\beta = \alpha/(\alpha - 1)$$

Similarly, if we know the value of beta we can easily find the value of alpha by using this equation:

$$\alpha \ \beta/(\beta + 1)$$

The Common-Emitter Circuit

There are three basic transistor amplifier circuits. In each of these, one of the transistor's three leads is referenced to the circuit's ground, or common point.

The common-emitter circuit illustrated in Fig. 1-7, is probably the most widely used. As the name suggests, the emitter is used as the common element. It is common to both the input and output circuits. The input signal is applied to the circuit across the base

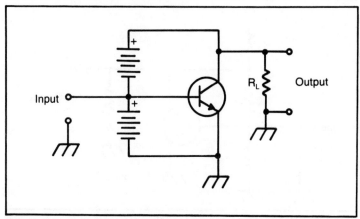

Fig. 1-7. The common-emitter circuit is probably the most commonly used transistor circuit.

and the emitter, while the output signal is tapped off across the collector and the emitter.

In most practical circuits, separate power supplies usually aren't used for the base (input) and collector (output) circuits. Instead, a common voltage source is used for both, as shown in Fig. 1-8. Resistors R2 and R3 drop the voltage down to the necessary level.

The output of a transistor amplifier is in current form. In the common-emitter amplifier, the output signal is the collector current (I_c). Several factors determine the level of this current, including, the transistor's beta, the base supply voltage (E1), the base resistor (R_b), the emitter resistor (R_e), and the internal voltage drop across the emitter-base junction. This voltage drop is usually about 0.7 volt for silicon transistors. Germanium transistors have a smaller voltage drop across the junction (typically about 0.2 to 0.3 volt).

The approximate value of the collector current (I_c) can be found with this formula. It is not exact, but it will be close enough for most purposes:

$$I_c = \frac{V_b - V_{be}}{\dfrac{R_b}{\beta} + R_e}$$

where V_b is the input signal voltage applied to the base, V_{be} is the voltage drop across the base-emitter junction, R_b is the base resis-

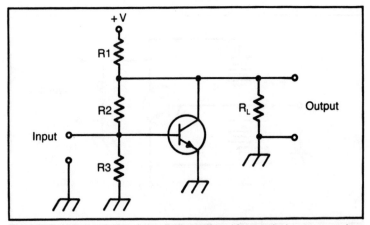

Fig. 1-8. A single power supply is usually employed for practical common-emitter circuits.

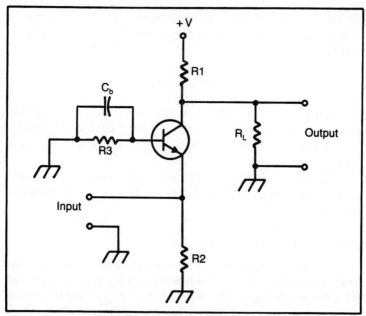

Fig. 1-9. This is the basic common-base transistor circuit.

tor, β is the beta, and R_e is the emitter resistor.

Let's say we are using a silicon transistor with a beta of 100. Since this is a silicon device. V_{be} will be 0.7 volt. In our sample circuit we will assign a value of 5000 ohms to R_b and 300 ohms to R_e. Plugging these values into the equation, we get:

$$\begin{aligned} I_c &= V_b - 0.7/(5000/100) + 300 \\ &= V_b - 0.7/50 + 300 \\ &= V_b - 0.7/350 \end{aligned}$$

In a circuit of this type, the values of V_{be}, R_b, R_e, and β are constants, so the collector current (I_c) is controlled by the voltage being fed to the base of the transistor (V_b).

Current gain, voltage gain, and power gain are all high for the common-emitter amplifier. The output signal is inverted, or 180° out-of-phase with the input signal.

The input impedance is low and the output impedance is high.

The Common-Base Circuit

In the common-base circuit, shown in Fig. 1-9, the input is applied across the emitter and the base, and the output is taken from

13

the collector and the base. In this configuration, the signal gain is defined by the ratio of the collector current (I_c) to the emitter current (I_e):

$$\text{Gain} = I_c/I_e$$

This is the same as the value for alpha. Therefore, the current gain must always be less than unity, but this circuit is capable of medium voltage gain, and high power gain. The output signal is in-phase with the input signal.

The input impedance is very low, and the output impedance is very high. This circuit is often used for impedance matching applications.

The Common-Collector Circuit

The third configuration for a transistor circuit is the common-collector amplifier, which is shown in Fig. 1-10. In this circuit, the input signal is fed across the base and the collector, and the output is tapped off across the emitter and the collector.

Notice that the positive terminal of the voltage source is grounded so all operating voltages within the circuit must be negative. The emitter is normally held at the most negative level.

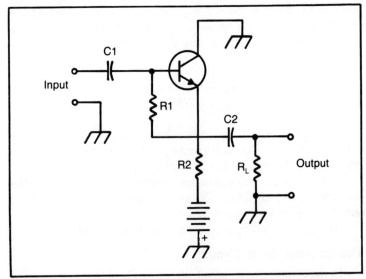

Fig. 1-10. Transistor circuits can also be arranged in a common-collector configuration.

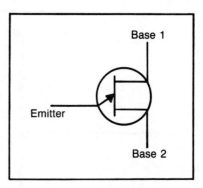

Fig. 1-11. A UJT is a transistor with a single pn junction.

The voltage gain for a common-collector amplifier is always less than 1 (below unity). The current gain is fairly high, but the power gain is low. This configuration actually does not make a very good amplifier.

The input impedance is moderately high, and the output impedance is low, so the common-collector circuit is often used for impedance matching in multiple-stage transistor circuits. The output signal is in-phase with the input signal.

Other Transistor Types

Generally, when we say "transistor" we are referring to the bipolar transistor, as described in the last few pages. Bipolar transistors are certainly the most common type of transistors. But there are other important types of transistors, each with their own unique internal structure.

The *unijunction transistor*, or UJT, has just a single pn junction. Its schematic symbol is shown in Fig. 1-11. The internal struc-

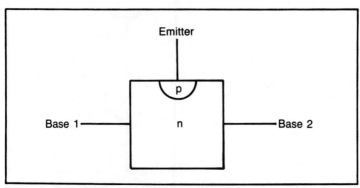

Fig. 1-12. The UJT has two base connections.

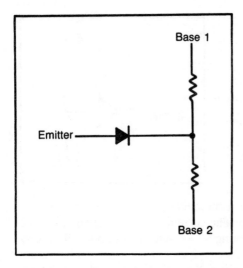

Fig. 1-13. This is a simplified equivalent circuit for a n-type UJT.

ture of the UJT is illustrated in Fig. 1-12. Notice that there are two base connections, on either side of the larger n-type section.

The n-section acts as a voltage divider resistor pair, with a diode (the pn junction) connected to the common end of the two resistances. A simplified equivalent circuit for an n-type UJT is shown in Fig. 1-13.

Closely related to the UJT is the PUT, or *Programmable Unijunction Transistor*. The schematic symbol for this device is shown in Fig. 1-14. Its internal structure is shown in Fig. 1-15. The PUT has three leads, labeled A (anode), C (cathode), and G (gate).

A voltage is placed across the anode and the cathode, with the anode positive with respect to the cathode. No current will flow

Fig. 1-14. A variation on the UJT is the PUT.

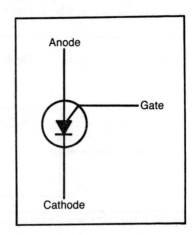

16

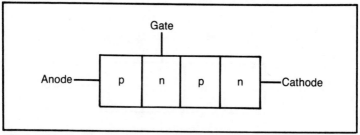

Fig. 1-15. The basic internal structure of the PUT.

between the anode and cathode until a negative (with respect to the anode) pulse is applied to the gate.

A silicon-controlled rectifier, or SCR, is essentially an electrically switched diode. It is very similar to the PUT. The schematic symbol for a SCR is illustrated in Fig. 1-16. As Fig. 1-17 illustrates, the main difference in the internal structure between the SCR and the PUT is the location of the Gate connection.

If a voltage is applied between the anode (+) and the cathode (−), and the gate is grounded (0 volts), no current will flow, even though the pseudo-diode is forward biased.

If an increasingly positive voltage is applied to the gate terminal, it will eventually reach a specific trigger voltage (which is dependent on the individual SCR used). Now, current can flow from the cathode to the anode, as if through an ordinary forward-biased diode.

If the gate voltage is now removed, current will continue to flow through the device. This current will continue to flow until the voltage between the anode and the cathode is interrupted.

Perhaps the second most commonly used type of transistor is

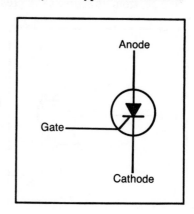

Fig. 1-16. A SCR is essentially an electrically switched diode.

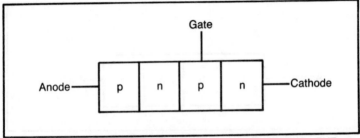

Fig. 1-17. The internal structure of the SCR is similar to that of the PUT, except for the location of the gate connection.

the FET, or *field-effect transistor*. The schematic symbol for the FET is shown in Fig. 1-18.

Many transistor circuits are variations on older vacuum tube circuits. There are many similarities in operation between transistors and vacuum tubes. However, the operation of a standard bipolar transistor doesn't quite correspond to that of a vacuum tube. Some transistor circuits won't work as well as vacuum tube circuits.

Does this mean we have to forego modern semiconductor technology and revert to bulky, expensive, and hot vacuum tubes? Not at all. The FET is a semiconductor device that can closely mimic the operation of a vacuum tube. In addition, it is capable of several unique tricks of its own.

The basic internal structure of a FET is illustrated in Fig. 1-19. Notice that there are again three leads. In this case they are labelled S (source), D (drain), and G (gate).

To get a general idea of how a FET works, consider the mechanical water system illustrated in Fig. 1-20. When the valve (gate) is fully opened, as in Fig. 1-20A, the water can flow through the pipe, from its source to where it can drain out. If, on the other

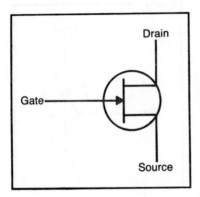

Fig. 1-18. FETs are almost as popular today as simple bipolar transistors.

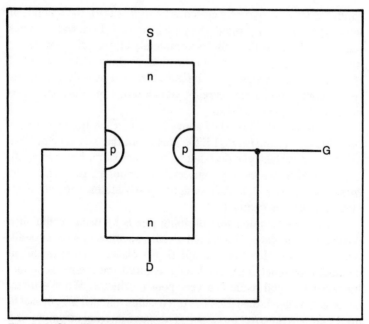

Fig. 1-19. Simplified diagram of a FET's internal structure.

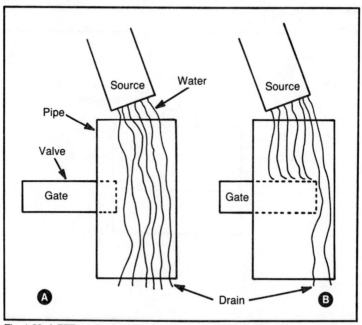

Fig. 1-20. A FET can be thought of as similar to a mechanical water pipe system.

hand, the valve is partially closed, as in Fig. 1-20B, the amount of water that can flow through the pipe is limited. Less water comes out of the drain. If the valve is completely closed off, no water at all will be able to flow through the pipe. Nothing will come out of the drain. In the same way, the gate terminal of a FET controls the amount of electrical current that can flow from the source terminal to the drain terminal.

The basic FET described above is more properly called a *junction field-effect transistor* (JFET). This is not the only type of FET available. Another type does not have an actual pn junction at all. These devices are known generically as *insulated gate field-effect transistors*, or IGFETs. As the name clearly states, the gate is insulated from the channel.

The most common way of doing this is by using a thin slice of metal as the gate (rather than a slab of semiconductor crystal). This metal is oxidized on the side that is placed against the semiconductor channel. This insulates the gate from the semiconductor because metal oxide is a very poor conductor. When a metal oxide gate is used, the IGFET is often called a MOSFET, or *metal-oxide-silicon field-effect transistor*. The basic internal structure of a MOSFET is illustrated in Fig. 1-21. The schematic symbol is shown in Fig. 1-22.

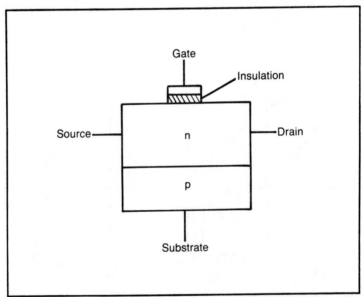

Fig. 1-21. A variation on the FET is the MOSFET.

20

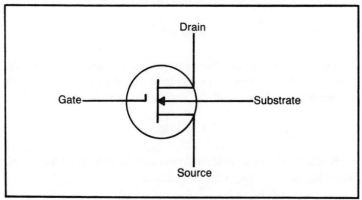

Fig. 1-22. The schematic symbol used to represent a MOSFET.

The IC

The transistor, and its relatives, made a lot of electronic applications practical that would not have been feasible using vacuum tubes. The transistor went a long way towards reducing the size and cost of electronic circuitry, but the industry still wasn't satisfied. Semiconductor techniques were improved and miniaturization was increased, leading to the development of the *integrated circuit*, of IC. Multiple transistors, and other components (such as resistors and capacitors) are etched onto a single slab of semiconductor material about the size of your thumbnail. The earliest ICs replaced just a handful of discrete components, which was impressive in and of itself, but modern ICs can be the equivalent of hundreds or even thousands of discrete components. It is the IC that makes the microcomputer possible.

In this book we will be concerned primarily with digital ICs. These devices will be discussed in more detail in Chapter 2.

OHM'S LAW

Anyone working with circuit design needs at least a basic grasp of a number of mathematical formulas. Fortunately, these aren't really as hard to use as you might suspect.

The most important and widely used formula in electronics work is also the simplest. You can't possibly do any serious work in the electronics field without knowing Ohm's law.

Ohm's law is a method for comparing the current, voltage, and resistance in a circuit. The basic formula states that the voltage (in volts) (E) equals the product of the current (in amperes) (I) multiplied by the resistance (in ohms) (R). That is:

$$E = IR$$

This formula can be easily rearranged to solve for any of the three variables involved. For example, to find the current when you know the voltage, and the resistance, use this formula:

$$I = E/R$$

Similarly, if you know the current and the voltage, you can find the resistance by using this equation:

$$R = E/I$$

Let's consider a few simple examples. If we have 20 mA (0.02 amp) across a 100-ohm resistor, the voltage drop will be equal to:

$$E = IR = 0.02 \times 100 = 2 \text{ volts}$$

Now, let's say we have 9 volts applied across a 2.2 kΩ (2200 ohm) resistor. The current flow works out to:

$$I = E/R = 9/2200 = 0.0041 \text{ amp} = 4.1 \text{ mA}$$

If we need a 15-volt drop and a current flow of 35 mA (0.035 amp), what size resistor do we need? The required resistance can be easily found using the Ohm's law formula:

$$R = E/I = 15/0.035 = 43 \text{ ohms}$$

POWER

The fourth most important parameter in electrical circuits (after voltage, current, and resistance) is the amount of power consumed. The standard unit for power is the *watt*. Power, in watts, equals the product of the voltage (in volts) multiplied by the current (in amps). That is:

$$P = EI$$

As a practical example, let's say we have 250 mA (0.25 amp) current flowing in a 10-volt circuit. The power consumption in this circuit would work out to:

$$P = EI = 10 \times .25 = 2.5 \text{ watts}$$

In some circumstances it may be convenient to combine the power formula with Ohm's Law. For instance, let's say we know the current and resistance, and we need to know the power, but we're not too concerned about the voltage. Ohm's law allows us to derive the voltage from the current and the resistance:

$$E = IR$$

We can substitute this formula for the value of E in the power equation:

$$P = EI = I \times R \times I = I^2 R$$

The power equals the current squared, multiplied by the resistance.

Similarly, we can find the power from the voltage and the resistance, without knowing the current:

$$I = E/R$$
$$P = EI = E \times (E/R) = E^2/R$$

COMBINING COMPONENT VALUES

Most practical electronics circuits are fairly complex, including several different resistances, capacitances, and inductances. In addition, in designing a circuit an unusual component value may be required even though it is not readily available. To deal with both these situations, we need to know how to combine component values.

Combining Resistances

We will probably be working most frequently with multiple resistances. Multiple resistances may be combined in series, as shown in Fig. 1-23 or in parallel, as shown in Fig. 1-24.

The series combination is perfectly straightforward. The resistances are simply added together:

$$R_t = R1 + R2 + R3 + \ldots + R_n$$

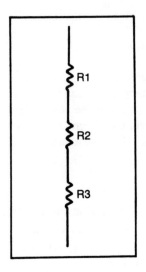

Fig. 1-23. Resistances in series add.

For example, let's say we have the following three resistances in series:

220 ohms
100 ohms
470 ohms

The total effective resistance would be equal to:

$$R_t = 220 + 100 + 470 = 790 \text{ ohms}$$

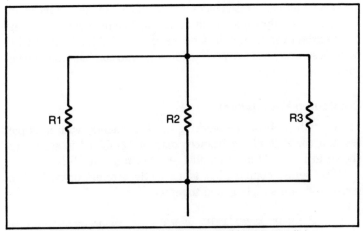

Fig. 1-24. Multiple resistances may also be combined in parallel.

24

The formula for parallel resistances is not quite so obvious:

$$1/R_t = 1/R1 + 1/R2 + 1/R3 + \ldots + 1/R_n$$

Using the same resistance values in the preceeding example, we find the parallel combination works out to:

$$1/R_t = 1/220 + 1/100 + 1/470 = 0.0045 + 0.01 +$$
$$0.0021 = 0.0166$$

$$R_t = 1/0.0166 = 60 \text{ ohms}$$

Most practical circuits include both series and parallel resistances. To combine the values, simply break up the circuit into simple series or parallel combinations in steps. A simple example is shown in Fig. 1-25. First add the series combination of R_a and R_b (R_{ab}), then figure the parallel combination of R_{ab} and R_c (R_{abc}). Finally, take the series combination of R_{abc} and R_d.

The series combination will always result in a total greater than any of the individual resistances making up the combination. A parallel combination always leads to a smaller total resistance than any of the individual resistances making up the combination.

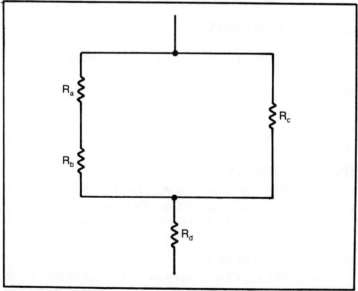

Fig. 1-25. In practical circuits we usually find both series and parallel resistances.

25

Combining Capacitances

Capacitances are combined in just the opposite way as resistances. For series combinations of capacitances, use this formula:

$$1/C_t = 1/C1 + 1/C2 + 1/C3 + \ldots + 1/C_n$$

Or, when there are just two capacitances in series:

$$C_t = (C1 \times C2)/(C1 + C2)$$

Capacitances in parallel simply add:

$$C_t = C1 + C2 + C3 + \ldots + C_n$$

Combining Inductances

Inductances don't figure too prominently into the types of circuits we will be discussing in this book, but it is worth mentioning that they combine in exactly the same way as resistances. That is, for series combinations:

$$L_t = L1 + L2 + L3 + \ldots + L_n$$

And, for parallel combinations:

$$1/L_t = 1/L1 + 1/L2 + 1/L3 + \ldots + 1/L_n$$

Or:

$$L_t = (L1 \times L2)/(L1 + L2)$$

KIRCHHOFF'S LAWS

Some circuits, like the one shown in Fig. 1-26, can't be reduced to convenient series and parallel combinations. Kirchhoff's laws are a set of handy tools for analyzing complex electronics circuits.

Kirchhoff's Voltage Law

Kirchhoff's voltage law is based on the concept of the loop. A loop is simply any closed conducting path. It may include voltage

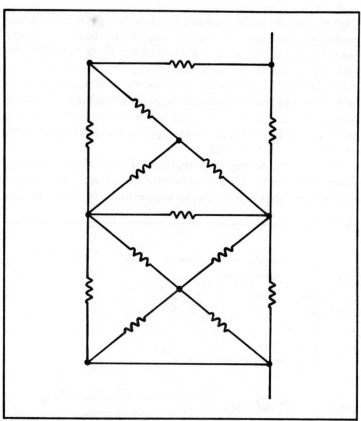

Fig. 1-26. Some circuits cannot be reduced to simple series-parallel combinations.

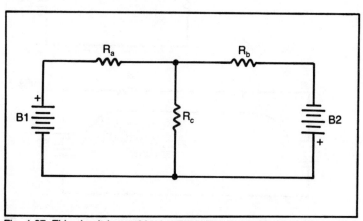

Fig. 1-27. This circuit is used in the discussion of Kirchhoff's laws.

27

sources (but not current sources), resistances, reactances, and conductors in any series combination. The circuit shown in Fig 1-27 has three loops, which are illustrated separately in Fig. 1-28. We only need to look at two of these to fully analyze the circuit. When using Kirchhoff's voltage law, you use the minimum number of loops that contain all of the circuit elements. Often there are several possibilities, and it doesn't matter which you use—you'll get the same results. Therefore, it makes sense to select the loops that will be the easiest to work with.

In Fig. 1-28 the loop currents are shown. A loop current is assumed to flow only within its associated loop. It is a mathematical fiction, which may or may not correspond to the real current actu-

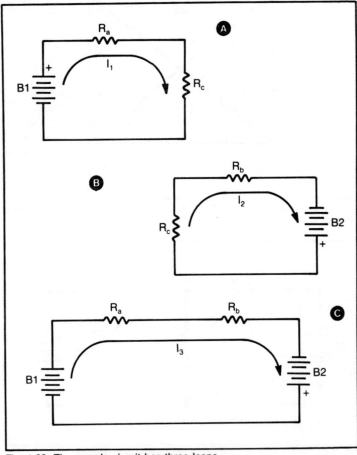

Fig. 1-28. The sample circuit has three loops.

ally flowing through that portion of the circuit. The loop current is assumed for mathematical convenience. The equations will work out and ultimately give us the correct results, and that's what matters.

Simply put, Kirchhoff's voltage law states that the algebraic sum of all voltage sources in any loop is equal to the algebraic sum of the voltage drops around the loop. The entire voltage is dropped within the loop. The voltage drops are considered to be caused not just by the loop's current, but by any other loop current flowing through the resistance element in question.

Select a direction (either clockwise or counterclockwise) for each loop current. It doesn't matter whether this relates to the direction of the actual current flow or not. If the "wrong" choice is made, the results will be negative rather than positive. The numerical values will be the same in either case.

It usually is simplest if all loop currents are assumed to flow in the same direction. I have arbitrarily selected a clockwise direction as a standard in the following examples.

The sign of the current flow through a resistance element determines the polarity of the voltage drop across that element. If the current through a resistance element is in the same direction as the loop current, the voltage drop is positive, otherwise, it is negative. Of course, voltage drops due to the loop current will always be positive, by definition. Voltage drops due to external loop currents may be either positive or negative.

If the loop current flows through a voltage source from the negative terminal to the positive terminal, the voltage is given a positive value, otherwise, it is negative.

Let's put Kirchhoff's voltage law to work analyzing the circuit shown in Fig. 1-27. Loops A and B in Fig. 1-28 contain all of the circuit elements, so they will be sufficient for our analysis. We can ignore loop C.

For our example, we will assume the following values for the circuit elements:

$$
\begin{aligned}
B1 &= 9 \text{ volts} \\
B2 &= 12 \text{ volts} \\
R_a &= 10 \text{ ohms} \\
R_b &= 50 \text{ ohms} \\
R_c &= 20 \text{ ohms}
\end{aligned}
$$

The circuit is redrawn in Fig. 1-29 with the two loop currents shown.

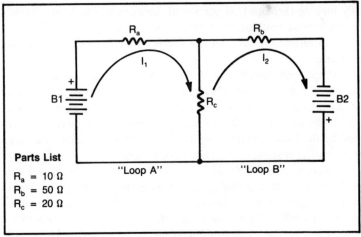

Fig. 1-29. The circuit is redrawn here for convenience, with two loop currents shown.

In loop A we have one voltage source (B1), and two resistance elements (R_a and R_c). Only loop current I_1 flows through R_a, so the voltage drop across this component is simply:

$$E_a = I_1 \times R_a$$

However, two loop currents (I_1 and I_2) flow through R_c. Since I_c is flowing in the opposite direction as I_1, it is given a negative value. The total voltage drop across this resistance element becomes:

$$E_c = (I_1 \times R_c) - (I_2 \times R_c)$$

According to Kirchhoff's voltage law, the sum of all voltage sources in the loop must be equal to the sum of all voltage drops in the loop. Therefore:

$$\begin{aligned} B1 &= E_a + E_c \\ &= (I_1 \times R_a) + (I_1 \times R_c) - (I_2 \times R_c) \\ &= I_1 \times (R_a + R_c) - (I_2 \times R_c) \end{aligned}$$

Plugging in the values from our parts list, we find:

$$\begin{aligned} g &= I_1 \times (10 + 20) - (I_2 \times 20) \\ &= (I_1 \times 30) - (I_2 \times 20) \end{aligned}$$

We can do the same thing with loop B:

$$
\begin{aligned}
B2 &= (I_2 \times R_b) + (I_2 \times R_c) - (I_1 \times R_c) \\
&= I_2 \times (R_b + R_c) - (I_1 \times R_c) \\
I_2 &= I_2 \times (50 + 20) - (I_1 \times 20) \\
&= (I_2 \times 70) - (I_1 \times 20)
\end{aligned}
$$

We now have a pair of simultaneous equations with two variables:

$$
\begin{aligned}
g &= (I_1 \times 30) - (I_2 \times 20) \\
I_2 &= (I_2 \times 70) - (I_1 \times 20)
\end{aligned}
$$

There are several methods for solving simultaneous equations. This is probably the simplest approach. First, rearrange one of the equations, as if solving for one of the variables. We will modify the second equation to give a formula for I_2:

$$
\begin{aligned}
I_2 &= (I_2 \times 70) - (I_1 \times 20) \\
I_2 + (I_1 \times 20) &= I_2 \times 70 \\
I_2 &= [I_2 + (I_1 \times 20)]/70
\end{aligned}
$$

Now, we can substitute this formula for I_2 in the first equation:

$$
\begin{aligned}
g &= (I_1 \times 30) - (I_2 \times 20) \\
&= (I_1 \times 30) - \{[(I_2 + (I_1 \times 20)]/70\} \times 20) \\
&= (I_1 \times 30) - \{[(I_2 \times 20) + (I_1 \times 20 \times 20)]/70\} \\
&= (I_1 \times 30) - \{(240/70) + [(I_1 \times 400)/70]\} \\
&= (I_1 \times 30) - [3.43 + (I_1 \times 5.71)] \\
&= (I_1 \times 30) - (I_1 \times 5.71) - 3.43 \\
&= [I_1 \times (30 - 5.71)] - 3.43 \\
&= (I_1 \times 24.29) - 3.43 = 9
\end{aligned}
$$

Because we have only one unknown variable in this equation now, we can rearrange the equation to solve for the unknown value:

$$
\begin{aligned}
9 &= (I_1 \times 24.29) - 3.43 \\
9 + 3.43 &= I_1 \times 24.29 \\
12.43/24.29 &= I_1 \\
0.51 &= I_1
\end{aligned}
$$

Loop current I_1 equals approximately 0.51 amp.

Now that we know the value of I_1 we can use our modified formula to solve for I_2:

$$
\begin{aligned}
I_2 &= [I_2 + (I_1 \times 20)]/70 \\
&= [I_2 + (0.51 \times 20)]/70 \\
&= (I_2 + 10.24)/70 \\
&= 22.24/70 \\
&= 0.32 \text{ amp}
\end{aligned}
$$

The next step is to use these current values to find the actual voltage drops across each of the resistance elements.

Resistor R_a is affected only by current I_1, so:

$$
\begin{aligned}
E_a &= I_1 \times R_a \\
0.51 \times 10 &= 5.1 \text{ volts}
\end{aligned}
$$

Resistor R_c, however, is affected by both the loop currents, so the voltage drop is slightly more complex:

$$
\begin{aligned}
E_c &= (I_1 \times R_c) - (I_2 \times R_c) \\
&= (0.51 \times 20) - (0.32 - 20) \\
&= 10.2 - 6.4 = 3.8 \text{ volts}
\end{aligned}
$$

Finally, R_b is affected only by loop current I_2, so its voltage drop works out to:

$$
\begin{aligned}
E_b &= I_2 \times R_b \\
&= 0.32 \times 50 = 16 \text{ volts}
\end{aligned}
$$

Wait a minute! How can more voltage be dropped than exists in the loop? Loop B contains only B2, which puts out 12 volts. The answer lies in our sign conventions. I_1 runs counter to I_2. So, for loop B, the voltage drop across R_c is:

$$
\begin{aligned}
E_{c2} &= (I_2 \times R_c) - (I_1 \times R_c) \\
&= (0.32 \times 20) - (0.51 \times 20) \\
&= 6.4 - 10.2 = -3.8 \text{ volts}
\end{aligned}
$$

B1 should equal the sum of the voltage drops in loop A (E_a and E_c) and B2 should equal the sum of the voltage drops in loop B (E_b and E_{c2}):

$$B1 = 9 = E_a + E_c = 5.1 + 3.8 = 8.9 \text{ volts}$$
$$B2 = I_2 = E_b + E_{c2} = 16 - 3.8 = 12.2 \text{ volts}$$

The slight differences here are due to cumulative roundoff errors in the calculations. Our results are close enough for most practical purposes.

Kirchhoff's Current Law

Besides his voltage law, Kirchhoff also came up with a law for analyzing currents in complex circuits. Remember that the loop currents we dealt with in Kirchhoff's voltage law were mathematical fictions, which may or may not correspond to the actual current flowing through the components. To deal with actual currents, rather than the mathematical fictions of Kirchhoff's voltage law, we use *Kirchhoff's current law.*

Again, we have to start off with a simple definition. A node is a connection point between two or more conductors. The nodes in our sample circuits are indicated in Fig. 1-30.

According to Kirchhoff's current law, the amount of current flowing into a node always exactly equals the current flowing out of that node. In other words, the algebraic sum of all currents through a node is zero. Current flowing into a node is assumed to be positive. Current flowing out of a node is assumed to be negative.

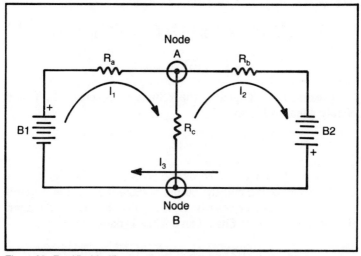

Fig. 1-30. For Kirchhoff's current law, circuit nodes are identified.

For voltage drops across resistance elements, the terminal where the current enters is assumed to be at a higher potential than the terminal where the current exits.

If a circuit has N nodes, we will need to examine $N-1$ nodes to completely analyze the circuit. In our sample circuit of Fig. 1-30, we only have two nodes, so we only need one to solve the circuit. We will use node A. There are three current paths into node A. These are marked in the diagram as I_1, I_2, and I_3. According to Kirchhoff's current law, the algebraic sum of these currents must be equal to zero. That is:

$$I_1 + I_2 + I_3 = 0$$

Current I_1 flows through resistor R_a. It is obviously equal to the voltage drop across R_a, divided by its resistance (Ohm's law—I = E/R).

Now, the voltage drop across R_a must be equal to the voltage going into the resistance element at the positive terminal (which is B1 in this case) minus the voltage at the negative terminal of the resistance element, which we will call E_a. The current direction of I_2 means node A is less positive (more negative) than node B, so voltage E_a takes on a negative sign. Putting this all together, we can create an Ohm's law equation for current I_1:

$$I_1 = [B1 - (-E_a)]/R_a$$

The two negative signs in front of E_a cancel out, leaving:

$$I_1 = (B1 + E_a)/R_a$$

Current I_2 is defined by the voltage drop across R_c. This is simply equal to E_a, so:

$$I_2 = E_a/R_c$$

Finally, I_3 is determined by the voltage drop across R_b. The input voltage is B2, and the output voltage is E_a. B2 is negative because of the battery polarity. E_a is negative because of the direction of the I_2 current flow. This makes I_3 equal to:

$$I_3 = [-B2 - (-E_a)]/R_b = (E_a - B2)/R_b$$

The next step is to substitute these formulas into the original node equation:

$$I_1 + I_2 + I_3 = 0$$
$$[(B1 + E_a)/R_a] + (E_a/R_c) + [E_a - B2)/R_b] = 0$$

We can simplify and rearrange the equation like this:

$$E_a \times [(1/R_a) + (1/R_b) + (1/R_c)] = (B2/R_b) - (B1/R_a)$$

Before we go any further we will need some specific component values to work with. We will use the same values we used in the Kirchhoff's voltage law example:

$$B1 = 9 \text{ volts}$$
$$B2 = 12 \text{ volts}$$
$$R_a = 10 \text{ ohms}$$
$$R_b = 50 \text{ ohms}$$
$$R_c = 20 \text{ ohms}$$

Plugging these values into this equation, we find:

$$E_a \times [(1/10) + (1/50) + (1/20)] = (12/50) - (9/10)$$
$$E_a \times (0.1 + 0.02 + 0.05) = 0.24 - 0.9$$
$$E_a = 0.17 = -0.66$$
$$E_a = -0.66/0.17 = -3.88 \text{ volts}$$

The negative sign simply indicates that the polarity is the opposite of the one we assumed.

We can now go back and solve for each of the currents in the circuit.

$$I_1 = (B1 + E_a)/R_a = (9 - 3.88)/10$$
$$= 5.12/10 = 0.512 \text{ amp} = 512 \text{ mA}$$
$$I_2 = E_a/R_c = -3.88/20 = -0.194 \text{ amp} = -194 \text{ mA}$$
$$I_3 = (E_a - B2)/R_b = (-3.88 - 12)/50 = -15.88/50 =$$
$$-0.318 \text{ amps} = -318 \text{ mA}$$

The negative values for I_2 and I_3 simply indicate that the actual direction of current flow is the opposite of that shown in Fig. 1-30.

Let's doublecheck our work by plugging the derived current value back into the node equation:

$$I_1 + I_2 + I_3 = 0$$
$$0.512 + (-0.194) + (-0.318) = 0$$
$$0.512 - 0.194 - 0.318 = 0$$

Yes. It works.

Of course, other circuits will result in different equations. The more nodes there are, the more equations you will have to work with.

AC VALUES

Formulas like Kirchhoff's laws and Ohm's law work very conveniently with dc voltages and currents. Everything is neat and straightforward. But, many electronics circuits carry ac voltages and currents. By definition, an ac signal continuously changes its value from instant to instant. How can we deal with constantly fluctuating parameters? What numbers can we plug into our equations.

There are several different methods of measuring ac signals. All are useful in some circumstances. The most straightforward approach is to simply identify the maximum level the signal reaches during each cycle. In the sine wave shown in Fig. 1-31, the *peak value* is 10 volts. Unfortunately, the peak value doesn't help us much in the circuit equations we are dealing with in this chapter. The actual voltage is 10 volts for only a small portion of each cycle. Usually the actual voltage will be lower than the peak value.

Closely related to the peak value is the *peak-to-peak value*. This is nothing more than the measurement of the distance from the positive peak to the negative peak. In our sample sine wave, the peak-to-peak value is 20 volts (+ 10 volts to − 10 volts). For sine waves, the peak-to-peak value will always be twice the peak value.

An obvious solution would be to calculate the average value of the ac signal. To do this, you use only half the cycle (either positive or negative, it doesn't matter). If the entire cycle is used, the mathematical average will always work out to zero because the two opposite half-cycles will cancel each other out. For sine waves, the average value will be equal to:

$$\text{Average} = 0.636 \times \text{Peak}$$

This equation is not valid for other waveshapes.

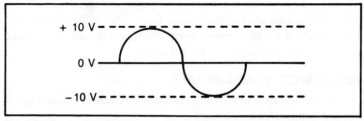
Fig. 1-31. Even a simple sine wave can be measured in several different ways.

The average value gives us a better idea of the ac parameters. Unfortunately, it cannot be used in standard circuit equations, such as Ohm's law.

What we need is a way to determine the equivalent dc value for the ac signal. This can be experimentally determined by passing the signals through a resistance element. The ac voltage that heats up the resistance element the same amount as the dc voltage is assumed to be "equal" to the dc voltage.

A complex mathematical formula can be used to calculate the equivalent value. The system is called *root-mean-square*, or RMS. Fortunately, we don't have to bother with the derivation. The RMS value of a sine wave can be calculated directly from the peak value by using this formula:

$$RMS = 0.707 \times Peak$$

The RMS value can also be found by starting with the average value, using this equation:

$$RMS = 1.11 \times Average$$

Remember that these equations are valid for sine waves only.

RMS values can be plugged directly into Ohm's law, Kirchhoff's laws, and other dc formulas, and will give the correct results.

Here is a summary of the basic ac values and their relationships:

$$RMS = 0.707 \times Peak$$
$$RMS = 1.11 \times Average$$
$$Average = 0.9 \times RMS$$
$$Average = 0.636 \times Peak$$
$$Peak = 1.41 \times RMS$$
$$Peak = 1.57 \times Average$$
$$Peak\text{-}to\text{-}Peak = 2 \times Peak$$

37

These equations are for sine waves only. They will not give correct results for other waveforms. Fortunately, for the circuit designer sine waves are by far the norm.

RESISTANCE IN AC CIRCUITS

Ac resistance is even more complex, because it is made up of several components:

- ☐ Resistance
- ☐ Capacitive Reactance
- ☐ Inductive Reactance

The *resistance component* is the same as dc resistance. It is a constant, and does not change with the frequency of the ac signal. The *reactance components* are frequency dependent. *Capacitive reactance* decreases with increases in frequency. It is defined as the ac resistance of a purely capacitive component. The formula is:

$$X_c = 1/(2 \pi FC)$$

Capacitive reactance is infinite at dc (0 Hz).

Inductive reactance is the ac resistance exhibited by a purely inductive component (coil). It increases with increases in frequency. The formula for inductive reactance is:

$$X_l = 2 \pi FL$$

Practical circuits include a combination of capacitive reactance, inductive reactance, and resistance. The total ac resistance at a specific frequency is called the impedance. Remember that impedance is a frequency specific value. It will change with the applied frequency.

Capacitive and inductive reactances are, by definition, out-of-phase with each other. This means that they can not simply be added together. The formula for calculating impedance is:

$$Z = \sqrt{R^2 + (X_l - X_c)^2}$$

where Z is the impedance, R is the dc resistance, X_l is the inductive reactance, and X_c is the capacitive reactance. All values are in ohms.

The circuit shown in Fig. 1-32 includes an ac voltage source,

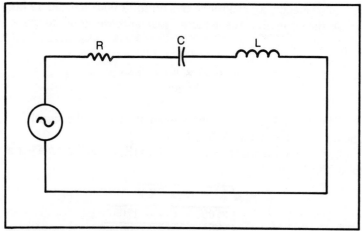

Fig. 1-32. For ac resistances we have to consider capacitors, and inductors, as well as simple resistors.

a capacitor, a coil, and a resistor. For simplicity, we will assume that each of the components is theoretically perfect—that is, the capacitor is purely capacitive (no resistive or inductive elements) the resistor is purely resistive, and the coil is purely inductive. All practical components will exhibit some dc resistance and both capacitive and inductive reactance. Fortunately, in most cases the leakage values (resistance and inductance in a capacitor, for instance) are usually so small they don't have any noticeable effect on the circuit's operation, so they may be reasonably ignored.

For our sample problems, we will assume the following component values:

Ac voltage	120 volts
R	2700 ohms (2.7 kΩ)
C	0.22 μF (0.00000022 farad)
L	150 mH (0.15 henry)

We can't perform any of the calculations without knowing the signal frequency. We will start by assuming that it is 60 Hz. This makes the capacitive reactance equal to:

$$\begin{aligned} X_c &= 1/(6.28 \text{ FC}) \\ &= 1/(6.28 \times 60 \times 0.00000022) \\ &= 1/0.0000829 \\ &= 12057 \text{ ohms} \end{aligned}$$

39

For convenience, we can round this off to 12,000 ohms, or 12 kΩ.

At the same time, the inductive reactance works out to about:

$$X_l = 6.28 \ FL$$
$$= 6.28 \times 60 \times 0.15$$
$$= 56 \ ohms$$

The dc resistance, of course, is unaffected by the signal frequency. It is a constant 2700 ohms.

Combining the three resistive values (R, X_c, and X_l) we get a total impedance of:

$$Z = \sqrt{R^2 + (X_l - X_c)^2}$$
$$= \sqrt{2700^2 + (56 - 12057)^2}$$
$$= \sqrt{7290000 + (-12001)^2}$$
$$= \sqrt{7290000 + 144024000}$$
$$= \sqrt{151314000}$$
$$= 12301 \ ohms$$

at 60 Hz.

Finally, we can now use Ohm's law to find out how much current is flowing through this circuit at 60 Hz:

$$I = E/Z = 120/12301 = 0.0098 \ amp = 9.8 \ mA$$

Next, let's see what happens when we increase the signal frequency to 250 Hz:

$$X_c = 1/(6.28 \times 250 \times 0.00000022)$$
$$= 1/0.0003456$$
$$= 2894 \ ohms$$

$$X_l = 6.28 \times 250 \times 0.15 = 236 \ ohms$$

$$Z = \sqrt{2700^2 + (236 - 2894)^2}$$
$$= \sqrt{7290000 + 2364^2}$$
$$= \sqrt{7290000 + 7065532}$$
$$= \sqrt{1435532}$$
$$= 3789 \ ohms$$

$$I = 120/3789 = 0.0317 = 31.7 \ mA$$

Now we will increase the signal frequency to 1000 Hz. (We won't bother to show the intermediate steps of the calculations):

$$X_c = 723 \text{ ohms}$$
$$X_1 = 942 \text{ ohms}$$
$$Z = 2709 \text{ ohms}$$
$$I = 0.0443 \text{ amp} = 44.3 \text{ mA}$$

One last example. This time the signal frequency is 5000 Hz:

$$X_c = 145 \text{ ohms}$$
$$X_1 = 4172 \text{ ohms}$$
$$Z = 5306 \text{ ohms}$$
$$I = 0.0226 \text{ amp} = 22.6 \text{ mA}$$

Notice how the impedance in this circuit starts out high (low current), then decreases as the signal frequency increases (current flow increases), until a certain point is passed, then the impedance starts to increase (and current flow decreases) as the signal frequency is further increased. The crossover point is of considerable significance. It is called resonance.

Series Resonance

Because the capacitive reactance decreases as the signal frequency increases, and the inductive reactance increases with the signal frequency, at some specific frequency the capacitive reactance will be exactly equal to the inductive reactance. Something very interesting happens at this frequency:

$$Z = \sqrt{R^2 + (X_1 - X_c)^2} = \sqrt{R^2 + (0)^2}$$
$$= \sqrt{R^2 + 0} = \sqrt{R^2} = R = Z$$

The capacitive and inductive reactances cancel each other out. The ac impedance simply equals the dc resistance. If you think about it for a minute, it becomes clear that this is the minimum value the impedance of the circuit can ever have.

The condition when the capacitive reactance equals the inductive reactance is called resonance. The frequency where this occurs is called the resonant frequency. There is always one (and only one) resonant frequency for any capacitance/inductance series combination.

At resonance, a capacitance and an inductance in series exhibit their minimum impedance. At frequencies above or below resonance, the impedance will be greater. The further away from the resonant frequency the signal frequency is (in either direction) the higher the circuit impedance.

The resonant frequency for any capacitance/inductance combination can be found with this formula:

$$F = 1/(2 \pi \sqrt{LC})$$

where F is the frequency in hertz, L is the inductance in henries, and C is the capacitance in farads. Of course, 2π is about 6.28.

Let's find the resonant frequency for the sample circuit we have been using for the last few pages. Remember, C = 0.00000022 and L = 0.15:

$$
\begin{aligned}
F &= 1/(6.28 \times \sqrt{(0.15 \times 0.00000022)}) \\
&= 1/(6.28 \times \sqrt{0.000000033}) \\
&= 1/(6.28 \times 0.001817) \\
&= 1/0.0011414 \\
&= 876 \text{ Hz.}
\end{aligned}
$$

The resonant frequency formula can be rearranged to solve for either of the component values. Notice that the dc resistance has absolutely no effect on the resonant frequency.

Let's say, for example, we need a circuit that is resonant at 1000 Hz. We will keep our 150 mH coil. What value should we change the capacitor to for the required resonant frequency? First, we rearrange the equation, which becomes:

$$C = 1/(4 \pi^2 F^2 L)$$

$4 \pi^2$ equals approximately 39.48, so the equation may be simplified to:

$$C = 1/(39.48 \ F^2 L)$$

Plugging in the values for our sample problem, we find we need a capacitance of about:

$$
\begin{aligned}
C &= 1/(39.48 \times (1000)^2 \times 0.15) \\
&= 1/(39.48 \times 1000000 \times 0.15)
\end{aligned}
$$

$$= 1/5921762.6$$
$$= 0.000000169 \text{ farad}$$
$$= 0.169 \ \mu\text{F}$$

Similarly, the resonance equation may also be rearranged to solve for the inductance value:

$$L = 1/(39.48 \ F^2C)$$

Parallel Resonance

So far we have been dealing solely with circuits in which the capacitive element and the inductive element are in series, as shown in Fig. 1-32. But they may also be connected in parallel, as illustrated in Fig. 1-33. This change has a number of effects. For one thing, the impedance equation becomes somewhat more complex:

$$Z = \sqrt{R^2 + [(X_l \times X_c)/(X_l - X_c)]^2}$$

To study the effects of this, we will use the same values from our previous example problems:

$$
\begin{aligned}
\text{Ac voltage} &= 120 \text{ volts} \\
R &= 2700 \text{ ohms} \\
C &= 0.22 \ \mu\text{F} \ (0.00000022 \text{ farad}) \\
L &= 150 \text{ mH} \ (0.15 \text{ henry})
\end{aligned}
$$

There is no need to repeat the reactance calculations for individual frequencies, since they are exactly the same as before:

$$60 \text{ Hz} \quad X_c = 12057 \quad X_l = 56$$

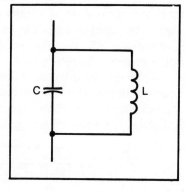

Fig. 1-33. In a parallel resonant circuit, the ac resistance is theoretically infinite at resonance.

43

$$
\begin{array}{llll}
250 \text{ Hz} & X_c = 2894 & X_l = 236 \\
1000 \text{ Hz} & X_c = 723 & X_l = 942 \\
5000 \text{ Hz} & X_c = 145 & X_l = 4712 \\
\end{array}
$$

The impedance at 60 Hz is therefore equal to:

$$
\begin{aligned}
Z &= \sqrt{2700^2 + [(56 \times 12057)/(56 - 12057)]^2} \\
&= \sqrt{7290000 + (675192/-12001)^2} \\
&= \sqrt{7290000 + (-56.26)^2} \\
&= \sqrt{7293165.3352} \\
&= 2700.5861 \text{ ohms}
\end{aligned}
$$

Skipping the intermediate steps of the calculation, we find that raising the signal frequency to 250 Hz changes the impedance to:

$$Z = 2712.2 \text{ ohms}$$

Now, if the signal frequency is 1000 Hz, the impedance works out to:

$$Z = 4118.42 \text{ ohms}$$

Finally, when the signal frequency is raised to 5000 Hz the impedance becomes:

$$Z = 2704.1415$$

Notice that as the frequency increases, the impedance increases, until a specific point is reached. Then the impedance starts to decrease with increasing frequency. Once again, the crossover point is the resonant frequency. The resonant frequency is the same for a parallel circuit as for a series circuit, assuming the same components are used in both. The calculations are exactly the same in either case. The only difference is in the behavior of the circuit as the resonant frequency.

We've already determined that resonant frequency for this particular combination of components is 876 Hz when the capacitive reactance and the inductive reactance each equal approximately 826 ohms. Let's see what happens to the impedance in this case:

$$
\begin{aligned}
Z &= \sqrt{2700^2 + [(826 \times 826)/(826 - 826)]^2} \\
&= \sqrt{7290000 + (682276/0)^2}
\end{aligned}
$$

44

$$= \sqrt{7290000 + \infty}$$
$$Z = \infty$$

In a parallel circuit, the impedance is theoretically infinite at resonance.

To summarize: in a series circuit, the impedance is at its minimum value (R) at resonance, and in a parallel circuit, the impedance is at its maximum value (∞) at resonance.

TRIGONOMETRIC FUNCTIONS

Many electronics calculations require basic trigonometric functions. Essentially, trigonometry is nothing more than a set of rules for defining relationships between angles and side lengths in triangles. A triangle has only three sides and angles, so only a limited number of combinations are possible.

We are primarily concerned with right triangles, which have one 90° (right) angle. A typical right triangle is shown in Fig. 1-34. The longest side (c) is called the hypotenuse. It is always directly opposite the right angle. The length of the sides of a right triangle always bear a specific mathematical relationship:

$$C^2 = a^2 + b^2$$

This is true for all right triangles.

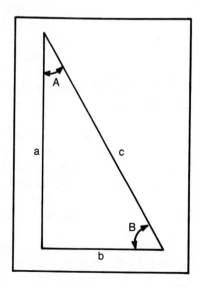

Fig. 1-34. Trigonometric functions are defined as the relationships between various angles and side lengths of a right triangle.

Similarly, there are six basic relationships between the angles and the side lengths. Each is given a specific name, as follows:

> sine
> cosine
> tangent
> arctangent
> secant
> cosecant

For angle A in Fig. 1-34, we can find the values for each of these relationships:

> sine A = b/c
> cosine A = a/c
> tangent A = b/a
> arctangent A = a/b
> secant A = c/a
> cosecant A = c/b

The same relationships hold true for angle B, except that sides a and b are reversed:

> sine A = a/c
> cosine A = b/c
> tangent A = a/b
> arctangent A = b/a
> secant A = c/b
> cosecant A = c/a

Notice that the B angle can be figured from A, because of the following relationships:

> sine B = cosine A
> cosine B = sine A
> tangent B = arctangent A
> arctangent B = tangent A
> secant B = cosecant A
> cosecant B = secant A

In most practical electronics work, we will be working from the angle, not side lengths of a hypothetical right triangle. There are mathematical equations for solving the trig functions of an angle, but they are long and complicated. Generally, it is more practical to just use a standard trig table. A table of natural sines from 0 to 90 is given in Table 1-1. Table 1-2 lists cosines, and Table 1-3 lists tangents. These three functions are by far the most commonly encountered in electronics work. Arctangents, secants, and cosecants are rarely used.

Most scientific calculators and computers also include trigonometric functions, so there won't be many occasions when the circuit designer will have to perform these calculations for himself. Usually a table, calculator, or computer will be available to do the work.

LOGARITHMS

Some functions vary smoothly and evenly, giving us a nice straight line when we try to graph them. Others tend to have many values jammed together in one part of the scale, while other parts of the scale have values that are widely spaced, as shown in Fig.

Table 1-1. Table of Natural Sines.

0—0.0000	25—0.4226	50—0.7660	75—0.9659
1—0.0175	26—0.4384	51—0.7771	76—0.9703
2—0.0349	27—0.4540	52—0.7880	77—0.9744
3—0.0523	28—0.4695	53—0.7986	78—0.9781
4—0.0698	29—0.4848	54—0.8090	79—0.9816
5—0.0872	30—0.5000	55—0.8192	80—0.9848
6—0.1045	31—0.5150	56—0.8290	81—0.9877
7—0.1219	32—0.5299	57—0.8387	82—0.9903
8—0.1392	33—0.5446	58—0.8480	83—0.9925
9—0.1564	34—0.5592	59—0.8572	84—0.9945
10—0.1736	35—0.5736	60—0.8660	85—0.9962
11—0.1908	36—0.5878	61—0.8746	86—0.9976
12—0.2079	37—0.6018	62—0.8829	87—0.9986
13—0.2250	38—0.6157	63—0.8910	88—0.9994
14—0.2419	39—0.6293	64—0.8988	89—0.998
15—0.2588	40—0.6428	65—0.9063	90—1.000
16—0.2756	41—0.6561	66—0.9135	
17—0.2924	42—0.6691	67—0.9205	
18—0.3090	43—0.6820	68—0.9272	
19—0.3256	44—0.6947	69—0.9336	
20—0.3420	45—0.7071	70—0.9397	
21—0.3584	46—0.7193	71—0.9455	
22—0.3746	47—0.7314	72—0.9511	
23—0.3907	48—0.7431	73—0.9563	
24—0.4067	49—0.7547	74—0.9613	

Table 1-2. Table of Cosines.

0—1.0000	25—0.9063	50—0.6428	75—0.2588
1—0.9998	26—0.8988	51—0.6293	76—0.2419
2—0.9994	27—0.8910	52—0.6157	77—0.2250
3—0.9986	28—0.8829	53—0.6018	78—0.2079
4—0.9976	29—0.8746	54—0.5878	79—0.1908
5—0.9962	30—0.8660	55—0.5736	80—0.1736
6—0.9945	31—0.8572	56—0.5592	81—0.1564
7—0.9925	32—0.8480	57—0.5446	82—0.1392
8—0.9903	33—0.8387	58—0.5299	83—0.1219
9—0.9877	34—0.8290	59—0.5150	84—0.1045
10—0.9848	35—0.8192	60—0.5000	85—0.0872
11—0.9816	36—0.8090	61—0.4848	86—0.0698
12—0.9781	37—0.7986	62—0.4695	87—0.0523
13—0.9744	38—0.7880	63—0.4540	88—0.0349
14—0.9703	39—0.7771	64—0.4384	89—0.0175
15—0.9659	40—0.7660	65—0.4226	90—0.0000
16—0.9613	41—0.7547	66—0.4067	
17—0.9563	42—0.7431	67—0.3907	
18—0.9511	43—0.7314	68—0.3746	
19—0.9455	44—0.7193	69—0.3584	
20—0.9397	45—0.7071	70—0.3420	
21—0.9336	46—0.6947	71—0.3256	
22—0.9272	47—0.6820	72—0.3090	
23—0.9205	48—0.6691	73—0.2924	
24—0.9135	49—0.6561	74—0.2756	

Table 1-3. Table of Tangents.

0—0.0000	25—0.4663	50—1.1918	75— 3.7321
1—0.0175	26—0.4877	51—1.2349	76— 4.0108
2—0.0349	27—0.5095	52—1.2799	77— 4.3315
3—0.0524	28—0.5317	53—1.3270	78— 4.7046
4—0.0699	29—0.5543	54—1.3764	79— 5.1446
5—0.0875	30—0.5774	55—1.4281	80— 5.6713
6—0.1051	31—0.6009	56—1.4826	81— 6.3138
7—0.1228	32—0.6249	57—1.5399	82— .1154
8—0.1405	33—0.6494	58—1.6003	83— 8.1443
9—0.1584	34—0.6745	59—1.6643	84— 9.5144
10—0.1763	35—0.7002	60—1.7321	85—11.43
11—0.1944	36—0.7265	61—1.8040	86—14.30
12—0.2126	37—0.7536	62—1.8807	87—19.08
13—0.2309	38—0.7813	63—1.9626	88—28.64
14—0.2493	39—0.8098	64—2.0503	89—57.29
15—0.2679	40—0.8391	65—2.1445	90— ∞
16—0.2867	41—0.8693	66—2.2460	
17—0.3057	42—0.9004	67—2.3559	
18—0.3249	43—0.9325	68—2.4751	
19—0.3443	44—0.9657	69—2.6051	
20—0.3640	45—1.0000	70—2.7475	
21—0.3839	46—1.0355	71—2.9042	
22—0.4040	47—1.0724	72—3.0777	
23—0.4225	48—1.1106	73—3.2709	
24—0.4452	49—1.1504	74—3.4874	

1-35. This is a logarithmic function. Typical logarithmic functions in electronics work include changes in acoustic volume and the charging rate of a capacitor, among others.

Logarithmic functions can be treated like a linear function, but the wide spread of values can leave you with a lot of numbers that can be very awkward to work with. Working with these functions using logarithms is much more convenient. Moreover, logarithms can greatly simplify math when very large and/or very small numbers are involved. The old-fashioned slide rule worked on the principle of logarithms.

The logarithm of any specific number is an exponent that indicates the power to which the given base must be raised to equal the given number. To clarify this, let's try a simple example. Let's assume our logarithmic base is 10. This is often called the common logarithm. What if we needed to know the common logarithm

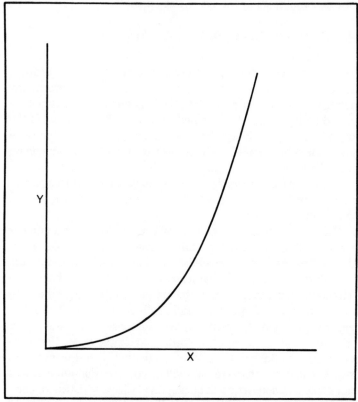

Fig. 1-35. Logarithmic functions are awkward if you try to graph them linearly.

of 1000? We want to raise 10 by some unknown power to give us 1000. That is:

$$\text{Log}_{10} (1000) = X$$
$$\text{where } 10^x = 1000$$

This particular example is simple enough, because most of us are well aware that 1000 is 10 cubed:

$$1000 = 10 \times 10 \times 10 = 10$$

So the common logarithm of 1000 is 3:

$$\text{Log}_{10} (1000) = 3$$

Solving a logarithm gets more complicated with values that are not exact multiples of the base. For example:

$$\text{Log}_{10} (657) = 2.8175654$$

The math here can be fairly complex and tedious. Fortunately, the odds are quite good that you will never have to perform any such operations directly. As with the trigonometric functions described earlier, logarithmic tables allow us to bypass most of the busy-work. We can interpolate for values that fall between table entries, or simply round off to the nearest table entry, depending on the level of accuracy required in the specific application.

Scientific calculators and computers usually feature logarithmic functions. The slide rule can still come in handy for solving logarithmic problems.

Table 1-4 lists the common (base 10) logarithms for a number of values. If you look over this table carefully, you should see certain patterns in the structure of the logarithms. Each logarithm consists of two parts—the characteristic and the mantissa. The characteristic is the portion of the number to the left of the decimal point. Practical logarithm tables, like the one in Table 1-5, generally give only the mantissa, because these values will repeat for different characteristics, according to simple rules. For numbers from 1 to 9.9999, the characteristic will be 0. For numbers greater than 0, the characteristic will be positive. For numbers less than 1, the characteristic will be negative. Characteristics for common logarithms are summarized in Table 1-6.

Table 1-4. Some Common Logarithms for Some Typical Values.

N	log₁₀ (N)	N	log₁₀ (N)
0	$-\infty$	40	1.6021
1	0.0000	45	1.6532
2	0.3010	50	1.6990
3	0.4771	55	1.7404
4	0.6021	60	1.7781
5	0.6990	65	1.8129
6	0.7782	70	1.8451
7	0.8451	75	1.8751
8	0.9031	80	1.9031
9	0.9542	85	1.9294
10	1.0000	90	1.9542
11	1.0414	95	1.9777
12	1.0792	100	2.0000
13	1.1139	110	2.0414
14	1.1461	120	2.0792
15	1.1761	130	2.1139
16	1.2041	140	2.1461
17	1.2304	150	2.1761
18	1.2553	160	2.2041
19	1.2787	170	2.2304
20	1.3010	180	2.2553
25	1.3979	190	2.2787
30	1.4771	200	2.3010
35	1.5441	300	2.4771
400	2.6021	500000	5.6990
500	2.6990	1000000	6.0000
600	2.7781	10000000	7.0000
700	2.8451	100000000	8.0000
800	2.9031	1000000000	9.0000
900	2.9542	10000000000	10.0000
1000	3.0000		
2000	3.3010		
3000	3.4771		
4000	3.6021		
5000	4.6990		
6000	3.7781		
7000	3.8451		
8000	3.9031		
9000	3.9542		
10000	4.0000		
20000	4.3010		
30000	4.4771		
40000	4.6021		
50000	4.6990		
60000	4.7781		
70000	4.8451		
80000	4.9031		
90000	4.9542		
100000	5.0000		

Table 1-5. The Mantissa of a
Logarithm Is Taken from A Standard Log Table.

1.0	.0000	3.6	.5563	6.2	.7924	8.8	.9445
1.1	.0414	3.7	.5682	6.3	.7993	8.9	.9494
1.2	.0792	3.8	.5798	6.4	.8062	9.0	.9542
1.3	.1139	3.9	.5911	6.5	.8129	9.1	.9590
1.4	.1461	4.0	.6021	6.6	.8195	9.2	.9638
1.5	.1761	4.1	.6128	6.7	.8261	9.3	.9685
1.6	.2041	4.2	.6232	6.8	.8325	9.4	.9731
1.7	.2304	4.3	.6335	6.9	.8388	9.5	.9777
1.8	.2553	4.4	.6435	7.9	.8451	9.6	.9823
1.9	.2787	4.5	.6532	7.1	.8513	9.7	.9868
2.0	.3010	4.6	.6628	7.2	.8573	9.8	.9912
2.1	.3222	4.7	.6721	7.3	.8633	9.9	.9956
2.2	.3424	4.8	.6812	7.4	.8692	10.0	1.0000
2.3	.3617	4.9	.6902	7.5	.8751		
2.4	.3802	5.0	.6990	7.6	.8808		
2.5	.3979	5.1	.7076	7.7	.8865		
2.6	.4150	5.2	.7160	7.8	.8921		
2.7	.4314	5.3	.7243	7.9	.8976		
2.8	.4472	5.4	.7324	8.0	.9031		
2.9	.4624	5.5	.7404	8.1	.9085		
3.0	.4771	5.6	.7482	8.2	.9138		
3.1	.4914	5.7	.7559	8.3	.9191		
3.2	.5051	5.8	.7634	8.4	.9243		
3.3	.5185	5.9	.7709	8.5	.9294		
3.4	.5315	6.0	.7782	8.6	.9345		
3.5	.5441	6.1	.7853	8.7	.9395		

To find the common logarithm for any decimal number, simply find the characteristic for the appropriate range from Table 1-6. Then move the decimal point in the original number, until its value is between 1 and 10, and find the mantissa in Table 1-5. Combine your characteristic and mantissa, and there you have your common logarithm.

For example:

$$Log\ (1700)$$

Notice that if no base is specified, common logarithms are generally assumed. This value (1700) is greater than 1000, but less than 10000, so the characteristic is 3.

Next, we move the decimal point, giving us:

$$1.700$$

Looking up this value in Table 1-5, we find the mantissa should be:

.2304

Putting it all together, we find:

Log (1700) = 3.2304.

The common logarithm of any decimal value can be found with relative ease, using this method.

The common logarithm is not the only type of logarithm in regular use. Another common system of logarithms is the natural or Napierian system. This system uses e as its base. The e is a mathematical constant with a value of approximately 2.718. As with π, this awkward value corresponds directly to certain natural phenomena, so natural logarithms are often very convenient to work with. A table of natural logarithms is given in Table 1-7.

Natural logarithms are often written as:

ln(N)

Table 1-6. Typical Characteristics for Logarithms Are Summarized Here.

Range	Characteristic
0.0000000001 to 0.000000000999	– 10
0.000000001 to 0.000000009999	– 9
0.00000001 to 0.00000009999	– 8
0.0000001 to 0.0000009999	– 7
0.000001 to 0.000009999	– 6
0.00001 to 0.00009999	– 5
0.0001 to 0.0009999	– 4
0.001 to 0.009999	– 3
0.01 to 0.09999	– 2
0.1 to 0.9999	– 1
1 to 9.999	0
10 to 99.99	1
100 to 999.9	2
1000 to 9999	3
10000 to 99999	4
100000 to 999999	5
1000000 to 9999999	6
10000000 to 99999999	7
100000000 to 999999999	8
1000000000 to 9999999999	9
10000000000 to 99999999999	10

1.0	0.0000	3.6	1.2809	6.2	1.8245	8.8	2.1748
1.1	0.0953	3.7	1.3083	6.3	1.8405	8.9	2.1861
1.2	0.1823	3.8	1.3350	6.4	1.8563	9.0	2.1972
1.3	0.2624	3.9	1.3610	6.5	1.8718	9.1	2.2083
1.4	0.3365	4.0	1.3863	6.6	1.8871	9.2	2.2192
1.5	0.4055	4.1k	1.4110	6.7	1.9021	9.3	2.2300
1.6	0.4700	4.2	1.4351	6.8	1.9169	9.4	2.2407
1.7	0.5306	4.3	1.4586	6.9	1.9315	9.5	2.2513
1.8	0.5878	4.4	1.4816	7.0	1.9459	9.6	2.2618
1.9	0.6419	4.5	1.5041	7.1	1.9601	9.7	2.2721
2.0	0.6931	4.6	1.5261	7.2	1.9741	9.8	2.2824
2.1	0.7419	4.7	1.5476	7.3	1.9879	9.9	2.2925
2.2	0.7885	4.8	1.5686	7.4	2.0015	10.0	2.3026
2.3	0.8329	4.9	1.5892	7.5	2.0149		
2.4	0.8755	5.0	1.6094	7.6	2.0281		
2.5	0.9163	5.1	1.6292	7.7	2.0412		
2.6	0.9555	5.2	1.6487	7.8	2.0541		
2.7	0.9933	5.3	1.6677	7.9	2.0669		
2.8	1.0296	5.4	1.6864	8.0	2.0794		
2.9	1.0647	5.5	1.7047	8.1	2.0919		
3.0	1.0986	5.6	1.7228	8.2	2.1041		
3.1	1.1314	5.7	1.7405	8.3	2.1163		
3.2	1.1632	5.8	1.7579	8.4	2.1282		
3.3	1.1939	5.9	1.7750	8.5	2.1401		
3.4	1.2238	6.0	1.7918	8.6	2.1518		
3.5	1.2528	6.1	1.8083	8.7	2.1633		

where N is the original number.

Antilogarithms

The reverse of a logarithm is an antilogarithm. Here we start out with a logarithmic value and convert it to a decimal number. Antilogarithms are usually written in this form:

Antilog (N)

You may occasionally see it notated like this:

Log^{-1} (N)

Once again, the most convenient approach is to use a Log table. This time we use the second (log) column to look up the given mantissa, and read the results in the first (value) column. If the characteristic has a nonzero value, we just need to add one more step:

$$\text{Antilog (C.mmmm)} = N \times B$$

where C is the characteristic. .mmmm is the mantissa, B is the system base (assumed to be 10 (common) if unspecified), and N is the value found in the Log table.

Combining Logarithms

Now let's put out logarithms and antilogarithms to work, and find out why they are so useful. Let's say we need to find the product of:

$$450000000 \times 7800000000$$

Numbers in this range can be awkward to work with. It's all too easy to make a mistake in the number of zeros, throwing the result off by a considerable amount. An interesting mathematical relationship among logarithms provides a more convenient solution:

$$\text{Log(A} \times \text{B)} = \text{Log(A)} + \text{Log(B)}$$

To find a product of any two numbers, we can add their individual logarithms. This gives the logarithm of the product. So, taking the antilogarithm gives us the direct result. This is the way multiplication is done on a slide rule. Let's work through our example:

```
Log(450000000) = 8.6532
Log(7800000000) = 9.8921
8.6532 + 9.8921 = 18.5453
Antilog (18.5453) = 3.51 × 10 = 3500000000000000000
```

This technique also comes in handy for combining very large numbers with very small numbers. For example:

```
63000000 × 0.000084
Log(63000000) = 7.79993
Log(0.000084) = −5.9243
7.7993 + (−5.9243) = 7.7993 − 5.9243 = −1.8750
Antilog (1.8750) = 7.5 × 10 = 75
```

The same kind of thing can work for division too, except we subtract instead of add the logarithm values:

$$Log(A/B) = Log(A) - Log(B)$$

Another useful application is in raising a value to a specific power. For example:

$$24^5$$

You could just manually multiply it out:

$$24 \times 24 \times 24 \times 24 \times 24$$

That's quite tedious at best, and it's very easy to make a mistake somewhere along the line. With logarithms, you can use this approach:

$$Log(A^B) = B \times Log(A)$$

For our example of 24^5, this works out to:

$$5 \times Log(24) = 5 \times 1.3802 = 6.9010$$
$$Antilog\ (6.9010) = 7.96 \times 10^6 = 7960000$$

Actually, 24^5 equals 7962624. The difference is due to rounding off values in the logarithmic method and interpolating between Log table entries. In this case, the total error worked out to be just slightly over 0.03%, which should be accurate enough for most practical applications.

Extracting roots is a particularly tough task for standard mathematics. It can be done, but the calculations are complex and time consuming. For example, how long would it take you to solve for the fourth root of 22?

$$\sqrt[4]{22}$$

Logarithms simplify the problem to one of straightforward division, which can be further reduced to simple subtraction. The logarithmic formula for root extraction is:

$$Log(\ \sqrt[A]{B}\ ) = Log(B)/A$$

So, for our sample problem:

$$\text{Log}(\sqrt[4]{22}) = \text{Log}(22)/4 = 1.3424/4$$

We could now go ahead and divide directly. But remember, logarithms allow us to reduce division to subtraction, so:

$$\text{Log}(1.3424/4) = \text{Log}(1.3424) - \text{Log}(4)$$
$$\text{Log}(1.3424) = 0.1271$$
$$\text{Log } 4 = 0.6021$$
$$0.1271 - 0.6021 = -0.4750$$
$$\text{Antilog } (-0.4750) = 0.3350$$

We just need to take the antilog of this value to find the fourth root of 22:

$$\text{Antilog}(0.3350) = 2.26$$

According to my scientific calculator, the fourth root of 22 is 2.1657368. The logarithmic method brought us very close, with a minimum of math.

If you have a scientific calculator or computer with the appropriate functions handy, you won't need to resort to logarithms to solve such problems because they can be solved directly by the machine.

Many of the values you will encounter in electronic design work will be logarithmic form, so you should be familiar with logarithms and antilogarithms, even if you don't use them to solve the types of problems described in this section.

Decibels

Many phenomena in nature and electronics conform to a logarithmic, rather than a linear scale. This makes direct comparisons between values somewhat difficult. One solution to this problem was the development of the decibel (dB) system. A decibel is actually one-tenth of a bel (B), but a bel is too large a unit to be practical for our purposes, so we work only with decibels.

The decibel system is a logarithmic method of comparing two values (powers, voltages, currents, or whatever). Decibels are frequently used in audio equipment, such as amplifiers, because our ears happen to perceive acoustic volume logarithmically, rather than linearly. A difference of 6 dB represents an approximate doubling of volume. A 1 dB difference would be almost imperceptible.

The formula for converting two powers to dB form is:

$$dB = 10 \times Log(P_2/P_1)$$

where P1 and P2 are the powers to be compared, and dB is the comparison factor in decibels. If the result is positive, P_2 is larger than P_1. If the result is negative, P_1 is larger than P_2.

Advertisements for audio amplifiers frequently emphasize the power ratings of the equipment. You'd think that a 50-watt amplifier would offer a considerable advantage over a 20-watt amplifier. But what is the real difference in decibels?

$$dB = 10 \times Log(50/20) = 10 \times Log(2.5)$$
$$= 10 \times 0.3979 = 3.979, \text{ or about 4 dB}$$

There hasn't even been a doubling of power.

Decibels can also be used to indicate voltage gain (the increase in amplitude from the input signal to the output signal). The formula is:

$$dB = 20 \times Log(E_0/E_1)$$

where E_0 is the output voltage, and E_1 is the input voltage.

This calculation assumes that the input and output impedances are equal. If this is not the case, the formula should be changed to look like this:

$$dB = 20 \times Log\ [(E_0 \times Z_0)/(E_i \times Z_i)]$$

It is important to remember that the decibel is a comparative, not an absolute value. An expression like, "the amplitude of that sound is 37 dB", is meaningless unless we know what it is being referenced to. In other words, we need to define the 0 dB point. Generally, in electronic equipment if no reference level is identified, a standard reference level of 6 millivolts (0.006 vol) across a 600-ohm impedance is assumed.

LAPLACE TRANSFORMS

Using the mathematical tools described so far in this chapter, we can analyze pretty thoroughly what is going on in a circuit if the signal flowing through it is a dc voltage or an ac sine wave. Unfortunately, many circuits we'll be dealing with in the real world are not so cooperative. The current flowing through many circuits varies with time, complicating the task of analysis greatly.

Even with a fairly simple dc circuit, like the one shown in Fig. 1-36, we sometimes have to concern ourselves with voltages and currents that change over time. When the switch is in position A, the circuit effectively functions like the one shown in Fig. 1-37. Moving the switch to position B changes the effective circuit to the one illustrated in Fig. 1-38. These changes in the circuitry must alter the voltages and currents flowing through the components in some way.

Circuits with changing conditions can be analyzed by using Laplace transforms. Once the correct transforms have been found, they can be substituted for the actual circuit values in Kirchhoff equations. The result is then converted into a meaningful value by using a transform table.

There are three major factors to be considered—the circuit elements and their transforms, the initial conditions within the circuit at time 0 (if appropriate), and the time-varying voltages and currents and their transforms.

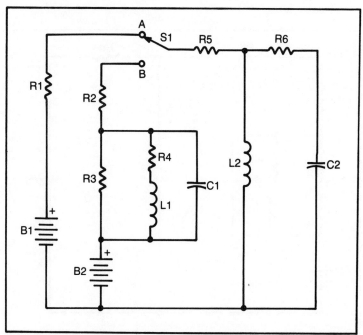

Fig. 1-36. Even in very simple dc circuits, we often have to be concerned with voltages and currents that change with time.

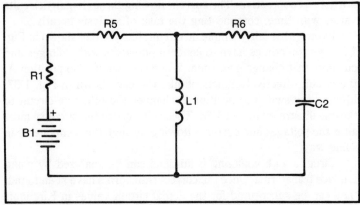

Fig. 1-37. When the switch in Fig. 1-36 is in position A, the effective circuit looks like this.

There are three types of passive components:

☐ resistors
☐ inductors (coils)
☐ capacitors

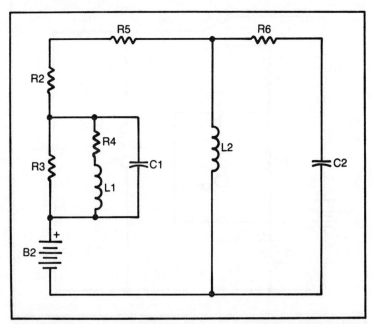

Fig. 1-38. When the switch in Fig. 1-36 is in position B, the effective circuit looks like this.

For a resistor, the Laplace transform is simply the value of that resistor in ohms. There is no time-varying aspect. The Laplace transform for a 2700-ohm resistor, for example, is 2700. With inductors and capacitors, we have to start working with a Laplace operator. It is represented in the equations as s. The Laplace transform of an inductor is the inductance multiplied by s:

$$sL$$

The Laplace transform for a capacitor is the reciprocal of the capacitance (in farads) multiplied by s:

$$1/sC$$

Consider the circuit illustrated in Fig. 1-39. At time $t = 0$, the switch is moved from position A to position B. Before $t = 0$, there was a voltage across the capacitor, and a current through the inductor, because there was a complete current path, powered by B1. In this case, the initial conditions of the circuit parameters are certainly of importance.

The initial condition transform for a voltage across a capacitor may be expressed as:

$$E_0/s$$

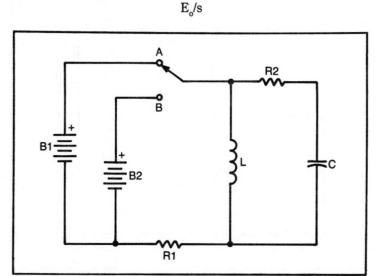

Fig. 1-39. This circuit is used for the Laplace transform example described in the text.

where E_o is the voltage across the capacitor at $t = 0$. Interestingly, the value of the capacitor is completely irrelevant to this initial condition transform, so there is no C value here.

For the current flowing through an inductor, the initial condition transform is written as:

$$LI_o$$

where L is the inductance in henries, and I_o is the current flowing at time $t = 0$. Notice that there is no s expression in this transform. For purposes of analysis, both of these transforms may be considered as voltage sources. This concept is illustrated in Fig. 1-40.

A time functions consists of a coefficient and a function of time. For example, $7e^{9t}$ is a time function in which the coefficient is 7, and the function of time is e^{9t}. For a second example, 8sine(5t) breaks down to a coefficient of 8, and a time function equal to sine(5t). The Laplace transform of any time-varying function is equal to the coefficient of that function multiplied by the function's transform.

The simplest possible function is 1 (or unit step). This function is applicable to a circuit that initially has no voltage current

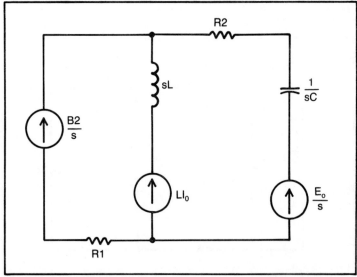

Fig. 1-40. Some of the components in the circuit of Fig. 1-39 are redrawn here as voltage sources for purposes of analysis.

Table 1-8. Common Laplace Transforms.

Time Function	Laplace Transform
1 (unit step)	$1/s$
t (ramp)	$1/s^2$
e^{at}	$1/(s-a)$
e^{-at}	$1/(s+a)$
te^{at}	$1/(s-a)^2$
te^{-at}	$1/(s+a)^2$
$1 - e^{at}$	$-a/s(s-a)$
$1/\omega \sin \omega t$	$1/(s^2 + \omega^2)$
$\cos \omega t$	$s/(s^2 + \omega^2)$
$1 - \cos \omega t$	$\omega^2 /s(s^2 + \omega^2)$

flowing through it. At time t = 0 a switch is closed, connecting a battery or other dc voltage source to the circuit. In this case the transform is:

$$1/s$$

Another simple function is the ramp. This is where the voltage starts zero at t = 0, then increases linearly with time. In this case, the transform is:

$$1/s$$

Additional common time functions and their transforms are given in Table 1-8. A few of the entries may require a little explanation for many readers.

The letter *e* is a mathematical constant like π. In this case, *e* is the base of the natural logarithm system (discussed earlier). The approximate value of e is about 2.718.

The term (n – 1)! indicates a factorial operation. A factorial is obtained by multiplying the given integer (n – 1, in this case) by each lower integer down to 1. That may be a bit confusing, so I will give an example. We will say n = 6, so (n – 1) = 5. Therefore, (n – 1)! = :

$$5! = 5 \times 4 \times 3 \times 2 \times 1 = 120$$

The next term in the table that may be unfamiliar is ψ. This symbol is used to represent radians-per-second. The radius (r) of a circle is the length from the center to the edge. The circumference (distance around the outside) of a circle is always equal to 2 π r. Now, imagine cutting out a segment of a circle so that the portion of the circumference included in the segment is equal to the radius (r). We then draw two radii from the ends of the circumference segment back to the circle's center. The two radii will form a specific angle which is equal to one radian. A complete circle, by definition, contains 2 π radians.

Radians-per-second is a function of frequency. The formula is:

$$\psi = 2 \pi F$$

where F is the frequency in hertz. The constant value 2 π is approximately equal to 6.28.

Returning to the table, the symbol ϕ represents a phase angle. If, for instance, a signal is 34° out-of-phase with a given reference, ϕ would be equal to 34.

While not included in this table, perhaps we should also mention the imaginary operator j, which is equal to the square root of -1:

$$j = \sqrt{-1}$$

No real number will fulfill the condition:

$$N \times N = -1$$

so j is said to be imaginary. But it can have a very real effect in many calculations.

Now that we know some of the most commonly used Laplace transforms, what do we do with them? Once we have the correct transforms for the various circuit elements, and have defined the initial conditions and driving functions, we can apply Kirchhoff's laws, just as we did with the dc circuits described earlier in this chapter.

To find the time-varying voltages and currents, it is necessary to rearrange the results of the Kirchhoff equations algebraically until they resemble one of the transforms in our table. Then we simply convert to find the results.

As an example of the use of Laplace transforms, let's consider the simple circuit shown in Fig. 1-41. We will assume the following component values:

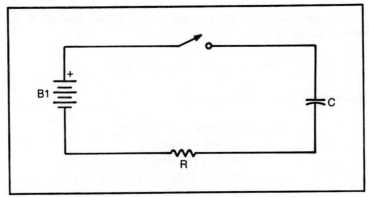

Fig. 1-41. This circuit is used for the second Laplace transform example described in the text.

    E1 = 6 volts
    R   = 2200 ohms
    C   = 10 μF (0.00001 farad)

The switch is closed at time t = 0. The circuit is redrawn in Fig. 1-42 to show the Laplace transforms of the circuit elements. The Laplace transform of the resistor is simply equal to the resistance (2200). The Laplace transform for the capacitor works out to:

$$1/sC = 1/(s \times 0.00001) = 100000/s$$

The Laplace transform for the voltage source (E1) is:

$$6/s$$

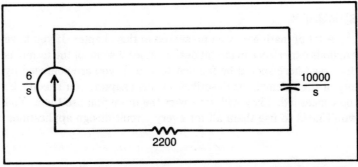

Fig. 1-42. At time t = 0, the circuit from Fig. 1-41 functions as if it looked like this.

65

We can combine these transforms into a form analogous to Ohm's law $(E = IR)$:

$$6/s = I \times (2200 + (100000/s)$$

Rearranging to solve for I, we get:

$$
\begin{aligned}
I &= (6/s)/[2200 + (100000/s)] \\
&= 6/(2200s + 100000) \\
&= 0.0027/(s + 45.4545) \\
&= 0.0027 \times [1/(s + 45.4545)]
\end{aligned}
$$

This closely resembles the second transform in the table:

$$1/(s + a)$$

with 0.0027 as the coefficient.

According to the table, the function for this particular transform is:

$$e^{-at}$$

The variable a holds it's original value (45.4545 in this case), so the total current flow in this circuit works out to:

$$I = 0.0027 \times e$$

Virtually any time-varying voltage or current in almost any circuit can be determined by using Laplace transforms.

SUMMARY

A lot of math has been presented in this chapter. If you have previous experience in circuit design, at least some of the formulas discussed here should be familiar to you. If you are confused by any of the calculations described in this chapter, you needn't be too concerned. They will get easier the more you use them. You won't need to use them all for every circuit design application.

Chapter 2

Digital Basics

M OST OF THE CIRCUITRY WE WILL BE DEALING WITH IN this book is digital. Digital circuitry can get very complicated in advanced applications, but it can always be broken down to fairly simply modules. Digital circuit design is almost a matter of combining modules in building-block fashion.

A *digital signal* may have only one of two possible states. Either the signal voltage is low, or it is high. No intermediate values are possible. Several names are used to describe digital signals, but they all mean exactly the same thing:

Low	High
0	1
Off	On
No	Yes

NUMBER SYSTEMS

Digital electronics uses what is called the *binary number system*, because there are two possible digits—0 and 1. We are more familiar with the decimal system, which has ten digits:

0 1 2 3 4 5 6 7 8 9

In the *decimal system*, if we need to express a value larger than the largest available digit (9), we add a second column. For exam-

67

ple, twenty-seven is written as 27, or $(2 \times 10) + (7 \times 1)$. This can be extended for as many columns as needed. For example:

$$3658 = (3 \times 10 \times 10 \times 10) + (6 \times 10 \times 10) + (5 \times 10) + (8 \times 1)$$

Each new column to the left is raised to the next power of ten.

The binary system works in the same way, except each column is raised to a power of two. For example:

$$11011 = (1 \times 2 \times 2 \times 2 \times 2) + (1 \times 2 \times 2 \times 2) + (0 \times 2 \times 2) + (1 \times 2) + (1 \times 1) = 16 + 8 + 0 + 2 + 1 = 27$$

The binary system is very awkward for human beings to work with, but it is very easy for machines (such as computers) because each digit may only be one or the other of two very unambigous values.

Compromise number systems are also available. One is the *octal* (base 8) *system*. If we break binary numbers into groups of three digits, eight values can be expressed:

Binary	Decimal
000	0
001	1
010	2
011	3
100	4
101	5
110	6
111	7

This makes the reading of large binary numbers more convenient for human beings. As an example, consider this binary number:

$$110011010001$$

It would be all too easy to make a mistake in copying a binary number like this. But if we break it up into octal chunks, it is much easier to conceptualize:

110	011	010	001
6	3	2	1

A similar numbering system is the *hexadecimal system*. This system has a base of sixteen. We run into a problem right away. The hexadecimal system requires 16 different digits, but we only know how to write ten. The solution is to use the letters A through F to represent values from eleven to fifteen.

Binary numbers are converted into hexadecimal by breaking up the digits into groups of four. Things become clearer when we compare binary, decimal, and hexadecimal values:

Binary	Decimal	Hexadecimal
0000	0	0
0001	1	1
0010	2	2
0011	3	3
0100	4	4
0101	5	5
0110	6	6
0111	7	7
1000	8	8
1001	9	9
1010	10	A
1011	11	B
1100	12	C
1101	13	D
1110	14	E
1111	15	F

Converting the same large binary number from our earlier example to hexadecimal, we get:

1100	1101	0001
9	A	1

BCD

Octal and hexadecimal numbers are a step up from the straight binary system. But we are used to using the decimal system, and it would be nice if we could get our electronic machinery to cooperate. Circuitry to perform the necessary conversion between number systems is called BCD or *binary-coded-decimal*.

To cover all the decimal digits from 0 to 9, we need at least four binary digits. Unfortunately, there are six extra combinations. These values are meaningless in a BCD system. These extra combinations are disallowed:

0000	0
0001	1
0010	2
0011	3
0100	4
0101	5
0110	6
0111	7
1000	8
1001	9
1010	disallowed
1011	disallowed
1100	disallowed
1101	disallowed
1110	disallowed
1111	disallowed

THE GATE

The heart of all digital circuitry is the gate. A gate is a circuit that accepts one or more digital input signals and puts out one or more digital output signals. The output values are determined by the input values.

Digital gate circuits are almost always in IC form, either as packages of simple gates, or as complex combinations of gating circuits in a single package.

The simplest possible digital gate would have a single input and a single output. There are four possible combinations:

	Input	Output
A	0	0
	1	0
B	0	0
	1	1
C	0	1
	1	0

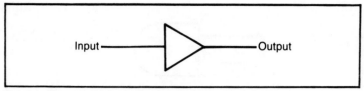

Fig. 2-1. The output of a buffer gate is the same as its input.

D	0	1
	1	1

A chart of the input and output combinations for a specific gate is called a truth table, or logic table.

A and D are clearly worthless as gates, because the output is constant. The input has no effect on the output. Simple hardwiring can be used in place of a gate circuit to achieve the same effect.

B might also look worthless, since the output is always the same as the input. Why not just use the input signal? Each digital signal (output from a previous gate) can drive just so many gate inputs. If we need to drive more inputs, we can add a gate of this type, called a buffer, to increase the "strength" of the output. The digital buffer gate is very similar in function to the analog buffer (unity gain) amplifier. The symbol used in schematic diagrams to represent buffer gates is shown in Fig. 2-1.

The pattern exhibited by gate C is probably the most useful signal input/single output gate. The output is the opposite of the input. This gate is called, not surprisingly, and inverter. It is also occasionally referred to as a NOT gate. The schematic symbol for this device is shown in Fig. 2-2. Notice that it is the same as the symbol for a buffer, except for the addition of a small circle at the output. In digital circuit diagrams, a small circle always indicates inversion.

Single input/single output gates are of limited value by themselves. Much more versatility is possible with multiple input gates. With two inputs and one output, there are sixteen possible combi-

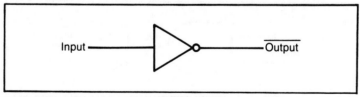

Fig. 2-2. The output of an inverter is the opposite of its input.

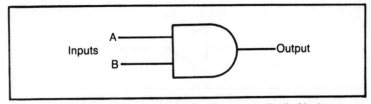

Fig. 2-3. The output of an AND gate is HIGH if, and only if, all of its inputs are HIGH.

nations. Several are trivial, or pointless. Some of the most commonly useful combinations are available in standard combinations.

Consider this combination:

Input A	Input B	Output
0	0	0
0	1	0
1	0	0
1	1	1

The output of this gate is a 1 if, and only if, both inputs (A AND B) are 1's. If either A or B (or both) is a 0, the output will be a zero. This is called an AND gate. The symbol is shown in Fig. 2-3.

If we add an inverter to the output, as shown in Fig. 2-4, the output pattern will be reversed:

Input A	Input B	Output
0	0	1
0	1	1
1	0	1
1	1	0

This time the output is a 1 if A and B are NOT both 1's. This is

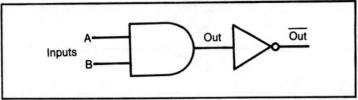

Fig. 2-4. Adding an inverter to the output of an AND gate creates a NAND gate.

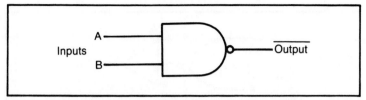

Fig. 2-5. This is the schematic symbol for a standard NAND gate.

called a NOT-AND gate, or a NAND gate. The NAND gate is probably the most commonly used type of gate in digital circuitry. It is
usually represented by the symbol shown in Fig. 2-5.

Another common type of gate is the OR gate. As the name suggests, the output is a 1 if input A is a 1 OR if input B is a 1. The
truth table is as follows:

Input A	Input B	Output
0	0	0
0	1	1
1	0	1
1	1	1

The schematic symbol for an OR gate is shown in Fig. 2-6.

As with the AND gate, the output of the OR gate is often inverted to create the NOR gate. The schematic symbol is illustrated
in Fig. 2-7, and the truth table is as follows:

Input A	Input B	Output
0	0	0
0	1	0
1	0	0
1	1	1

The output is a 1 if, and only if neither A NOR B is a 1.

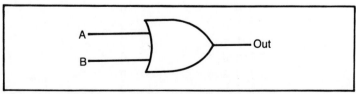

Fig. 2-6. Another commonly used digital gate is the OR gate.

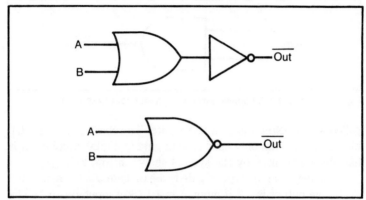
Fig. 2-7. A NOR gate is an OR gate with an inverted output.

Another variation on the basic OR gate is the Exclusive-OR gate. This is often shortened to X-OR gate. Here is the truth table:

Input A	Input B	Output
0	0	0
0	1	1
1	0	1
1	1	0

The output is a 1 if, and only if one input is a 1. If both inputs are 1's (or if both are 0's) the output will be 0. The X-OR gate may also be called a digital difference detector. The schematic symbol for this type of gate is shown in Fig. 2-8.

Any of the basic two input gates may be easily expanded to allow three or more inputs. For example, here is a truth table for a three input AND gate.

Inputs	Output
A B C	
0 0 0	0
0 0 1	0
0 1 0	0
0 1 1	0
1 0 0	0
1 0 1	0
1 1 0	0
1 1 1	1

Similarly, a three input X-OR gate would exhibit this logic pattern:

Inputs	Output
A B C	
0 0 0	0
0 0 1	1
0 1 0	1
0 1 1	0
1 0 0	1
1 0 1	0
1 1 0	0
1 1 1	1

Simple gates can be combined to create more complex gating patterns. For example, the circuit shown in Fig. 2-9 has four inputs and two outputs. The truth table for this circuit is:

Inputs	Outputs
A B C D	X Y
0 0 0 0	0 1
0 0 0 1	0 0
0 0 1 0	0 0
0 0 1 1	1 1
0 1 0 0	0 0
0 1 0 1	0 0
0 1 1 0	0 1
0 1 1 1	1 0
1 0 0 0	1 0
1 0 0 1	0 1
1 0 1 0	0 0
1 0 1 1	0 0

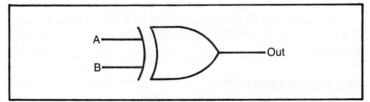

Fig. 2-8. A variation on the basic OR gate is the EXCLUSIVE-OR (or X-OR) gate.

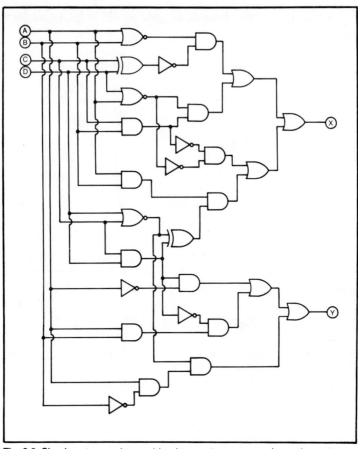

Fig. 2-9. Simple gates can be combined to create more complex gating patterns.

Inputs	Output
1 1 0 0	1 1
1 1 0 1	1 0
1 1 1 0	1 0
1 1 1 1	0 1

Any desired logic combination can be built up from a collection of basic digital gates. In most cases there are several possible approaches.

THE MULTIVIBRATOR

Most digital signals originate from some sort of multivibrator circuit. A multivibrator is a pulse wave generator. There are three basic types:

☐ Monostable
☐ Bistable
☐ Astable

Each of these is extremely useful for various tasks.

The Monostable Multivibrator

The *monostable multivibrator* has one stable state. When it receives an input pulse it temporarily snaps to the opposite logic state for a fixed period, then returns to its original stable state. In other words, there is one output pulse for each input pulse, as shown in Fig. 2-10.

The primary advantage of the monostable multivibrator is that the output pulse is always a specific length, regardless of the length of the input pulse. Generally this type of circuit is used to lengthen brief signal pulses. For this reason, the monostable multivibrator is often called a pulse stretcher.

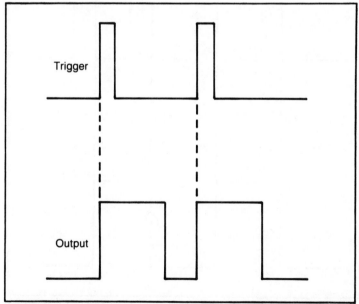

Fig. 2-10. A monostable multivibrator can be momentarily forced out of its single stable state by an input pulse.

The Bistable Multivibrator

The second type of multivibrator is the *bistable*. As the name suggests this circuit has two stable output states. It can remain in either state indefinitely. Each time an input pulse is received, the output reverse states. The action of a bistable multivibrator is illustrated in Fig. 2-11.

In a way, a bistable multivibrator is a form of one bit memory (see Chapter 4). It "remembers" its last state. Bistable multivibrators are also called *flip-flops* for reasons which should be fairly obvious.

The Astable Multivibrator

The third type of multivibrator is the *astable multivibrator*, which has no stable states. Its output switches continuously back and forth between the two possible output states, as shown in Fig.

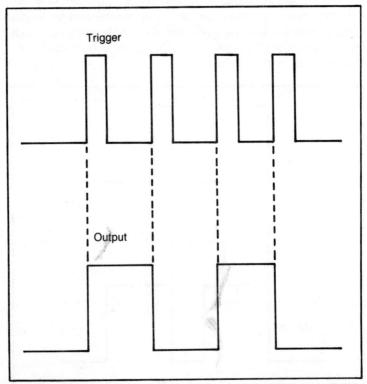

Fig. 2-11. A bistable switches between its two stable output states each time an input pulse is received.

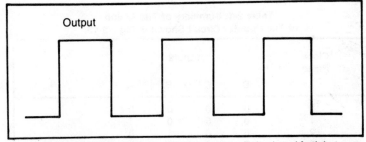

Fig. 2-12. An astable multivibrator switches continually back and forth between two unstable states.

2-12. In other words, the astable multivibrator is a rectangle wave generator.

COUNTERS

A binary counter can be created by stringing together several flip-flops, as shown in Fig. 2-13. The output of the first flip-flop (A) triggers the second (B), which triggers the third (C), which triggers the fourth (D).

The action of this circuit is outlined in Table 2-1. Note how the outputs count in binary from 0000 to 1111 (decimal 15), then the cycle is repeated. This is a sixteen-step, or modulo-sixteen counter.

Each time we add another stage to the counter, the modulo increases to the next power of two. For example:

3 stages	modulo-8
4 stages	modulo-16

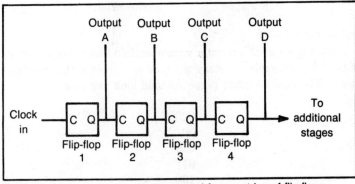

Fig. 2-13. A binary counter can be created from a string of flip-flops.

**Table 2-1. Summary of The Action
of The Counter Circuit Shown in Fig. 2-13.**

Clock Pulse	Outputs				
	D	C	B	A	
0	0	0	0	0	
1	0	0	0	1	
2	0	0	1	0	
3	0	0	1	1	
4	0	1	0	0	
5	0	1	0	1	
6	0	1	1	0	
7	0	1	1	1	
8	1	0	0	0	
9	1	0	0	1	
10	1	0	1	0	
11	1	0	1	1	
12	1	1	0	0	
13	1	1	0	1	
14	1	1	1	0	
15	1	1	1	1	
16	0	0	0	0	(Counter resets)
17	0	0	0	1	
18	0	0	1	0	
19	0	0	1	1	
20	0	1	0	0	

and so forth . . .

5 stages	modulo-32
6 stages	modulo-64
7 stages	modulo-128
8 stages	modulo-256

and so forth.

What if we need a counter with a modulo that is not a power of two? For example, let's say we need a counter with a modulo of six. The desired count pattern would look like this:

000
001
010
011
100
101

000
001
010

and so on.

Most flip-flops have a clear (or R or RESET input that can force the output back to logic 0. By using some digital gates, we can force the flip-flops to clear after a specific count value has been reached.

We start out with a simple counter with a modulo equal to the next higher power of two. In our example (six), we need a modulo-eight (three stage) counter, as shown in Fig. 2-14. Ordinarily, the output count pattern of this circuit will look like this:

000
001
010
011
100
101
110
111
000
001
010

and so on.

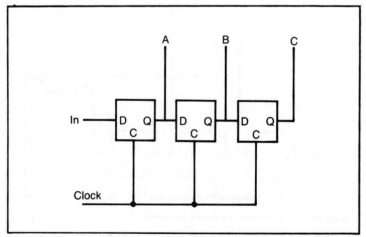

Fig. 2-14. A modulo-eight counter is made from three flip-flop stages.

For our modulo-six counter we want the count sequence to reset to 000 after 101. That is:

$$A = 1$$
$$B = 0$$
$$C = 1$$

We can get the result we want by ANDing together outputs A and C and feeding this signal back to the RESET input(s), as illustrated in Fig. 2-15. Note that output B doesn't matter in the gating, since the count of 111 can never be reached. If A and C are 1's, B must be a 0. By using the proper combination of gates, literally any whole number modulo can be achieved.

In most practical circuits, you won't have to work with individual flip-flop stages. Full counter circuits are available in IC form.

Some IC counters are designed to count out in a somewhat different manner than described here. As an example, we will consider the CD4017 counter/divider chip, which is a CMOS device. The pinout diagram for this IC is shown in Fig. 2-16.

This IC has ten outputs numbered from 0 to 9. On any specific count, only one of the inputs is high (logic 1), and the other nine will be low (logic 0). We can simulate this approach with flip-flops and gates, as illustrated in Fig. 2-17. Only one output can be a 1 at any time.

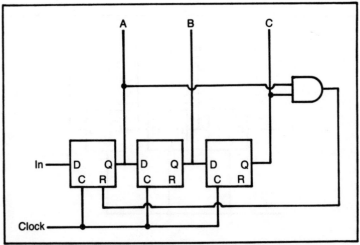

Fig. 2-15. A modulo-six counter resets itself after a count of five.

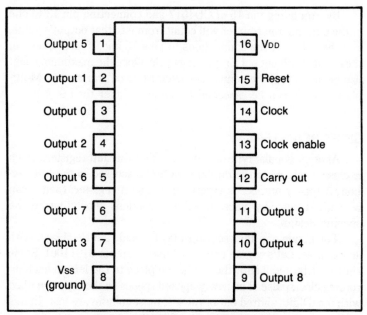

Fig. 2-16. The CD4017 is a dedicated counter/divider chip.

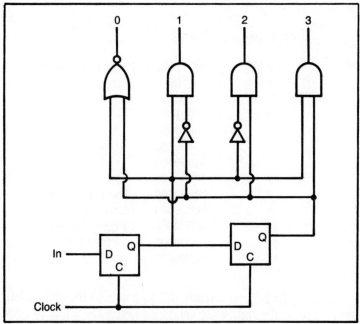

Fig. 2-17. This circuit simulates the operation of the CD4017.

83

By grounding pin 15 of CD4017 and connecting pin 13 to one of the outputs, the counter will count from 0 to that output's value, and then stop. If the connections to pins 13 and 15 are reversed, the counter will put out a repeating cycle. Once the maximum count has been passed, the count goes back to 0 and starts over. Multiple CD4017s can be cascaded for counts higher than 9.

SHIFT REGISTERS

Another popular type of digital circuit is the shift register, which is closely related to the digital counters discussed in the last section. A binary number is entered into a shift register, then it can be shifted place-by-place in either direction, depending on the specific design.

The action of a shift register may be made a little clearer with an example. Let's say we enter the binary number 01011001. Some shift registers will shift the digits one place to the left on each incoming clock pulse. The newly opened spaces on the right are filled with 0's. Digits shifted out of the left-most column are lost. In this case, the shift sequence will look like this:

Clock Pulse #	Number	
0	01011001	(original number)
1	10110010	
2	01100100	
3	11001000	
4	10010000	
5	00100000	
6	01000000	
7	10000000	
8	00000000	(The register is
9	00000000	cleared, so no
10	00000000	further changes
11	00000000	will take place.)
12	00000000	

Other shift register circuits will loop around the exiting left-most digit to the right-most column, causing the digits to cycle through each position, like this:

Clock Pulse #	Number	
0	01011001	(original number)
1	10110010	
2	01100101	
3	11001010	
4	10010101	
5	00101011	
6	01010110	
7	10101100	
8	01011001	(The original
9	10110010	number again.)
10	01100101	
11	11001010	
12	10010101	

In this case, the pattern will be repeated indefinitely.

There are also shift register circuits which shift the digits to the right instead of the left. For example, a shift to the right and clear shift register would exhibit the following pattern:

Clock Pulse #	Number	
0	01011001	(original number)
1	00101100	
2	00010110	
3	00001011	
4	00000101	
5	00000010	
6	00000001	
7	00000000	
8	00000000	(The shift
9	00000000	register is
10	00000000	now cleared.)
11	00000000	
12	00000000	

Finally, for a shift register with a right shift and recycle:

Clock Pulse #	Number	
0	01011001	(original number)

Clock Pulse #	Number	
1	10101100	
2	01010110	
3	00101011	
4	10010101	
5	11001010	
6	01100101	
7	10110010	
8	01011001	(The original
9	10101100	number again.)
10	01010110	
11	00101011	
12	10010101	

Once again, this pattern will repeat indefinitely.

The digits may be entered or read out of the shift register either serially (one digit at a time) or parallelly (all digits simultaneously), depending on the design of the circuit. There are four possible combinations:

- ☐ SISO   Serial In/Serial Out
- ☐ SIPO   Serial In/Parallel Out
- ☐ PISO   Parallel In/Serial Out
- ☐ PIPO   Parallel In/Parallel Out

Shift register applications include short term memories, digital delays, and mathematical operators. A left shift performs binary multiplication, and a shift right performs binary division.

MULTIPLEXERS AND DEMULTIPLEXERS

In some complex digital systems we will need one signal at a given point in the circuit part of the time, but other signals will be needed at other times. To build such a system, we obviously need some way to select between two or more possible inputs. A specialized digital subcircuit that has been developed for just this purpose is a *multiplexer*, or MUX for short.

Figure 2-18 shows how a simple multiplexer can be made from several NAND gates. This circuit has four data inputs (1 through 4), and two control inputs (A and B). The logic signals fed to the control inputs determine which of the data input signals will reach the output. Only one of the data inputs is active at any one time.

86

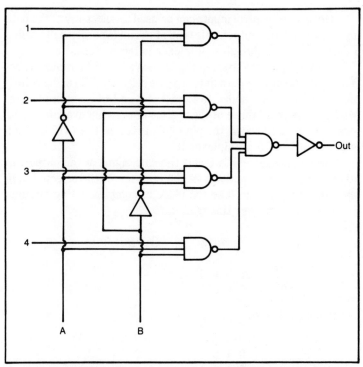

Fig. 2-18. The simple multiplexer can be constructed from several NAND gates.

The truth table for this circuit is as follows:

Control Inputs A B		Data Inputs 1 2 3 4				Output
0	0	0	x	x	x	0
0	0	1	x	x	x	1
0	1	x	0	x	x	0
0	1	x	1	x	x	1
1	0	x	x	0	x	0
1	0	x	x	1	x	1
1	1	x	x	x	0	0
1	1	x	x	x	1	1

where "x" represents "don't care." Notice how only one of the data input lines is of significance for any combination of values at the control inputs (A and B).

Because the control inputs can be used to select any of the data inputs to reach the output, this type of circuit is occasionally called a data selector, although multiplexer is the preferred name.

The multiplexer shown in Fig. 2-18 is a 1-of-4 multiplexer, because any one of four data lines may be selected. The same principle is commonly expanded to form 1-of-8 or 1-of-16 multiplexers. Multiplexers in all three of these sizes are readily available in IC form. Figure 2-19 shows the pinout diagram for the 74150, which is a typical 1-of-16 multiplexer IC.

Some multiplexer ICs invert the data signal at the output. In other words, the output will be the opposite of the selected data line. Multiplexers can take the place of complex gating circuits. For example, consider this truth table:

Inputs	Output
A B C D	
0 0 0 0	0
0 0 0 1	0
0 0 1 0	1
0 0 1 1	0
0 1 0 0	0
0 1 0 1	1
0 1 1 0	1
0 1 1 1	0
1 0 0 0	0
1 0 0 1	1
1 0 1 0	1
1 0 1 1	1
1 1 0 0	0
1 1 0 1	0
1 1 1 0	1
1 1 1 1	0

It would be inconvenient at best to generate this truth table with simple gates. Figure 2-20 shows how this truth table may be generated by a 74150 1-of-16 multiplexer IC.

A 1-of-16 multiplexer can generate 2^{16} different truth tables. In other words, there are 65,536 possible combinations of inputs and outputs.

A multiplexer can also come in very handy when unusual counting sequences are required. For example, combining the circuit of

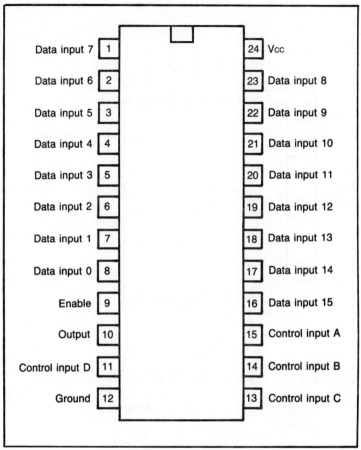

Fig. 2-19. The 74150 is a dedicated 1-of-16 multiplexer chip.

Fig. 2-20 with a four-stage modulo-sixteen counter, as shown in Fig. 2-21 would generate the following output sequence:

Clock Pulse #	Counter Outputs	Output
0	0000	0
1	0001	0
2	0010	1
3	0011	0
4	0100	0
5	0101	1

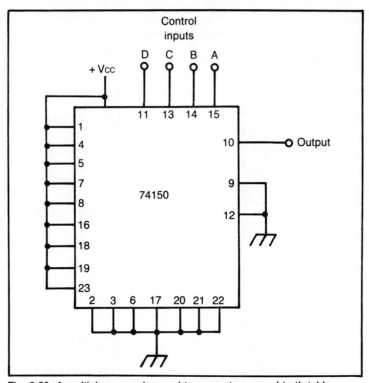

Fig. 2-20. A multiplexer can be used to generate unusual truth tables.

Clock Pulse #	Counter Outputs	Output	
6	0110	1	
7	0111	0	
8	1000	0	
9	1001	1	
10	1010	1	
11	1011	1	
12	1100	0	
13	1101	0	
14	1110	1	
15	1111	0	
16	0000	0	(The pattern
17	0001	0	repeats.)
18	0010	1	
19	0011	0	
20	0100	0	

and so on. Any pattern of binary digits can easily be generated using this method. Multiplexers are also used for keyboard scanning applications.

The opposite of a multiplexer is a *demultiplexer* of DEMUX. The control inputs of a demultiplexer determine which of several output lines will be activated by the single data input line. A typical demultiplexer IC is the 74154 1-of-16 demultiplexer, which is illustrated in Fig. 2-22.

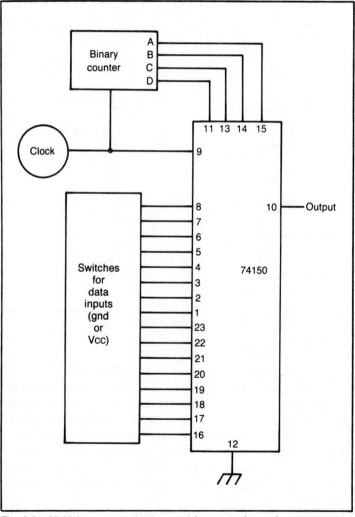

Fig. 2-21. Multiplexers can also be used for unusual counting sequences.

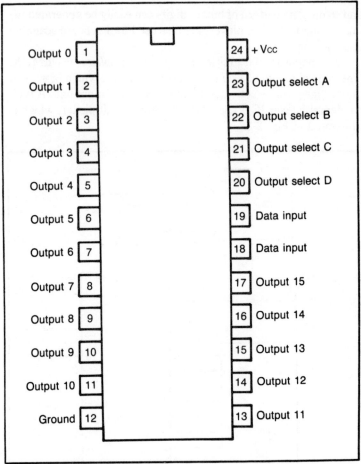

Output 0 — 1	24 — + Vcc
Output 1 — 2	23 — Output select A
Output 2 — 3	22 — Output select B
Output 3 — 4	21 — Output select C
Output 4 — 5	20 — Output select D
Output 5 — 6	19 — Data input
Output 6 — 7	18 — Data input
Output 7 — 8	17 — Output 15
Output 8 — 9	16 — Output 14
Output 9 — 10	15 — Output 13
Output 10 — 11	14 — Output 12
Ground — 12	13 — Output 11

Fig. 2-22. The 74154 is a 1-of-16 demultiplexer IC.

DISPLAY DRIVERS

Many digital devices use seven-segment LED or LCD displays as output devices. Obviously, some method of converting the binary signals into the appropriate lit displays is necessary. Individual gates may be used, but this tends to increase total circuit bulk and cost. Because this is such a common requirement in digital electronics, a number of display driver ICs have been made available.

A typical example is the CD4511 BCD to 7-Segment Latch/Decoder/Driver IC, which is illustrated in Fig. 2-23. As the rather lengthy name indicates, this chip fills a number of related functions. Basically it accepts a four digit BCD number and puts an output signal on the appropriate pins to light the desired display segments.

BILATERAL SWITCHES

It is often handy to have a digitally controlled switch. That is, a switch that may be open or closed, depending on the logic signal from another part of the circuit. This function can conceivably be served with a gating network, but this can often be awkward, bulky, and expensive. As you've probably anticipated, IC manufacturers have met this need with specialized chips.

Figure 2-24 shows the pinout diagram and functional internal structure of the CD4066 quad bilateral switch. This CMOS chip consists of four digitally controlled switches. The switches are called bilateral because they have no fixed polarity.

Digital switch units like the CD4066 are often used in hybrid circuits that use both digital and analog devices. Analog components such as resistors or capacitors may be selected or programmed via digital signals. Digital-to-analog signal conversion is one obvious application for this type of device.

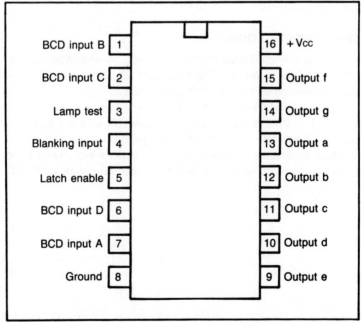

Fig. 2-23. Many output display interfacing tasks can be accomplished with the CD4511 BCD to seven-segment latch/decoder/driver IC.

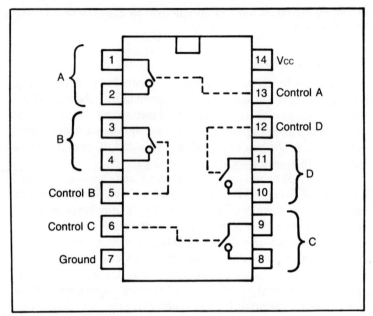

Fig. 2-24. The CD4066 quad bilateral switch IC contains four digitally controllable analog switches.

THREE-STATE LOGIC

We have been discussing two state logic. A somewhat similar concept is *three-state logic*. This technique can also be used for digitally controlled switching of digital signals.

Most digital circuits, of course, have two possible output conditions—either the output is a low voltage (0), or it is a high voltage (1). Three-state systems add a third possible output state. This is a high impedance condition, which is neither a logic 0 or a logic 1, and appears to the circuit as the absence of any signal at all.

Chapter 3

The CPU

T HE HEART OF ANY MICROCOMPUTER CIRCUIT IS THE CPU, or *Central Processing Unit*. This is the part of the computer that does the "thinking." CPUs are sometimes called *microprocessors*. For our purposes, the two terms are interchangeable.

The most important feature of a CPU is its programmability. That is, it can be instructed to perform different operations at different times. In Chapter 2, we saw how a multiplexer could be "programmed" to simulate a complex gating circuit. CPUs carry this concept much further.

A CPU could be made up from individual gating circuits. (This was done for the first computers, which were room-filling monsters.) Such a design would be extremely complicated, expensive, and bulky. Fortunately CPUs are available in relatively inexpensive IC form. This is what makes the kind of projects described in this book practical. Some CPUs can now be bought in single quantities for under $10. Therefore, it is reasonable to tie up a computer system for a single, dedicated purpose.

COMMANDS AND DATA

A CPU "understands" a number of commands. These are in binary form. For example, 01001101 or 11101001. Each binary number has a specific meaning for the CPU. A series of commands to perform a specific task is called a program. If you program the

CPU directly, using the binary number commands, this is called machine-language programming.

Translation programs are available to allow the user to program the CPU with a more convenient set of commands. Assembly language replaces each binary number command with an easy to remember mnemonic. For instance, ADD A,B for adding values A and B, instead of 10011100. For higher level languages, such as BASIC or Pascal, each user-entered command may correspond to several binary language commands in sequence. A special program is used to convert the commands entered by the user into the binary form understandable by the CPU.

COMPONENTS OF A COMPUTER

Figure 3-1 shows the basic structure of a typical computer circuit. Two or more of these stages may be included on a single IC, but for now we will consider them as separate entities. There are essentially four sections to a computer:

- ☐ Processor (CPU)
- ☐ Memory
- ☐ Input Port
- ☐ Output Port

The processor does the actual computing. The memory stores the program commands and data used in executing the program. The input and output ports allow the computer to communicate with the outside world (anything that is not an integral part of the computer itself). The input port permits data from some external device to be fed into the computer, and the output port lets the computer feed its results out to some external device. In a typical microcomputer, the keyboard is connected to the input port, and the display screen is connected to the output port.

Communication between the various internal sections of the computer are accomplished via buses. These are digital signal lines that can carry coded binary data. The binary data may represent numerical values, alphanumeric characters, or machine-language commands. The only difference is in how the CPU is instructed to interpret the binary information.

The data bus connects the processor section to everything else. The data bus goes from the CPU to the memory, the input port, and the output port. Data flows from the input port to the CPU,

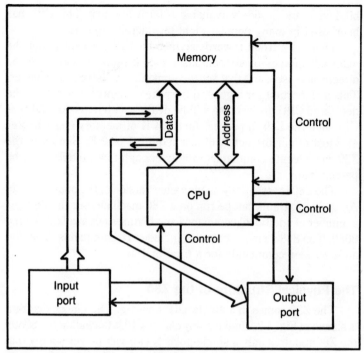

Fig. 3-1. Most practical computers include these stages.

from the CPU to the output port, or in either direction between the memory and the CPU. The CPU determines which piece of data goes where.

The address bus goes from the CPU to the memory. The data on this bus determines which portion of the memory the processor is using. The concept is simple enough if you think that the CPU needs to know the address of whatever it is looking for, just as you need to know the address to find a friend's home.

The third bus is used for system control and synchronization. The signals on this bus keep the various sections of the computer functioning simultaneously. For example, the input port uses this bus to let the CPU know there is some incoming data available from the external input device.

THE Z80

In the projects described in this book we will be working with the Z80 CPU chip. Certainly other CPUs could be used, but I feel the Z80 is probably the best choice. It is a reasonably powerful eight-bit device, and is widely available at fairly low cost. This CPU has been used in many popular eight-bit microcomputers.

There is a trend towards sixteen-bit CPUs recently, but the main advantages of sixteen-bits are that more memory can be directly accessed, and that some commands can be executed faster. This is important for a general-purpose computer, but not for the dedicated CPU projects we will be dealing with here. An eight-bit CPU like the Z80 can access up to 64 K of memory (see Chapter 4). Most of our projects will just require 1 or 2 K. Similarly, the Z80 can execute commands rapidly enough that no delay will be perceptible.

The Z80 is essentially an upgraded version of the popular 8080. All 8080 programs can be run on a Z80 machine, but the Z80 has a number of additional commands and features not available on the 8080. The 8080's instruction set includes 78 commands. The Z80 adds 80 new commands for a total of 158.

The Physical Structure of the Z80

The Z80 comes in a 40-pin DIP housing. The pinout diagram is shown in Fig. 3-2. Unlike many earlier CPUs (including the 8080), the Z80 requires only a single-polarity + 5-volt power supply (pin #11) and only a single-phase clock (pin #6). (The ground connection is made to pin #29.) Earlier CPUs often required 2 or 3 (or more) supply voltages, often dual polarity, and complicated clock circuits. The Z80 is far, far simpler to use.

The Z80 is designed to run at a clock speed of 2.5 MHz. This is about 25% faster than for the 8080. Some Z80s can be run at even higher clock rates, up to 4 MHz. For our purposes here, the boosted speed wouldn't be much of a noticeable improvement, so any standard Z80 may be used in the projects. As Fig. 3-2 shows, the Z80 has a 16-line address bus, labelled A0 to A15:

Address Line	Pin #
A0	30
A1	31
A2	32
A3	33
A4	34
A5	35
A6	36
A7	37

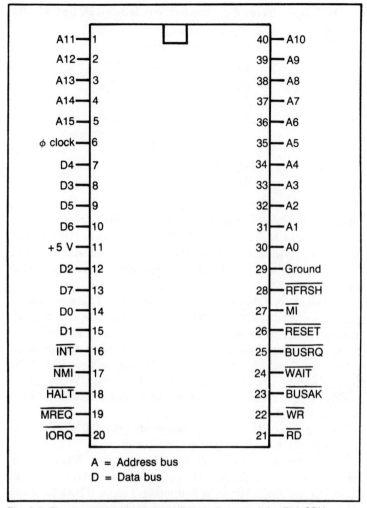

Fig. 3-2. The projects in this book will be built around the Z80 CPU.

Address Line	Pin #
A8	38
A9	39
A10	40
A11	1
A12	2
A13	3
A14	4
A15	5

The Z80 also has an eight line data bus, labelled D0 through D7:

Bus Line	Pin #
D0	14
D1	15
D2	12
D3	8
D4	7
D5	9
D6	10
D7	13

The other pins serve various specific functions.

RESET (pin #26) initializes the Z80. This means the program counter, along with the I and R registers are zeroed. All interrupts are disabled. The RESET function is activated by feeding a logic 0 into pin #26.

BUSRQ at pin #25 stands for "BUS ReQuest." This input allows an external device to request control of the address and data buses and control signals by inputting a logic 0 on this line. The Z80 relinquishes this control by bringing output BUSAK (pin #23) (BUS ACKnowledge) low. This changeover of control is done for DMA (*Direct Memory Access*) and similar special functions. When the external device is done, it puts a 1 on the BUSRQ line, and the CPU resumes control.

Output signal MI (pin #27) goes low when the Z80 is in the operation code fetch cycle of instruction execution.

IORQ (pin #20) stands for *Input/Output ReQuest*. When this pin goes low, it indicates that the address bus holds a valid I/O address for an I/O read (input) or write (output) operation. If both IORQ and MI are low, an interrupt acknowledge cycle is in progress.

This input labelled INT (pin #16) is an interrupt request line. In order for the interrupt to be acknowledged by the Z80, the interrupt enable flag (IFF) must be enabled (this is done under software control), and BUSRQ must be high. If the interrupt is activated, IORQ goes low during the MI signal to indicate an interrupt acknowledge to the external I/O device requesting the interrupt.

A second interrupt request line is NMI at pin #17. Perhaps this should be called an interrupt demand, rather than request, because this input cannot be disabled (masked). NMI stands for *nonmaskable Interrupt*. When this line is activated (with a logic zero), the CPU jumps to a specific memory location (&H0066). (&H before a number indicates the value is given in hexidecimal—see Chapter 2.)

MREQ (pin #19), RD (pin #21), and WR (pin #22) are three-state outputs. The names stand for *Memory REQuest, ReaD*, and *WRite*, respectively. The address bus holds a valid address for memory access when MREQ and either RD or WR are low.

When a MREQ signal is output to the external memory circuitry, the memory's logic circuits put a 0 on the WAIT input (pin #24) until the memory is finished. This is necessary because some memory devices may operate at a slower rate than the CPU.

RFRSH (pin #28) is used for memory refresh operations. This output lets the external memory circuit know that the contents of the R register are now on the address bus. A refresh read of dynamic memory (see Chapter 4) can now be done via the MREQ signal.

The HALT output (pin #18) is software activated. When the Z80 executes a HALT instruction, this pin goes low. An NMI, I/O interrupt, or control panel action must occur before normal operation can resume. Typically HALTs are used to wait for an interrupt, stop execution at the end of the program, or to indicate an error condition.

The internal structure of the Z80 is illustrated in Fig. 3-3.

Timing Signals

Each instruction requires a finite amount of time to be executed. Different types of instructions require different times. Execution times are measured in machine cycles (M), each made up of several clock cycles.

The first machine cycle (MI) is always an operation code fetch and decode. During this time period, the CPU gets the next instruction from external memory, and determines what it means.

The various instructions used in the Z80 can take anywhere from 4 cycles (1.6 μs) to 20 cycles (8 μs). Of course, the execution times would be lengthened if the CPU was interfaced with a slower external memory device.

Registers

A CPU includes several registers. These are built-in memory locations used for addressing, manipulating data, and loading commands. All CPUs have a program counter register. This is where the next address to be accessed in the external memory is held.

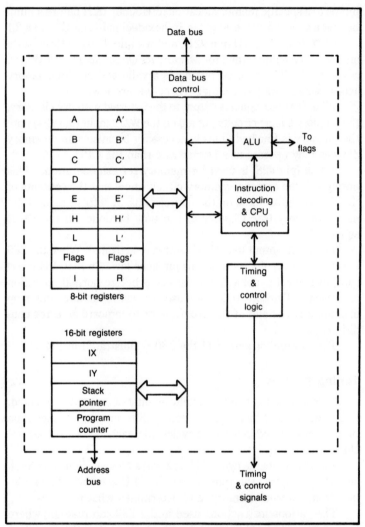

Fig. 3-3. This is a simplified block diagram of the Z80 microprocessor.

Without this register the computer would not be able to "keep its place" in the program. It would quickly become hopelessly lost.

The Z80 has 22 internal registers. Most of them (18) hold eight bits each. The eight-bit registers are names:

A (accumulator)
A'

B
B'
C
C'
D
D'
H
H'
L
L'
Flags
Flags'
I (Interrupt Vector)
R (Memory Refresh)

Notice that most of the eight-bit registers are duplicated (as indicated by the prime mark). The functions of the various registers will be discussed shortly.

An eight-bit register can store any one of 256 different values (from 0 to 255). Two eight-bit registers can be combined to act as a sixteen-bit register.

The Z80 also has four sixteen-bit registers. These are:

☐ IX Index Register
☐ IY Index Register
☐ Stack Pointer
☐ Program Counter

A sixteen-bit register can store any of 65,536 values (from 0 to 65,535). All of the registers in the Z80, except the Interrupt Vector and the Memory Refresh, may be utilized by the programmer.

The Program Counter, of course, is used to hold the current address in external memory. Because this is a sixteen-bit register, 65,536 (64K) memory location may be directly addressed by the Z80. This bus is brought out to the sixteen address bus pins (30 - 40, 1 - 5).

The Stack Pointer is similar to the Program Counter. It is used to locate a piece of data anywhere in external memory (65,536 possible locations). This register also uses the address bus pins. The "Stack" is a section of memory used to temporarily store variables (data) during the program. The Stack is also used to "remember" the previous value of the Program Counter during subroutines, and other register values during interrupt routines.

The CPU can be programmed to notice when certain conditions exist, and interrupt the program to perform a special interrupt routine (which may be located anywhere within the external memory). When the interrupt routine is completed, the main program will be resumed. Interrupts will be discussed in more detail later on. The eight most significant bits of an interrupt vector address are loaded into register I (Interrupt Page Register). The eight least significant bits of the address are supplied by the interrupting input device.

Register R is used for Memory Refresh of dynamic external RAM (memory). Dynamic RAM will forget everything if it is not periodically refreshed. Register R allows the Z80 to do this automatically, so the user doesn't have to worry much about it. This register uses seven bits to count every instruction fetch. Its contents (from 0 to 127) are transmitted through the seven least significant address bus lines while the current instruction is being decoded. External memory logic is used to complete the refreshing process.

The two index registers (IX and IY) allow the CPU to perform indexed type instructions. These instructions are primarily used for accessing data tables in memory.

Register A is a general-purpose register. That is, its current function is determined by the specific program. This register is also known as the accumulator. It is the primary register used to hold the results of arithmetic and logic operations in the Z80.

The Z80 has several other general-purpose registers (B, C, D, E, H, and L) that can be used along with register A for temporary storage of various values throughout the program. These additional general-purpose registers can be combined in pairs to create a 16-bit register if required. The pair arrangements are as follows:

B—C
D—E
H—L

A complete second set of general-purpose arrays is also available in the Z80 (A', B', C', D', E', H', and L'). A single instruction can be used to switch between the two sets of registers. This is particularly useful to increase speed during interrupt operations. The temporary results can be stored in the second set of registers rather than external memory. This allows the CPU to retrieve these values faster.

The FLAGS register (sometimes called F) is a set of eight yes/no condition indicators. The flag bits can be checked by the CPU to determine various effects of arithmetic and logic operations. The eight flags are:

☐ Bit #0	C	Carry Flag	This flag indicates whether or not an overflow occurred in the last arithmetic operation. It is like a mathematical carry.
☐ Bit #1	N	Subtract Flag	This flag is used internally for BCD subtract operations. It is not used by the programmer.
☐ Bit #2	P/V	Parity/Over-flow Flag	This flag has a dual purpose. It is used to check parity for logic operations or overflow for arithmetic operations.
☐ Bit #3	X		Not used.
☐ Bit #4	H	Half-Carry Flag	This flag is used internally for BCD operations. It is not used by the programmer.
☐ Bit #5	X		Not used.
☐ Bit #6	Z	Zero Flag	This flag is set (1) if the result is zero, otherwise it is reset (0).
☐ Bit #7	S	Sign Flag	This flag is set (1) if the result is negative, otherwise it is reset (0).

A second FLAGS register (FLAGS′ or F′) is provided for use with the primed set of general purpose registers.

The Instruction Set

The power of any CPU is in its instruction set. The instruction set is simply all the binary commands the CPU can understand and execute. A CPU that understood only ten or so commands could theoretically be programmed to do anything a more powerful CPU could do, but the programming would be awkward and tedious and take up an unnecessary amount of memory space.

The Z80's instruction set is made up of 158 commands, which is quite a powerful collection. For convenience, the commands can be divided into eight basic categories:

☐ Arithmetic and Logical
☐ Bit Manipulation
☐ Block Transfer and Search
☐ CPU Control
☐ Input/Output
☐ Jump, Call and Return
☐ Load and Exchange
☐ Rotate and Shift

The Arithmetic and Logical category should be fairly self-explanatory. This category includes instructions for performing mathematical operations such as add, subtract, and multiply, and for performing logical operations such as AND, OR, and NOT.

These logical operations are performed on a bit-by-bit basis for the contents of two registers. For example:

$$A = 10100101$$
$$B = 11001001$$
$$A \text{ AND } B = 10000001$$
$$A \text{ OR } B = 11101101$$
$$A \text{ XOR } B = 01101100$$

The Z80 always places the results of its arithmetic and logical operations into register A. Any previous contents of this register will be lost unless they have previously been stored elsewhere (in another register, or in external memory).

The Z80 has several special instructions for performing mathematical operations directly on BCD values, eliminating several steps in many applications.

The Z80's bit manipulation instructions allow the programmer to check or change the value of any individual bit in a number stored in one of the registers or external memory. This class of commands was not included in the 8080's instruction set.

The Block Transfer and Search commands are also unique. Such commands are not supported on most other CPUs. The functions can be accomplished with any computer, of course, but usually they take many separate instructions. On the Z80 a single command can be used to transfer a block of data from one memory location to another, or to search a block of memory for a specified character.

The CPU Control category is sort of a miscellaneous catchall for several commands that control the operation of the CPU itself. This category includes HALT and enable/disable instructions. There are also three instructions to set various interrupt modes, and a "no-operation" instruction.

The commands in the Input/Output category control the interaction between the CPU and external I/O devices. Data may be transferred between the CPU and an external device either one bit at a time, or one byte (8 bits) at a time. Block transfers of data can also be accomplished with I/O devices.

The JUMP, CALL, and RETURN commands are used for unconditional and conditional branches to other sections of the program (rather than the next consecutive instruction according to the Program Counter). A conditional jump is made only if the data being examined has certain characteristics. For example, a conditional jump might be made if the contents of register A are greater than the contents of register B.

This class of commands also includes instructions for using program subroutines. A subroutine is a section of a program that may be called from any point within the main program. When the subroutine is completed, the main program is resumed from where it left off.

Load and Exchange instructions are used to transfer data between the CPU's internal registers, or between registers and external memory. Data is moved eight or sixteen bits at a time.

Finally, the Rotate and Shift commands perform operations similar to the shift register circuits described in Chapter 2. Arithmetical and logical shifts are supported by the Z80. Any CPU register or memory location may be shifted. The value to be shifted does not necessarily have to be in the accumulator (register A). The

Z80 even includes two instructions for rotating BCD digits.

Addressing Modes

The Z80 can use several different addressing modes to find stored data. Each has its advantages in different programming applications. The nine addressing modes of the Z80 are:

- ☐ Register Addressing
- ☐ Implied Addressing
- ☐ Register Indirect Addressing
- ☐ Extended Addressing
- ☐ Immediate Extended Addressing
- ☐ Modified Page Zero Addressing
- ☐ Relative Addressing
- ☐ Indexed Addressing

All of these addressing modes are carried over from the 8080 except for Relative Addressing and Indexed Addressing.

The simplest addressing mode is Register Addressing. In this mode one of the CPU's internal registers is being addressed. The appropriate register name is included in the instruction itself. For example, INC B tells the CPU to increment (add one to) the value currently stored in register B.

Implied Addressing is similar, except the appropriate register is not specifically mentioned in the instruction. It is implied. For example, the command ADD B tells the CPU to add the contents of register B to the contents of register A, and store the result in register A, even though register A is not mentioned in the command. Its use is implied, since this register is normally used in all arithmetic and logic operations.

In Register Indirect Addressing, the value held in the specified register pair (16 bits) identifies a specific location in external memory. Usually the HL pair is used for this function, but the BC or DE pairs may also be used.

Extended Addressing might be called Direct External Addressing. The full instruction is made up of three bytes. The first byte is the actual command code. The other two bytes are the actual memory address desired. For example, if the value in the second and third bytes is the binary equivalent of 375, the 375th memory location will be addressed.

In the Immediate Addressing mode, external memory and the

CPU registers are ignored. An eight-bit (one byte) value is entered as part of the instruction. This value is used as the operand of the required operation.

Extended Immediate Addressing is similar to the Immediate Addressing mode. The difference is that in this mode, a 16-bit (two byte) immediate value is entered along with the instruction code.

Modified Page Zero Addressing is used to call a commonly used subroutine or interrupt routine processing for multi-interrupt capability. The command is called a restart, and transfers the program pointer to a page 0 location. Page 0 is defined as memory locations 0 through FF_{16} (255_{10}). The advantage here is that only a single byte is required for the CALL function. This reduces the amount of memory consumed by the program, and speeds up the execution.

The seven addressing modes described so far were also included in the 8080. Relative Addressing is a new mode added to the Z80's instruction set. This mode is used only for jump type instructions. A two-byte instruction is used. The first byte is the actual command code. The second byte is an eight bit signed displacement value from -128 to $+127$. A Relative Addressing command can cause the program pointer to jump back up to -126 locations or forward up to $+129$ locations from its current position. Once again the advantage is reducing the memory space consumed by the program, and to speed up the execution of the instruction.

Indexed Addressing was another new feature for the Z80, which was not part of the 8080's instruction set. In this addressing mode, the contents of one of the two index registers (IX or IY) is added to an eight-bit displacement value included in the instruction. This mode is basically an expanded form of the Relative Addressing mode.

Interrupt Processing

One of the most important features determining the power of a CPU is its interrupt processing capabilities. Interrupts allow the CPU to respond to external conditions and alter its programming accordingly. The Z80 has strong interrupt processing capabilities.

Two interrupt inputs are included on the Z80 chip—INT and NMI. INT is the standard interrupt from an external I/O device. NMI is used for a Nonmaskable Interrupt. Nonmaskable simply means that this interrupt line cannot be disabled by software. If a logic 0 is applied to this pin, the CPU will always respond to the interruption. This type of interrupt should be used for critical conditions that should be acted upon immediately, such as system reset, or power failure.

When a Nonmaskable Interrupt is triggered (logic 0), the Z80 will execute a RESTART to memory location &H0066 (the &H prefix, remember, represents a hexadecimal value). The contents of the Program Counter are automatically saved by PUSHing the contents onto the Stack. (The NMI feature is not included on the earlier 8080.)

The standard INT type interrupt can be enabled (EI) or disabled (DI) via software commands. When disabled, an interrupt signal presented to the INT pin will be ignored.

Three interrupt modes are also software selectable:

- ☐ IM0
- ☐ IM1
- ☐ IM2

Of course, when the DI (disabled) command has been called, none of the interrupt modes can function.

The IM0 mode is the only interrupt mode that was available on the 8080. In the IM0 mode when a logic 0 is presented to INT, the CPU goes into an interrupt state. It signals the interrupting external I/O device via the IORQ and MI outputs. These signals tell the interrupting device that the CPU is ready for it. The current contents of the Program Counter are PUSHed onto the Stack. A RESTART instruction includes a three-bit value from 0 to 7. Depending on this value, control of the CPU will be automatically transferred to one of the following memory locations:

Binary Value	Decimal Value	Memory Location
000	0	&H00
001	1	&H08
010	2	&H10
011	3	&H18
100	4	&H20
101	5	&H28
110	6	&H30
111	7	&H38

These eight memory locations are closely spaced (only eight bytes apart). Generally, they will include instructions for JUMPs to other areas of memory.

At the end of the interrupt routine, a return (RET) instruction should be used to POP the address of the interrupted instruction from the Stack to the Program Counter, and the CPU picks up where it left off. As you can see, several different interrupt routines may easily be set up to respond appropriately to various interrupting I/O devices.

The IM1 mode functions similarly to the NM1 input, except it can be software enabled. When an interrupt is received in this mode, the Program Counter's contents are PUSHed onto the Stack, and a RESTART is executed. Program control jumps to &H38. The chief advantage of this mode is that no external hardware is required to jam the RESTART instruction onto the data bus at the proper time. The disadvantage is that only a single interrupt handling routine can be set up.

The third interrupt mode (IM2) is extremely powerful. Up to 128 different interrupt levels can be defined in this mode. A table of addresses for the various interrupt processing routines can be stored anywhere in memory. The most significant eight bits of the starting address for this table are previously stored in register 1. In the IM2 mode, the IORQ and MI outputs respond in the same way as in mode IM0. The interrupting I/O device then transmits an eight-bit value representing the lower eight bits of the interrupt vector. This value is combined with register I to complete the interrupt table address. CPU control is transferred to the appropriate address in the table for the specific device currently interrupting.

The last bit of the device number must always be 0. This is because each stored address in the table takes up two bytes, so the odd bytes should be skipped. This leaves 128 possible values that can be input by the interrupting device.

External logic should be used to establish the priority of the various external devices to ensure that only one interrupt can occur at any one time.

Chapter 4

Semiconductor Memory

ANY COMPUTER REQUIRES SOME KIND OF MEMORY CIRCUIT to function. Memory circuits store binary numbers in electrical form. The stored numbers may represent program commands (in machine language), numerical data, or alphanumerical characters.

The simplest digital memory circuit is the flip-flop (see Chapter 2). It can "remember" one bit (binary digit) indefinitely, until it is triggered into the opposite state, or power is interrupted. A binary word or byte can be stored in a shift register.

Unfortunately, these devices are very limited as memory circuits in a computer. Unless the amount of data to be stored is extremely small, a collection of flip-flops or shift registers will probably be completely inadequate for the task. Fortunately, specialized digital circuits, called memories, have been developed. Many different types and sizes of digital memory circuits are widely available in IC form. For our purposes, memory devices can be divided into two broad classes:

☐ RAM
☐ ROM

RAM (*Random Access Memory*) can be read from or written to. That is, the CPU can examine or change the stored data.

ROM (*Read Only Memory*), on the other hand, can only be read from. It cannot be written to. The CPU can examine data stored in ROM, but it cannot alter it in any way. Within each of these broad categories, there are several variations.

RAM

RAM is short for *Random Access Memory*. This name indicates that any specific location in the memory can be contacted without stepping through any other locations. This permits very fast exchange of data between memory and the CPU.

A shift register, on the other hand, is an example of a sequential memory. For instance, let's say we need to know the logic state of bit number 5 in an eight-stage SISO shift register. Before we can look at bit 5, we have to step through bits 1, 2, 3, and 4. Obviously, this will take some finite amount of time. When dealing with thousands of bits of data, the disadvantages of sequential memory becomes obvious.

However, in some cases sequential memory still has its uses. Most microcomputers, especially low cost models, can store programs and data on cassette tapes for later use. All data on the tape must be accessed sequentially. It is not as convenient as the more random access floppy disc, but it is considerably cheaper and mechanically simpler. (Floppy discs are not entirely random access, but they come reasonably close.)

A random access memory assigns a unique address to each individual memory location, with each location holding one piece of memory (generally either one bit or one byte). This type of memory can be considered analogous to a post office box system. Any box (or memory location) can be uniquely defined by an address identifying its column and row. This concept is illustrated in Fig. 4-1. There is no need to go through any intermediate locations. If we know the address we can go directly to the desired location.

In a RAM we can either look at the value stored at a given address without changing it (read), or we can replace the old value with a new value (write). For this reason, RAM is occasionally called Read/Write Memory, or RWM. Some technicians feel this is a better name since ROM (discussed shortly) can also be randomly accessed. However, RAM is the established name in common usage.

There are two basic types of RAM depending on the circuitry used. They are called static RAM and dynamic RAM.

Static RAM

A static RAM is basically made up of a series of addressable

	A	B	C	D	
1	A1	B1	C1	D1	
2	A2	B2	C2	D2	
3	A3	B3	C3	D3	
4	A4	B4	C4	D4	

Fig. 4-1. Memory addressing can be thought of as a post office box system.

flip-flops. Data can be stored in a static RAM virtually indefinitely, unless the stored values are erased or changed, or the power supply is interrupted. A static RAM cannot store data without continuously applied power. A typical static memory cell using CMOS technology is illustrated in Fig. 4-2.

Static RAM retains stored data as long as power is supplied to the chip. CMOS devices usually have a special low-power mode. Only enough power is drawn to prevent the memory from being erased, but not enough to operate the entire chip for full READ/WRITE operations. Battery back-up can be used, because only 1 μA (0.000001 amp), or less, is drawn in the low-power mode. Essentially the battery life span is about the same as its unused shelf-life.

The internal structure of a typical static RAM IC is shown in Fig. 4-3. There are three primary sections:

☐ Memory cell array
☐ Address decoding
☐ I/O block

Each memory cell stores a single bit of data. The cells are arranged in an array of rows and columns. The address decoding circuitry determines the appropriate row and column positions (address) for each cell as it is called by the CPU. As long as a cell is unselected by the address decoder, its output is not connected to anything at all.

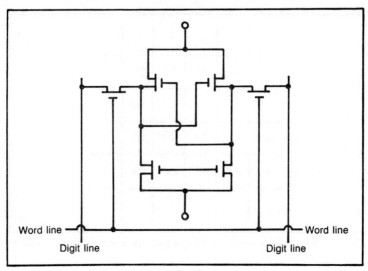

Fig. 4-2. This is a typical static RAM cell.

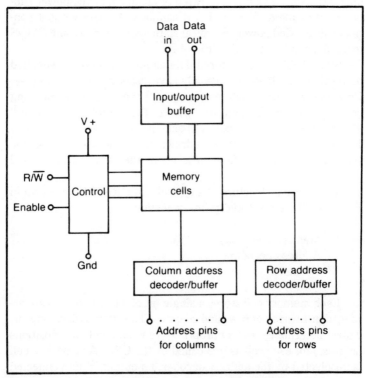

Fig. 4-3. A typical static RAM IC has three primary sections.

116

The I/O (Input/Output) block interfaces the memory cells with circuitry outside the IC. This section determines whether a READ or a WRITE operation is to be performed. An output buffer amplifier is also included in the I/O block to prevent unnecessary drain on the memory cell outputs. The output buffer is usually called the *sense amplifier.*

Most modern RAM ICs have a CHIP ENABLE pin. This allows a three-state output, which is an advantage when several memory devices share the same data.

Dynamic RAM

The other type of RAM is *dynamic RAM.* In a dynamic RAM circuit, each bit is stored in a capacitor (or, usually, the etched equivalent in an integrated circuit). A charged capacitor represents a logic 1, while a discharged capacitor would represent a logic 0.

A dynamic memory cell is much simpler than a static memory cell. Compare the dynamic memory cell circuit in Fig. 4-4 with the static memory cell circuit shown in Fig. 4-2. This means that, all other factors being equal, a dynamic memory of a given storage capability will tend to be much smaller and less expensive than a comparable static memory.

Dynamic RAM is certainly not without its disadvantages. The most important limitation is that no capacitor can hold a charge indefinitely. Eventually the charge will tend to leak off, erasing the stored data.

Electronically reading the value stored in a dynamic memory cell tends to recharge partially charged capacitors, refreshing the

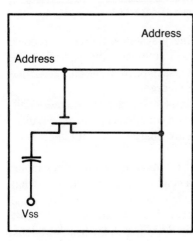

Fig. 4-4. Dynamic RAM cells are simpler than static RAM cells.

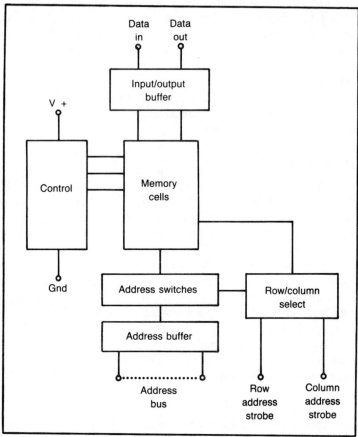

Fig. 4-5. Block diagram of a typical dynamic RAM IC.

memory. Practical dynamic memory systems, therefore, require special refreshing circuits that will automatically read all of the memory locations at regular intervals to prevent the charged capacitors from leaking off so much voltage.

A dynamic memory cell is simpler than a static memory cell, but dynamic memories require more complex supporting circuitry (to periodically refresh the capacitor charges), so a trade-off is inevitable.

Improvements in technology have allowed for more static memory cells to be contained within a single IC chip, and at somewhat lower manufacturing costs. At the moment, the balance of the scale tips somewhat towards static over dynamic memories in most general applications. But dynamic RAM is still far from obsolete.

A block diagram of a typical dynamic RAM IC is shown in Fig. 4-5. Most modern dynamic RAM ICs includes built-in refresh circuitry. The entire IC is refreshed during a READ operation, or a whole row can be refreshed by simply addressing it.

To save on the number of pins, the same pins are generally used for both row and column addressing. Two more control pins determine the current function. Row and column strobes indicate which address is currently on the bus.

Making The Choice

Static and dynamic RAM each have their own advantages and disadvantages. Static RAM requires simpler support circuitry, and is easier to use. The circuitry of the cells themselves is more complex. Fewer cells can be contained within an IC of a given size. Also, a static RAM chip will tend to cost more than a comparable dynamic RAM IC.

Because each dynamic RAM cell is really nothing more than a capacitor, dynamic RAMs tend to be relatively inexpensive and compact, compared to static RAMs. But the need for periodic refreshing of the stored data calls for more complex support circuitry design.

For the projects in this book, I have decided to concentrate on static RAMs. IC technology has improved to a point where these devices are not too expensive. Since the projects will only require a fairly small amount of memory, the difference in costs wouldn't amount to much more than a dollar or so. Dynamic RAM wouldn't offer much advantage for our purposes here, although it may still be desirable in a complete microcomputer.

ROM

Data can be read out of or written into a RAM. The user can store his own data, freely changing it at any time. Unfortunately, if the power to the system is ever cut off for any reason, any and all data stored in RAM will be irretrievably lost. In some applications it may be desirable that some data or programming be stored in memory in such a way that the user cannot inadvertently erase or change it.

It is extremely convenient to have some programming automatically boot up when the system is turned on. All computer systems need some kind of operating system. Most microcomputers also have a high-level language translation program (usually BA-

SIC) that is immediately available upon power up.

The solution to these problems and special requirements is a type of memory that can be read from but not written to. This type of memory is called ROM or *Read Only Memory*.

Like RAM, ROM is usually supplied in IC form. All of the data in a ROM chip is permanently determined by the manufacturer when the device is made. Obviously, this means that ROMs are only practical for applications where many identical units are required. Otherwise the manufacturing costs would be too high.

A typical use of ROM chips would be in a commercial microcomputer system. The operating system and the BASIC programming language are included in ROM, so the user won't have to load this software into the computer each time he turns it on.

Some popular microcomputers, such as the Tandy Color Computer have a special port where external ROM packs can be plugged in. Each ROM pack contains software for a specific application. Video game systems are dedicated microcomputers. Usually the software (game programs) are supplied in ROM packs.

Because the data stored in a ROM is permanently hard-wired within a chip, each ROM memory cell can be far simpler than either a static or dynamic RAM cell. Several typical ROM cells are illustrated in Fig. 4-6. The data stored in each cell is determined

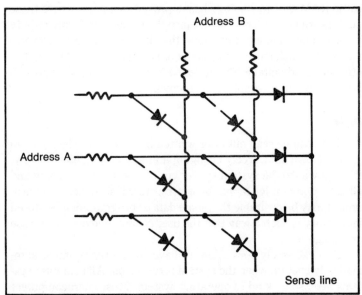

Fig. 4-6. ROM cells are very simple in concept.

by the presence (logic 1) or the absence (logic 0) of a connecting diode element at the appropriate address location. The user has no way of ever changing any of the data stored in a ROM. If even a single bit must be changed, the entire ROM chip must be replaced.

The chief advantage of ROM is its permanance. Stored data cannot be accidentally lost, even if system power is disconnected for years.

PROM

Since the data in a ROM must be irrevocably determined at the time of manufacture, this type of memory is really not very practical for applications where only a few copies are to be made. It certainly isn't very practical for the hobbyist. Unless you need a few hundred identically programmed ROM chips, the cost per unit would be too high.

Fortunately, a compromise is available. For applications where the permanent storage capabilities are needed, but only a few copies (or just a single prototype) will be used, a user-programmable ROM has been developed. This type of memory is called PROM, or *Programmable-Read-Only Memory*.

Each memory cell in a PROM is similar to a ROM cell. The difference is that the connecting diode elements are a special fused type. Every memory cell in a PROM contains a fused diode element at each and every address location (all 1's). The user can program the chip by selectively blowing out the fuses on unwanted diodes (0's).

Once programmed, a PROM behaves exactly like a ROM. Data can be read from it, but the stored data cannot be erased or changed by the microcomputer. Of course, additional fuses may be blown (special circuitry is required) to change more 1's to 0's. But there is no way to ever replace a blown diode (change a 0 back to a 1.

Once programmed, the data stored in a PROM cannot be changed by the CPU. This means if a mistake is made during programming the PROM, or even a small change is needed, the entire chip must be discarded and a new one must be programmed from scratch.

EPROM

There is a special type of PROM that allows the chip to be erased and reused. This type of memory is known as EPROM, or *Erasable-Programmable-Read-Only Memory*.

An EPROM works in essentially the same way as a regular PROM except for the fact that the entire chip can be cleared (all of the stored data erased) by exposing the chip to a strong ultraviolet light source. A small plastic window is embedded in the IC package for this purpose.

Note that the entire chip must be erased at once. There is no way to change just a few bits selectively. It is an all or nothing proposition.

Because sunlight and most other visible light sources contain some ultraviolet energy, a programmed EPROM should be carefully shielded from all light to avoid accidental erasure of data. As long as the erase window is kept covered, there should be no problem.

A more recent variant is the EEPROM, or *Electrically-Erasable-Programmable-Read-Only Memory*. In this type of device, a special electrical signal is used to clear (erase) the stored data in the chip as a whole. Again, individual bits cannot be selectively altered.

MEASURING MEMORY SIZE

Since binary numbers are used to define the memory location addresses, the number of cells in a memory system is almost invariably a power of 2, like 256 (2^8), 1024 (2^{10}), or 4096 (2^{12}).

In large practical systems, memory size is usually defined as being so many K. The letter K is normally used to indicate a factor of one thousand. However, 1000 is not a power of 2. The nearest power of 2 is 1024, so in memory systems K actually represents a factor of 1024. That is:

$$
\begin{array}{rcl}
1\ \text{K} &=& 1024 \\
4\ \text{K} &=& 4096 \\
16\ \text{K} &=& 16384 \\
64\ \text{K} &=& 65536 \\
128\ \text{K} &=& 131072 \\
256\ \text{K} &=& 262144 \\
1000\ \text{K} &=& 1\ \text{Meg} = 1024000
\end{array}
$$

You do have to be careful about just what is being counted. For many memory ICs, 1 K indicates a storage capability of 1024 bits, while in computer systems, the quantity in question is the number of bytes that can be stored. A 4 K memory in this instance would hold 4096 sets of 8 bits each, or 32,768 individual bits (0's or 1's).

The variable terminology can cause some confusion if you're not careful.

As IC technology has been improved over the years, more and more memory cells can be crammed onto a single bit. Many modern memory ICs use multiple bit locations. Usually it will be specified as, for example, 4 K × 8 bits. In this device, 4096 bytes could be stored. Each memory location will be eight arrays deep. Each array must have its own individual set of I/O circuitry. A 4096 × 1 memory and a 256 × 8 memory will each hold 4096 individual bits, but the single dimensioned unit will tend to be significantly less expensive because of the lesser I/O requirements.

The number of memory cells that can be placed on a single chip has increased significantly over the last few years. The required number of pins can easily become extremely unwieldy. The solution is to use the same address lines for both row and column addresses. Decoder pins are used to identify which type of address is currently on the line. Matrixing circuitry is included on-chip to keep everything straight. This increases the complexity and cost of the individual chip, but even so, a single 256 K bit chip is going to be cheaper than four separate 64 K ICs.

OTHER MEMORY DEVICES

A number of other forms of memory have been developed over the last few years. Some, such as bubble memories and CCDs (Charge-Coupled Device) show considerable promise for the future. Currently, however, they are prohibitively expensive for the experimenter. It would not be appropriate to discuss them in detail here. Hopefully, a future edition of this book will be able to discuss the availability of such devices.

Chapter 5

Interfacing

T HE MOST POWERFUL CPU IN THE WORLD WON'T DO A BIT of good if it can't communicate with the outside world. In this chapter we will cover the basics of interfacing. Interfacing is nothing more than the methods used to connect a CPU with various Input and/or Output devices.

MEMORY MAPPED I/O

Most CPUs treat Input/Output ports as memory locations. Certain memory addresses are used as I/O ports, rather than actual memory locations. Data can be READ from or you can WRITE to an I/O port in the exact same way as regular memory. This method of interfacing is called Memory Mapped I/O.

I/O ports are addressed like ordinary memory locations, but they generally don't function in quite the same way. Some I/O registers are READ ONLY (input). These registers are used to input data, and to indicate the status of the I/O device. Other I/O registers are WRITE ONLY (output), including data output and control signals from the CPU to the I/O device. If the CPU needs to know what was previously fed to a WRITE ONLY port, the data should have been saved to another memory location.

Because no special I/O instructions are needed by the CPU, using Memory Mapped I/O frees up operation codes for other purposes. However, most CPUs don't use all possible operation codes anyway. For an eight bit CPU, there are 256 possible codes. The Z80, for example uses less than 200. Therefore, saving op-codes is a limited advantage.

Memory Mapped I/O does, however, offer some real advantages. Programming is slightly simplified. Memory reference commands can be used to manipulate the I/O registers, rather than being limited to simple LOAD and STORE operations.

In a high-level language, such as BASIC, memory mapped I/O can also come in handy. PEEK and POKE commands can be used to interact with any I/O port. I/O ports can be addressed directly without resorting to machine-language routines.

There are also some minor disadvantages. Specialized I/O commands would make some functions a little more convenient. Also, in most full microcomputers, memory space is at a premium. Memory Mapped I/O uses up some of the memory locations (typically 256 to 4096 addresses). Most CPUs use only Memory Mapped I/O. It works just fine. In many applications it is highly desirable, in others it is simply adequate.

DIRECT I/O

The Z80 (and the earlier 8080) offers another interfacing mode. I/O ports are addressed directly, separate from memory locations. Specialized commands are used for I/O:

☐ In   Read Input
☐ Out   Write Output

An eight bit I/O address is included with the IN or OUT commands. This adds up to a total of 256 possible I/O ports. Some complex I/O devices will use up more than a single port, so the number isn't quite as large as it might seem at first glance. Floppy-disc controllers typically use about eight interface registers.

Direct I/O requires a slightly more complex system bus, because I/O READ and I/O WRITE control signals are needed in addition to the address and data bus lines. The nice thing about the Z80's approach is that either Direct or Memory Mapped I/O can be used. It is up to the designer to select the method best suited to the specific application at hand.

Z80 INTERFACE TIMING

To design CPU circuits and I/O interfaces, you need to know

the timing signals. You have to know what will happen and when. A typical memory read by the Z80 takes three clock periods, as illustrated in Fig. 5-1. If the memory cannot respond quickly enough, it will issue a WAIT signal to make the CPU not move on before it has acquired the desired data. The way the WAIT signal affects the timing of a READ operation is illustrated in Fig. 5-2. The basic pattern is the same, but during the WAIT cycles, the CPU is

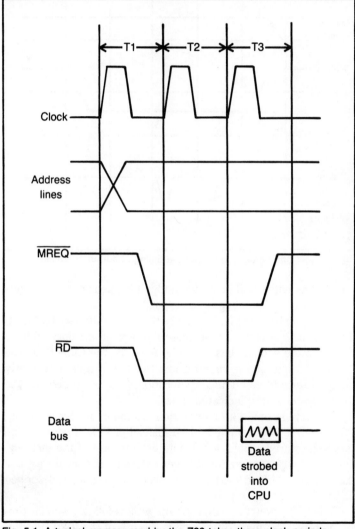

Fig. 5-1. A typical memory read by the Z80 takes three clock periods.

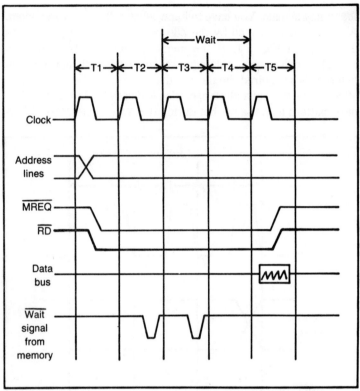

Fig. 5-2. WAIT can be used to extend the timing of a READ operation.

in a holding pattern. Essentially, nothing happens until the external memory device is ready to respond.

Referring back to Fig. 5-1, notice the MREQ (Memory REQuest) signal. This line is used to indicate that a valid memory address is now on the address bus lines (A0-A15). At the same time, the RD (ReaD) line is also brought low to READ the data currently stored at the addressed memory location. Data is strobed into the CPU register at the indicated time.

The timing of a WRITE operation is similar, as shown in Fig. 5-3. The WR (WRite) line is used instead of RD, of course. The data to be stored is held on the data bus for most of the three cycles of the WRITE operation. Slower external memory device can also force the CPU to WAIT during a WRITE operation, as described earlier for READ operations.

The Z80's INPUT and OUTPUT operations follow a similar timing pattern. The main difference is the use of the IORQ (I/O Re-

Quest) line, instead of MREQ. The timing signals for an IN (input) operation are shown in Fig. 5-4. An OUT (output) operation's timing signals are illustrated in Fig. 5-5. I/O devices can issue WAIT signals to extend the timing as necessary, just as discussed earlier for external memory.

Note that the IN and OUT operations are normally four clock periods long, rather than the three clock periods of READ and WRITE operations. This is because the Z80 automatically adds a WAIT cycle. Virtually all I/O devices are slower than semiconductor memories.

BUS INTERFACE CIRCUITRY

A typical I/O bus interface is made up of an address recognizer (so the port knows when the CPU is addressing it) along with ap-

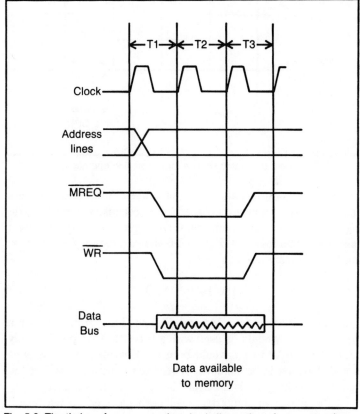

Fig. 5-3. The timing of WRITE operations is similar to that of READ operations.

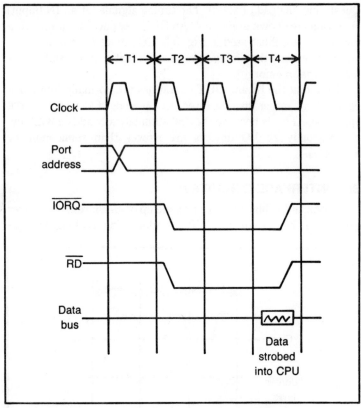

Fig. 5-4. These are the timing signals for a typical IN operation.

propriate input buffers and/or output latches. Address recognizers are not really complicated. An address recognizer is really nothing much more than a multi-input (16-input lines) AND gate with selected inputs inverted. Figure 5-6 shows a circuit for recognizing the following address:

1100 1010 1110 0111

This circuit is set up for a Memory Mapped I/O system. The same type of circuitry could be used with a Direct I/O system, but only address lines A0 to A7 would be used. Control and status lines would also have to be included. When the proper address is on the bus, the clock signal is brought high to activate the port.

Often a number of interfaces will be included on a single board. In this case, most of the address bits can be ANDed together once

130

and factored into a more limited decoder/gating system. This reduces the IC count of the circuit, lowering the cost and space requirements of the interface board.

To interface I/O signals, of course, we need to know the electrical characteristics of the signals. In most cases, a logical 1 is about +5 volts, and a logic 0 is approximately ground potential (0 volts). Most digital circuitry will fill these requirements easily.

Current is a little trickier in some cases. Input is rarely a problem. Only a very small current is drawn by the CPU's input line(s). There can be some difficulty in interfacing output signals. Typically a CPU can only put out a mere 1 mA or so. This is definitely insufficient to drive most practical output devices. It is not even enough to light up a simple LED.

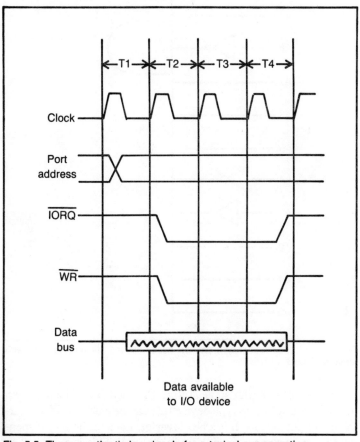

Fig. 5-5. These are the timing signals for a typical OUT operation.

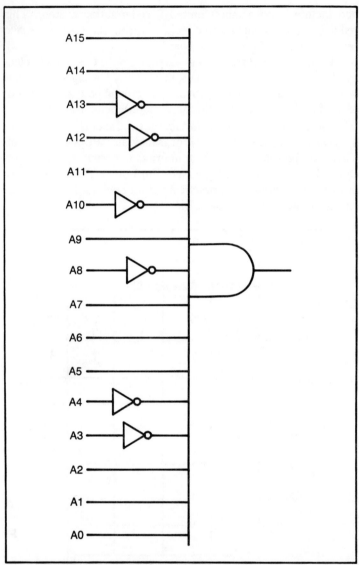

Fig. 5-6. Address recognition can be accomplished via an AND gate with selected inputs inverted.

Some sort of buffer stage is clearly needed. The 75492, shown in Fig. 5-7, is a CMOS type device that can be a useful aid in interfacing output signals. It is a hex inverter. Each of the six independent inverter stages can sink up to 200 mA. This is sufficient to

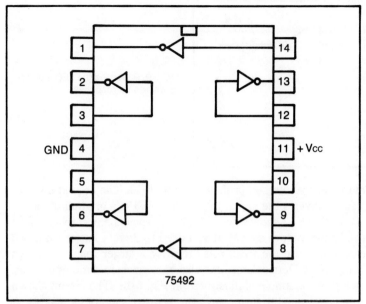

Fig. 5-7. The 75492 is a good choice for buffering I/O signals.

drive LEDs or small electromechanical relays, solenoids, and other such devices. The 75492 can share its power supply with the CPU.

Figure 5-8 shows a simple interface circuit for driving an LED. The LED will light when the CPU outputs a logic 1. It will be dark for a logic 0 (or for no output).

In some applications we may want the output device to respond in the opposite way (on for 0, off for 1). There are two ways to do this. One is to simply reverse the polarity of the LED, as illustrated in Fig. 5-9. This will work, but it is only applicable for LEDs. A

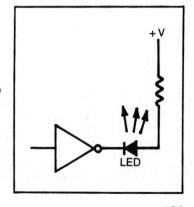

Fig. 5-8. This output circuit can be used to light up a LED.

133

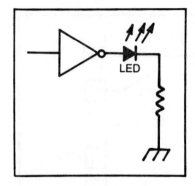

Fig. 5-9. Reversing the LED's polarity inverts its response.

more general method is shown in Fig. 5-10. The second inverter stage reinverts the signal to match the CPU's original output.

Figure 5-11 shows how a small electromechanical relay can be used as an output device. If you need to drive a larger load, you can simply use the small relay to drive a larger relay, as shown in Fig. 5-12. Optoisolators can also be very useful for output interfacing. An example is illustrated in Fig. 5-13. The circuit shown here is designed to turn a cassette recorder's motor on and off. A CPU's output can be used to control an ac appliance. An interface circuit for this application is illustrated in Fig. 5-14.

So far in this section we have been dealing with 1-bit output devices. There is no reason at all why we can't use the entire 8-bit data bus of the CPU. Figure 5-15 shows how we can use four BCD encoded bits from the data bus to drive a seven-segment LED display that can display any of the ten standard digits. The IC labelled

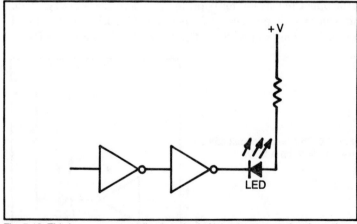

Fig. 5-10. This is a more generalized method of inverting output signal reactions.

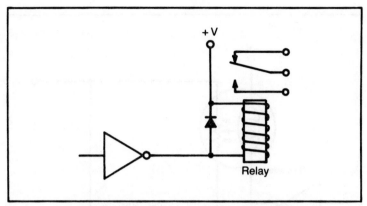

Fig. 5-11. A computer can control a small electromechanical relay.

7475 is a latch. This component allows the computer to do other things, while the LEDs continue to display the output data. The number displayed will remain unchanged until the port is accessed again (with a new OUT command) and new data is fed into the latches. (Of course, if power is interrupted, the latches will "forget" what the stored display data was.)

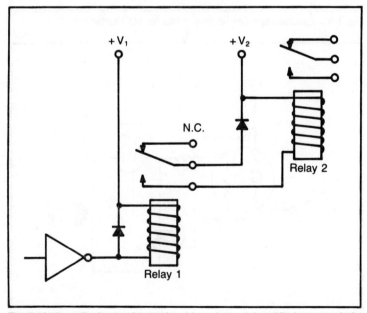

Fig. 5-12. A small relay can be used to drive a larger relay to limit current drain on the OUT line.

135

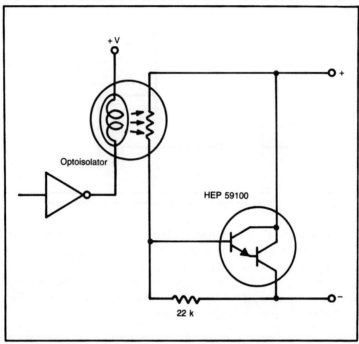

Fig. 5-13. Optoisolators can be very useful for I/O interfacing.

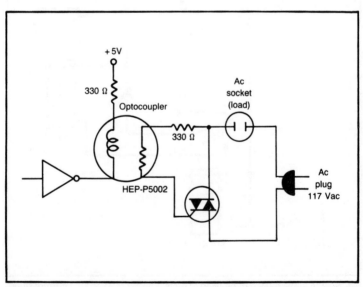

Fig. 5-14. This circuit can be used to allow the CPU to turn any ac appliance on and off.

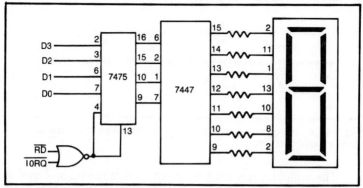

Fig. 5-15. Four BCD-encoded bits can drive a seven-segment LED unit.

The 7447 is a seven-segment decoder/driver IC. Both the 7475 and the 7447 are TTL devices. Their power supply should be a tightly regulated + 5 volts. Similar CMOS devices could be substituted, if you prefer.

INTERFACING ANALOG SIGNALS

There is one basic problem with interfacing computers with many external devices. Computers are, by definition, digital devices. They deal with strings of simple on/off signals. There are never any intermediate values. But, it's an analog world outside the computer. Most circuitry deals with a continuous linear range of values. There are no neat, clear-cut steps.

To use an analog device as an input for a computer, we need some way to transform the analog signal into a digital signal. Circuitry to accomplish this task is called, not surprisingly, an A/D (analog-to-digital) converter. Similarly, to use an analog device for output purposes, a D/A (digital-to-analog) converter is used. Both types of converter will be discussed shortly.

An analog signal is made up of a continuously varying series of levels. A digital signal is made up of a series of discrete values. If we sample the analog waveform at various discrete moments within its cycle, we can digitally express the instantaneous level for each sample, as illustrated in Fig. 5-16. By the same token, if we output a string of digital values at a regular rate, we can roughly simulate an analog waveform. Obviously, the greater the number of samples per cycle, the better the accuracy. Figure 5-17 shows the crude results obtained when only a small number of samples per cycle is used.

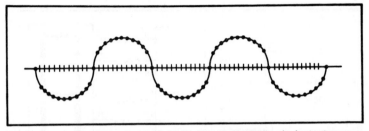

Fig. 5-16. An analog waveform can be digitized by sampling its instantaneous level at rapid intervals.

The sampling rate must be at least twice the highest analog frequency to be converted. Figure 5-18 illustrates why this is so. If the sample rate is less than twice the sampled frequency, the separation between cycles will be lost. A lower phantom frequency will be created. This is called aliasing. If we need to preserve the original waveshape, instead of just the signal frequency, higher sampling rates may be required.

In our examples we have been showing sine waves. A sine wave is the simplest analog ac signal. It consists of a single frequency component. More complex waveforms are made up of many different frequency components called harmonics, which are multiples of the base frequency. To preserve the waveshape in the conversion process, the sampling rate must be at least twice the highest frequency component of interest.

Another problem with the digital representation of analog signals is called *quantization error*. An analog signal can take any value along a continuous range. Digital signals can only take on specific discrete values. Intermediate values cannot be expressed, and must be rounded off. This rounding off can create a certain amount of distortion, as illustrated in Fig. 5-19. The conversion process (in

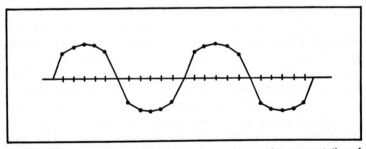

Fig. 5-17. If the sampling rate is relatively low, only a crude representation of the original waveform will be digitized.

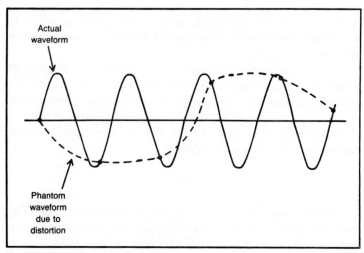

Fig. 5-18. If the sampling rate is less than twice the frequency being sampled, aliasing can result.

either direction) takes some finite amount of time. This is called the conversion time (T_c).

Some A/D converters are called *successive approximation* types. The conversion time is equal to $n + 1$ clock (sample) periods, when

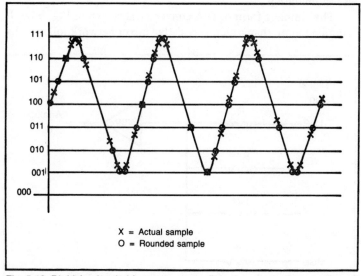

X = Actual sample
O = Rounded sample

Fig. 5-19. Digitizing inevitably causes some distortion, due to the rounding off of intermediate values.

n is the bit length of the digital output. For example, an 8-bit successive approximation A/D converter would have a conversion time equal to 9 clock periods.

Other A/D converters require a conversion time equal to 2^n, where n is again equal to the number of bits in the output. This type of converter is slower than the successive approximation type.

Conversion time influences the maximum number of samples that can be taken per unit of time. The absolute maximum number of cycles per second is equal to:

$$1/T_c$$

Another time factor to be considered is the *aperture time*. This is the total time losses throughout the system influencing the maximum possible sampling rate. The primary component of the aperture time is the conversion time, but there are other factors, including *output settling time* and the *slew rate* of the input amplifier.

D/A Converters

We will first look at D/A (digital-to-analog) converters because they tend to be somewhat simpler than A/D (analog-to-digital converters). Once we understand D/A conversion. A/D conversion is less intimidating.

The simplest form of D/A converter is shown in Fig. 5-20. It is nothing more than a simple resistive mixer network followed by

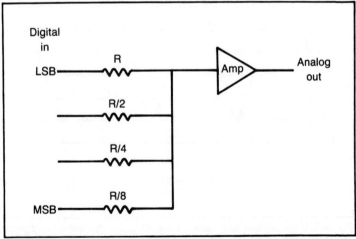

Fig. 5-20. A simple resistive mixer network can serve as a D/A converter.

a buffer amplifier (to prevent loading down the digital output circuitry). Only four bits are shown for simplicity. The same principles can be applied to any number of bits.

The resistor values are of importance, of course. This is because the various bits in a binary number have different values. The most-significant-bit (further to the left) is weighted heavier than the least-significant-bit (further to the right):

MSB   LSB

1   0   1   0

Each successive bit is an increase of a power of two. Therefore, the resistance values are also set up in factors of two.

R1	R	MSB
R2	2R	
R3	4R	
R4	8R	LSB

For small digital values (few bits), this isn't a problem. For example, for a 4-bit system, if R is equal to 1 k (1000 ohms), the resistor for the least-significant bit would have to be equal to 8R, or 8 k. For an 8-bit system, the resistance values would have to run up to 128 k. For a sixteen bit D/A converter, the LSB resistor would need a value of 32,768,000 ohms. It is next to impossible to get a reasonable amount of stability over such a range of resistances.

Another problem is the odd-ball resistance values required. For an 8-bit system, you will need the following resistance values (assuming R = 1 k):

1 k	
2 k*	(2.2 k)
4 k*	(3.9 k)
8 k*	(8.2 k)
16 k*	(15 k)
32 k*	(33 k)
64 k*	(62 k)
128 k*	(120 k)

The values marked * are not standard values. The standard values given in parentheses may be used, but at a loss of accuracy.

A better approach is the R/2R ladder network, illustrated in

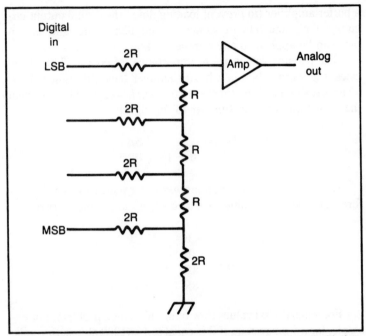

Fig. 5-21. The R-2R ladder D/A converter is usually easier to work with than the circuit shown in Fig. 5-20.

Fig. 5-21. Only two resistance values are required—R and 2R. Each bit sees a different resistance between ground and the buffer amplifier.

To digitally simulate (or recreate) an analog waveform, a string of digital values is fed through the D/A converter in sequence, as shown in Fig. 5-22. A better approximation can be achieved by

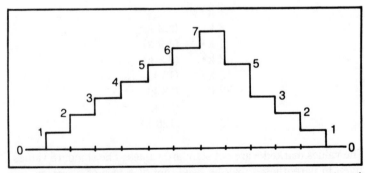

Fig. 5-22. An analog waveform can be simulated by feeding out a string of binary values through a D/A converter.

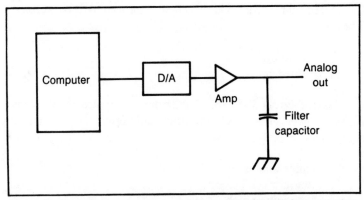

Fig. 5-23. The analog output can be improved with a simple filter capacitor.

smoothing out the output signal with a low-pass filter. A moderately large capacitor across the output, as shown in Fig. 5-23, will do the trick fairly well. The results are illustrated in Fig. 5-24.

A/D Converters

Analog-to-digital (A/D) conversion is a somewhat more complicated proposition than digital-to-analog (D/A) conversion. This is because of the timing and resolution problems described earlier in this chapter.

There are several possible approaches to A/D conversion. One basic method is based on the integrator. An integrator is an op-amp (operational amplifier) circuit that creates a ramp voltage from the input voltage. A simple integrator circuit is illustrated in Fig.

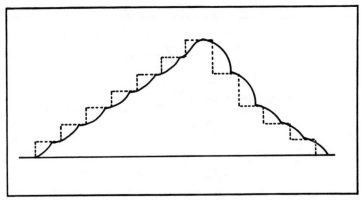

Fig. 5-24. Here we see the results of using a filter capacitor at the output of a D/A converter.

5-25. Integrators are used in two popular forms of A/D converters. They are:

☐ Single-slope
☐ Double-slope

Figure 5-26 shows the block diagram for a typical single-slope A/D converter circuit. Note that it is made up of several simpler subcircuits:

☐ Sample and Hold
☐ Integrator
☐ Electronic Switch
☐ Voltage Comparator
☐ Reference Voltage
☐ Gate
☐ Clock
☐ Gate Generator (Timing Coordinator)
☐ Counter

A *sample and hold* is a circuit that samples the instantaneous value of an analog input signal when triggered, and holds the sampled value at the output until retriggered. This stage gives the integrator a constant input voltage to work with for each conversion.

The switch is used to clear the circuit to zero. When it is closed, the capacitor is allowed to discharge. Usually this is an electronic rather than a mechanical switch. Often a FET (field-effect transistor) is used for this purpose. It is controlled by the gate generator.

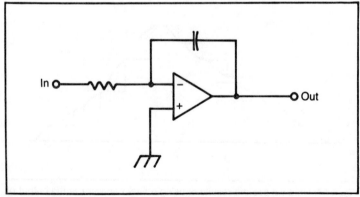

Fig. 5-25. Most A/D converters are based on the integrator.

144

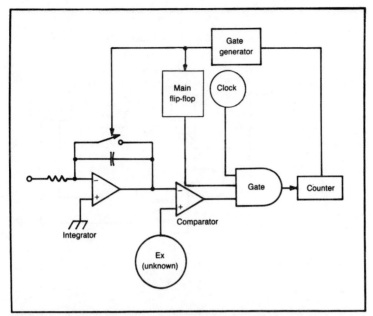

Fig. 5-26. A block diagram of a typical single-slope A/D converter.

The output of the integrator rises from zero in a linear fashion, at a rate determined by the input voltage.

The next stage after the integrator is the comparator. A comparator is a circuit that compares two analog input voltages and issues an output to indicate which one is higher. The output of the integrator is compared with a reference voltage.

The clock puts out a continuous stream of evenly spaced pulses. As long as the output of the comparator is high (reference voltage is greater than the integrator's output voltage) the clock pulses can pass through the gate to the counter. The counter simply counts how many clock periods occur before the integrator voltage exceeds the reference voltage. This produces a binary value that is proportional to the analog input voltage.

The single-slope A/D converter is relatively simple (in fact, it is the simplest type of A/D converter) and fairly low cost, but it suffers somewhat in terms of accuracy. The last digit will tend to bobble because partial clock pulses may be included in the timing period, "confusing" the counter circuitry. An improvement in accuracy and stability can be obtained by using a dual-slope A/D converter circuit. The block diagram for this type of device is shown in Fig. 5-27.

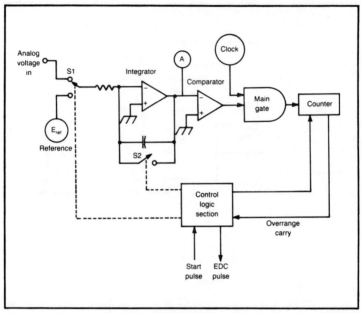

Fig. 5-27. A dual-slope A/D converter is more accurate and stable than a single-slope circuit.

A dual-slope A/D converter is made up of the following sub-circuits:

☐ Sample and Hold *
☐ Reference
☐ Electronic Switch *
☐ Integrator *
☐ Comparator *
☐ Clock *
☐ Gate *
☐ Logic Control
☐ Counter *

Most of these subcircuits are essentially the same in function as in the single-slope A/D converter discussed earlier. These duplications are marked with asterisks. The reference is a precision voltage or current source. It is used as a comparison standard for the unknown analog input signal.

At the beginning of the cycle, the input voltage is fed through the integrator and the number of clock pulses is counted, as in the single-slope A/D converter until the counter overflows. At this point the output of the integrator is proportional to the input signal. Now the *control logic section* will change the integrator's input to the Reference, which has the opposite polarity as the original analog signal. Therefore, the new integration process will discharge the capacitor. The integrator's ramp will slope downwards, rather than upwards. The signals are illustrated in Fig. 5-28. Because the Reference has a constant value, the discharge slope will have a constant rate. The steepness of the slope will be proportional to the analog input signal.

Because the counter has just overflowed before the discharge process, the count is 0000. The count will continue to increment during the downward slope until the integrator output reaches zero

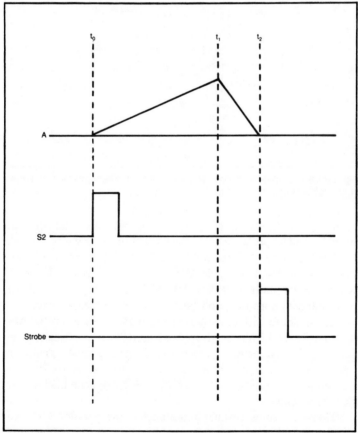

Fig. 5-28. These are the internal signals from the circuit shown in Fig. 5-27.

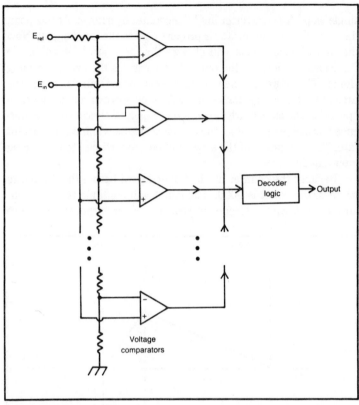

Fig. 5-29. The parallel A/D converter is often called a flash converter because of its high speed conversions.

(ground), cutting off the comparator/gate network. The count at this point will be proportional to the level of the analog input signal.

The dual-slope A/D converter is relatively immune to noise errors in the input signal and clock frequency inaccuracies. However, this type of circuit is relatively slow (although still fast enough for most practical purposes) and fairly complex and expensive.

A completely different approach to A/D conversion is the *parallel converter*, which is illustrated in Fig. 5-29. It is basically a series of voltage comparators, comparing the analog input signal with a dc reference voltage. A precision resistor network is used to bias the comparator stages. Each comparator is biased one LSB higher than its neighbor.

There are some serious limitations to the parallel A/D converter, especially in terms of the number of output bits. The num-

148

ber of comparator stages can rapidly become extremely unwieldy. Plus, there is a practical limit to how small an LSB the comparators can recognize. The chief advantage of this type of A/D converter is speed. Conversion takes place virtually instantly. Parallel A/D converters are often called *flash converters* for this very reason.

Section II

Projects

Chapter 6

CPU Breadboard

N OW THAT WE HAVE THE BASICS DOWN, WE CAN GET TO work on the actual projects. The basic computer at the heart of the projects will be virtually the same in each case, so we will cover the common circuitry in this chapter. In addition, we will set up a convenient breadboarding system for experimenting with the various CPU-based circuitry.

For best results, you should etch PC boards for the circuits. Because these projects are intended only as starting points for your own customization, foil patterns for PC boards cannot be included here. An alternative approach would be to use wire-wrapping techniques. Just don't try to get away with any kind of point-to-point wiring. Computer circuitry is too precise for that.

COMPONENTS OF THE SYSTEM

Several subcircuits will be used in most of the projects. Our breadboarding system will include permanent versions of each. The subcircuits described in this chapter include:

☐ Power supply
☐ CPU
☐ Clock/Signal Generator
☐ Memory
☐ Hexadecimal Keypad
☐ LED readouts

153

☐ Input port
☐ Output port
☐ Breadboard

All of the circuitry will be designed with the Z80 CPU in mind. If you use a different CPU chip, additional support circuitry may be required.

POWER SUPPLY

The power supply requirements are not complex. The Z80 requires a reasonably well-regulated +5 volt voltage source. This same voltage can be used to drive virtually all of the support circuitry. The power supply circuit should be able to supply a hefty amount of current, because a number of different circuits may be operating at the same time.

The 7805, shown in Fig. 6-1, is a widely available 5-volt regulator IC. With adequate heatsinking, it can supply up to 1.5 amp. To limit the current drain, we will use three 7805's in parallel. The first will supply the CPU and memory chips. The second powers the input circuits, and the third supplies the output circuits. This division of labor will help limit the chances of overloading one of the voltage regulator chips. However, don't make the mistake of

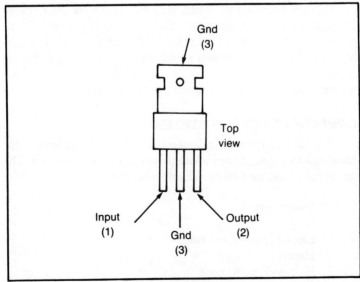

Fig. 6-1. The 7805 is a popular 5-volt regulator IC.

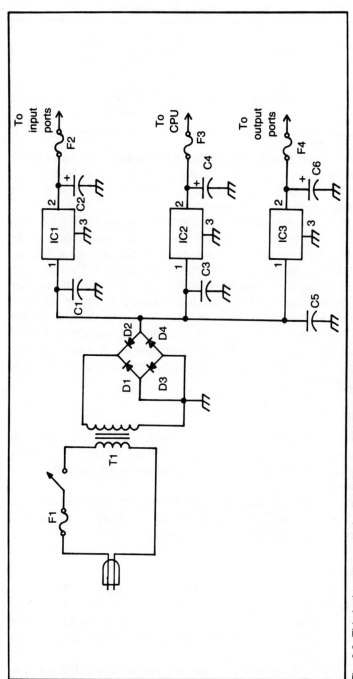

Fig. 6-2. This is the power supply circuit for our CPU breadboard.

Table 6-1. Parts List for Fig. 6-2.

IC1-IC3	7805 5-volt Regulator
D1-D4	1N4004 Diode
T1	6.3 Vac Transformer
F1	3-amp Fuse
F2-F4	1-amp Fuse
C1, C3, C5	0.1-μF Capacitor
C2, C4, C6	470-μF Capacitor

skimping on heatsinking. Adequate heatsinking is assumed in the design. If you're not sure, include a little extra heatsinking. You can't have too much. A three amp input fuse will also help prevent blowing any of the regulators.

The complete power supply circuit is illustrated in Fig. 6-2. The parts list is given in Table 6-1. The output fuses for each of the regulators are optional. If used, it will be virtually impossible (or, at least, extremely unlikely) to burn out a regulator. The input fuse is *not* optional. It must be used to ensure the safety of your circuitry and yourself. It doesn't pay to scrimp on simple safety. A fuse and holder doesn't cost that much. Not having the system fused when problems show up, could cost a lot. In some cases, it could cost your life. Include the input fuse, and use a grounding plug, especially if a metal chassis is used to house *Any* of the circuitry supplied by the power supply.

THE CPU

As stated earlier, the CPU used is the Z80. This is not a terribly expensive IC, but still, do yourself a big favor, and use a socket (40 pins). It will make construction and later servicing much, much easier.

For your convenience, the pinout diagram of the Z80 is shown in Fig. 6-3. The Z80 is reasonably self-contained, so no external circuitry is required for the CPU section.

CLOCK

Any CPU requires some sort of clock to drive it. All operation timings are defined in terms of clock cycles. We need a source of clean square waves with fairly precise frequency stability. Most computer systems use a crystal-controlled clock, because of the degree of precision offered.

The clock circuit we will be using is illustrated in Fig. 6-4. The

156

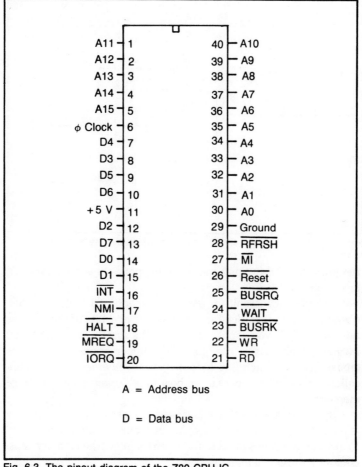

Fig. 6-3. The pinout diagram of the Z80 CPU IC.

parts list is given in Table 6-2. Notice that the clock output is made available for use of other circuitry, in addition to the CPU itself. Also, note that connections to the CPU will be indicated by a circle containing the appropriate pin number. This convention will be employed throughout this book.

MEMORY

For the on-board memory, I have decided to use the MM74C920. The pinout for this device is shown in Fig. 6-5. This IC is arranged as 256 × 4 bits. If we use two MM74C920's in parallel we can have a 256 byte RAM. This should be sufficient for

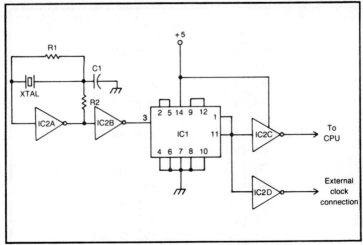

Fig. 6-4. This is the clock circuit for our breadboarding system.

the projects used in this book. Both memory chips are addressed in unison.

The memory circuit for our CPU breadboard system is illustrated in Fig. 6-6. Notice that only the lower 8 bits of the address bus are used. If you choose to expand the system with additional memory devices, you can utilize the upper memory addresses (above &HFF). Each 256 byte section of memory is commonly called a page. Figure 6-7 shows how to address a second page of memory.

Because static RAM is being used, no special support circuitry is required. If you choose to employ dynamic RAMs, you will need to include provisions for automatic refreshing of the memory cells.

HEXADECIMAL KEYPAD

The circuits described so far in this chapter make up a fairly complete computer. There's just one problem—there's no way for the user to communicate with the CPU. Without input and output

Table 6-2. Parts List for Fig. 6-4.

IC1	CD4013 Flip-Flop
IC2	CD4069 Hex Inverter
R1	10 MΩ Resistor
R2	330 Ω Resistor
C1	22 pF Capacitor
XTAL	3.58 MHz Crystal (3.579545 MHz)

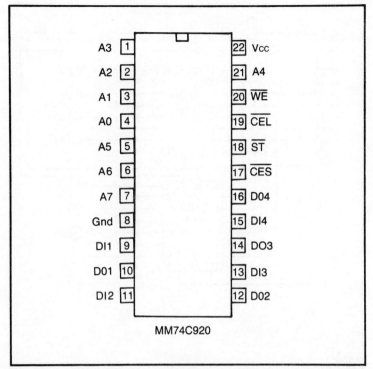

Fig. 6-5. The MM74C920 is used for on-board RAM in our breadboarding system.

devices, the computer system is absolutely worthless.

The most common method of entering data (and commands) into a computer is some form of keyboard. For our projects, we don't need a full alphanumeric keyboard. We will be working exclusively with machine-language commands, and numerical data. For convenience, we will use the hexadecimal (base sixteen) numbering system. Each byte on the data bus is made up of two hexadecimal digits.

A hexidecimal keypad has sixteen key switches:

$$0 - 1 - 2 - 3 - 4 - 5 - 6 - 7 -$$
$$8 - 9 - A - B - C - D - E - F$$

It is generally convenient to arrange the keys in a row/column format, as illustrated in Fig. 6-8. You can obtain a suitable hexadecimal keypad for just a few bucks from many surplus dealers. Alternatively, you can cannibalize the keys from a pocket calculator.

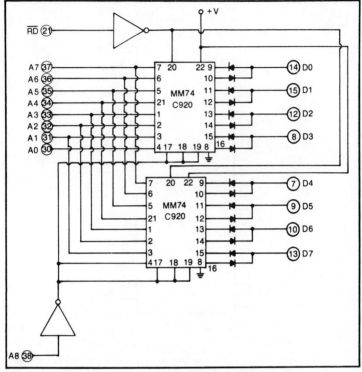

Fig. 6-6. This is the complete on-board RAM circuit.

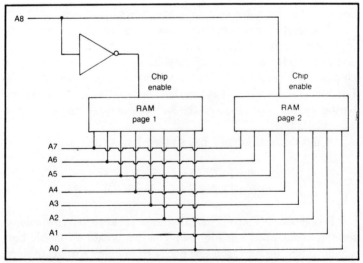

Fig. 6-7. Here we see how to address a second page of memory.

160

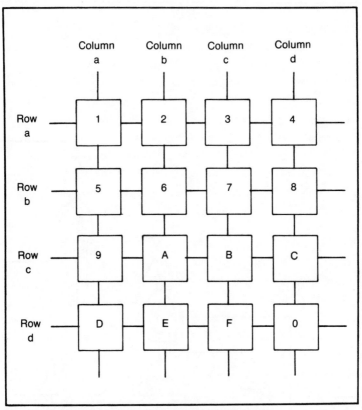

Fig. 6-8. The keypad is arranged in a row/column format.

A circuit for encoding the hexadecimal switches into binary form is shown in Fig. 6-9. The parts list is given in Table 6-3. Switch debouncing is included in the circuit to prevent false data entry.

The flip-flop labelled U/L determines whether the next key pressed will be placed on the upper four bits or the lower four bits of the data bus. It will automatically reverse its state after each key press.

Closely related to the keypad is the memory stepper shown in Fig. 6-10. Table 6-4 gives the parts list. This circuit allows you to step forward or backward through the memory addresses. Each time S1 is closed, the address will be increased by one. S2 will decrease the address by one. This allows the user to gain access to any memory location.

Because our basic system has only 256 bytes of memory, the counter is designed to only count from 0 to 255. If you use a larger

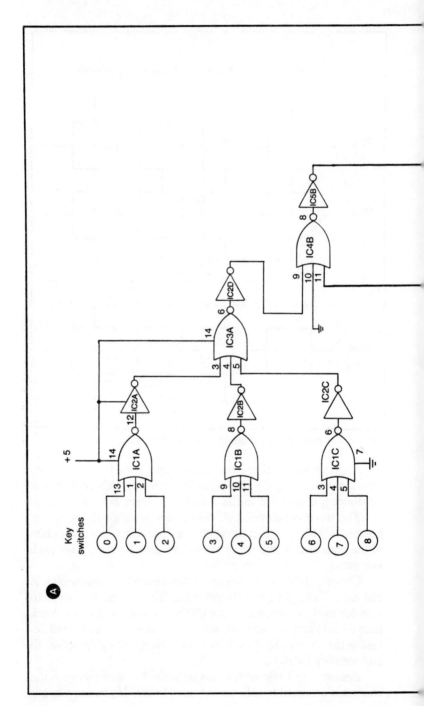

162

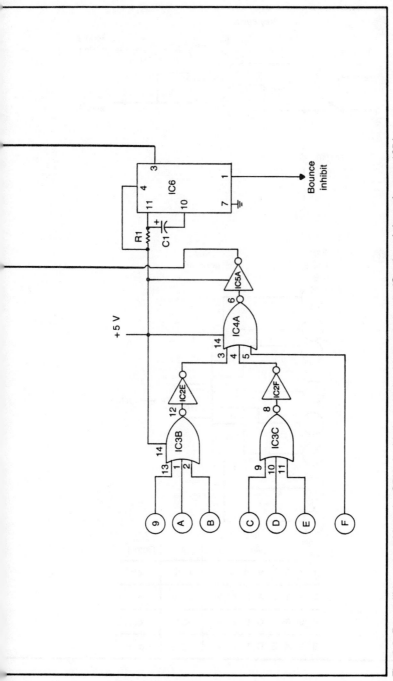

Fig. 6-9. Data will be entered into the CPU via this hexadecimal keypad circuit. (Continued through page 165.)

163

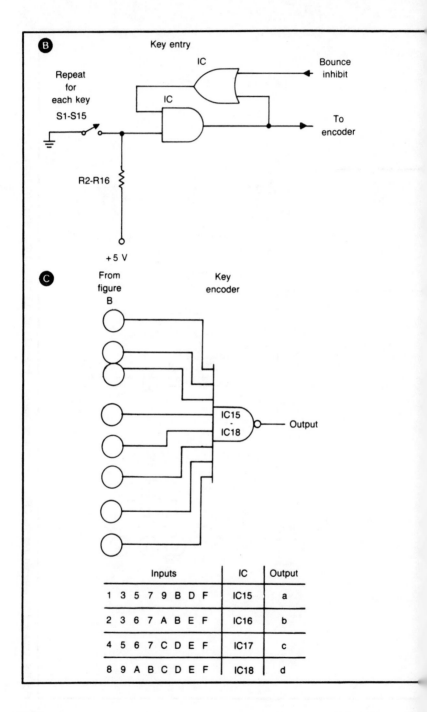

Inputs									IC	Output
1	3	5	7	9	B	D	F		IC15	a
2	3	6	7	A	B	E	F		IC16	b
4	5	6	7	C	D	E	F		IC17	c
8	9	A	B	C	D	E	F		IC18	d

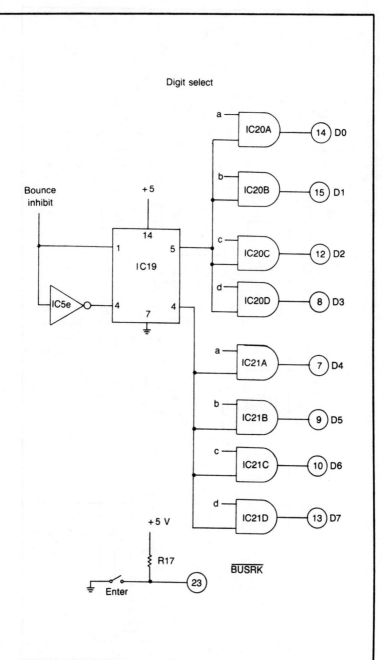

Digit select

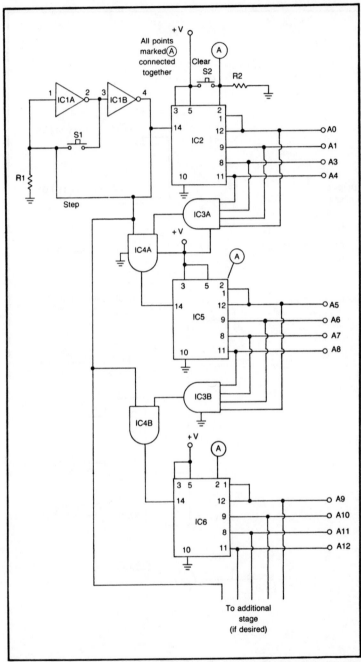

Fig. 6-10. The memory stepper circuit.

166

Table 6-3. Parts List for Fig. 6-9.

IC1, IC3, IC4	74C27 Triple 3-Input NOR Gate
IC2, IC5	CD4009 Hex Inverter
IC6	74C121 One Shot
IC7-IC10, IC20, IC21	74C08 Quad 2-Input AND Gate
IC11-IC14	74C32 Quad 2-Input OR Gate
IC15-IC18	74C30 8-Input NAND Gate
IC19	74C74 Dual D-Type Flip-Flop
R1	22 kΩ Resistor
R2-R17	4.7 kΩ Resistor
C1	47 μF Capacitor

Table 6-4. Parts List for Fig. 6-10.

IC1	7404 Hex Inverter
IC2, IC5, IC6	7493 Binary Counter
IC3	Dual 4-Input AND Gate
IC4	Quad 2-Input AND Gate
R1, R2	10 kΩ Resistor
S1, S2	NO Push Switches

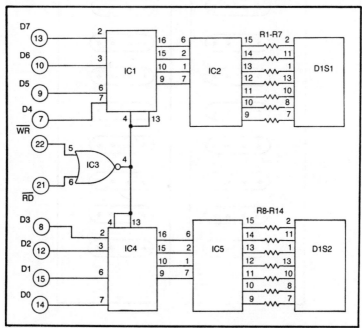

Fig. 6-11. Output data is displayed on two seven-segment LED units.

167

Table 6-5. Parts List for Fig. 6-11.

IC1, IC4	7475
IC2, IC5	7447
IC3	7402
DIS1, DIS2	7-Segment LED Display (MAN71, or equivalent)
R1-R14	270 Ω Resistor

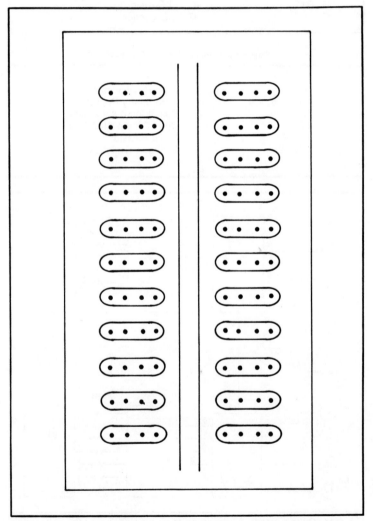

Fig. 6-12. A typical interconnection pattern for a breadboarding socket.

memory, you will need to increase the range of the counter. The eight LEDs indicate the current memory address in binary. For larger memories, more LEDs will have to be added.

LED DATA READOUT

Figure 6-11 shows the circuitry required to display data in hexadecimal form on two seven-segment LED units. The parts list is

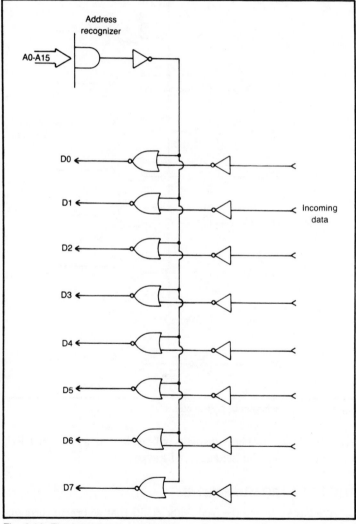

Fig. 6-13. The basic input port circuit.

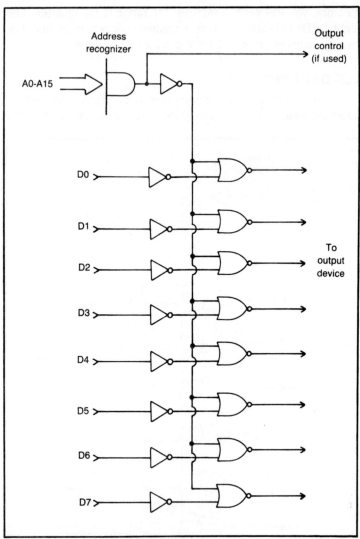

Fig. 6-14. The basic output port circuit.

given in Table 6-5. These displays will readout data from the CPU, and entries from the hexadecimal keypad.

THE BREADBOARD SYSTEM

We have covered the basic subcircuits that will recur throughout the projects. Now, we need some method of interfacing these circuits with additional circuitry to create the individual dedicated projects described in the next few chapters.

A breadboarding socket can be mounted on the system chassis to allow easy experimentation. This is simply a multipin solderless socket that the various component leads and jumper wires can quickly be plugged into or pulled out of. The various socket holes are electrically interconnected in a specific pattern. A typical pattern is illustrated in Fig. 6-12.

Figure 6-13 shows the basic input port, and the basic output port is illustrated in Fig. 6-14. The specific project circuitry will be connected to the CPU through these ports.

Chapter 7

EPROM Programmer

T HE PROGRAMMING FOR EACH OF THE PROGRAMS CAN BE entered into RAM. But, each time you turn off the power, it will be completely lost. You'll have to re-enter the program the next time you want to use the project. This is a nuisance at best.

EPROMs are an ideal choice for permanent storage. The experimenter can store whatever data/programs he chooses. Further, the EPROM can be erased and reused if the project's hardware or software is changed. Moreover, some projects might lose their usefulness over time. If you're no longer using a project, you can erase the EPROM and reuse it in a new project.

In this chapter we will describe a circuit for programming EPROMs. The EPROM we will be using is the 2704. This chip holds 512 (1/2 K) bytes—more than enough for our purposes. The pinout for this IC is shown in Fig. 7-1.

Figure 7-2 shows how the EPROM can be addressed by the CPU along with the RAM featured in the preceeding chapter. Notice that the EPROM's addresses start at &H00 00 and runs to &H02 00. RAM addresses start at &H02 01 instead of &H00, as in the original design. This is because the CPU will look to the first location in memory when it is first turned on. This is where the program should begin. Unless we want to manually enter a JUMP command when power is applied, some form of ROM should be at the bottom of memory.

While the use of IC sockets is strongly advised throughout the

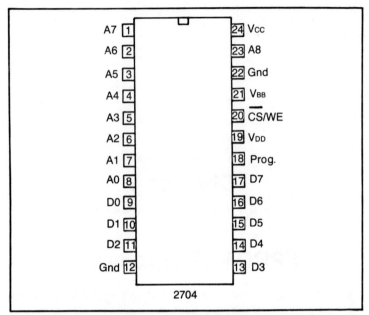

Fig. 7-1. The 2704 EPROM can store 1/2 K bytes.

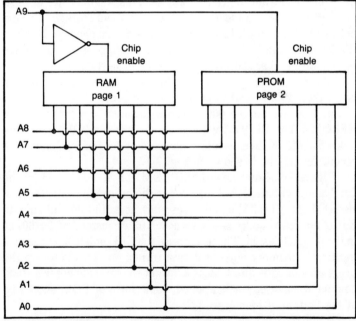

Fig. 7-2. The EPROM is addressed at a higher page over the system RAM.

174

projects, it is virtually mandatory for the EPROM(s). The only way to change the program is to physically exchange the EPROM chip. You certainly don't want to have to desolder for this.

The EPROM programming circuit is shown in Fig. 7-3. The parts list is given in Table 7-1. Notice that several supply voltages are needed to power this circuit, in addition to the standard +5 volts. Figure 7-4 shows a circuit for a supplemental power supply to provide the additional required voltages:

$$+30 \text{ volts}$$
$$+12 \text{ volts}$$
$$-5 \text{ volts}$$

The parts list for the supplemental power supply is given in Table 7-2. The +5 volts connections are made to the power supply circuit described in Chapter 6.

EPROMs have a small window in the DIP housing, as illustrated in Fig. 7-5. This window is used to erase the data stored in the chip. To prevent accidental erasure, cover the window with a piece of black electrical tape before programming.

To erase the EPROM, remove the black tape covering the window, and expose the chip to a strong ultraviolet light source for 15 to 30 minutes. An ultraviolet lamp can be purchased from many

Table 7-1. Parts List for Fig. 7-3.

IC1	Quad 2-Input OR Gate
IC2	8-Input NAND Gate
IC3	Hex Inverter
IC4	8255 Programmable Peripheral Interface
IC5	74151 Dual Peripheral AND Driver
IC6	LM723 Voltage Regulator
LED1	LED ("READ")
LED2	LED ("WRITE")
R1, R6, R7	2.2 kΩ Resistor
R2	5.6 kΩ Resistor
R3	10 kΩ Resistor
R4	10 Ω Resistor
R5	10 kΩ Trimpot
R8	220 Ω Resistor
R9, R10	330 Ω Resistor
C1, C3	0.1 μF Capacitor
C2	22 μF Capacitor

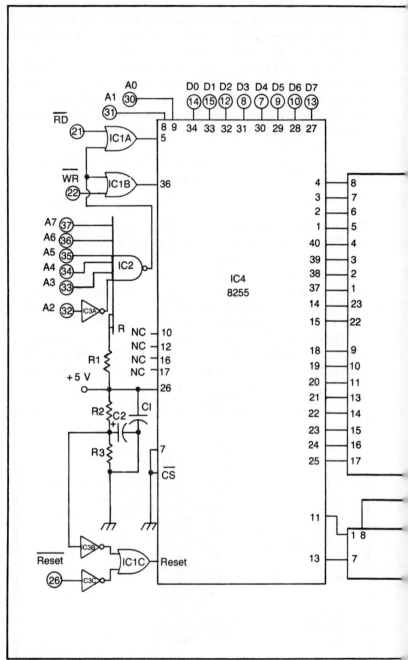

Fig. 7-3. This circuit is used to program EPROMs.

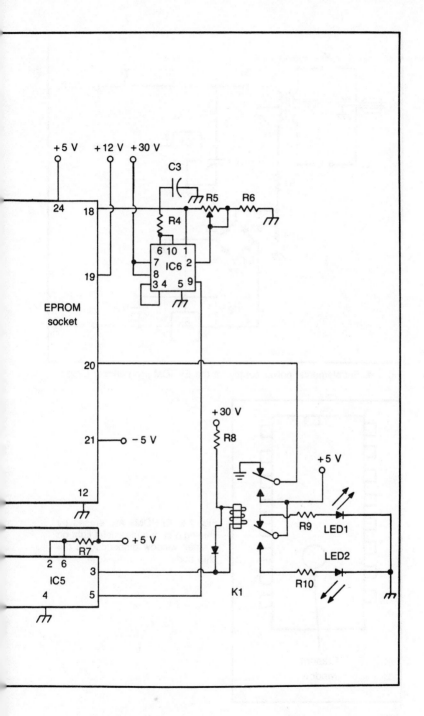

177

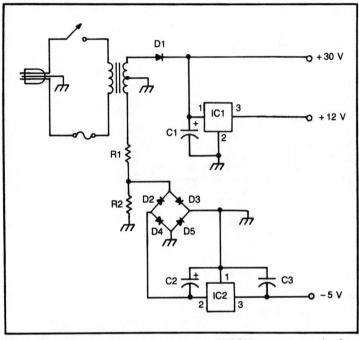

Fig. 7-4. Supplemental power supply for the EPROM programmer circuit.

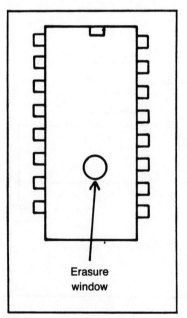

Fig. 7-5. EPROMs are erased by shining a strong ultraviolet light on a small window embedded in the chip body.

Erasure window

178

Table 7-2. Parts List for Fig. 7-4.

IC1	LM340-12 +12-volt Regulator
IC2	LM320-5 −5-volt Regulator
R1	1 kΩ 1/2-watt Resistor
R2	4.7 kΩ 1/2-watt Resistor
C1, C2	1000 μF Electrolytic Capacitor
C3	0.1 μF Capacitor
T1	30-V CT 300 mA Transformer
F1	0.5-amp Fuse and Holder

hardware, lighting, and novelty stores. In a real pinch, you could expose the chip's window to strong sunlight for a few hours, but it is better to have an ultraviolet light source that is under your control.

Chapter 8

Timer/Automation Systems

I N THE LAST TWO CHAPTERS WE BUILT A BASIC CPU SYSTEM
for our projects. Now, it's time to start putting it all to work
for practical applications. In this chapter we will explore the use
of the CPU as an ultimate control clock. Because of its precise clock
pulses driving all its functions, a CPU can serve as a very accurate
time-keeping device. The output ports can be used to control virtually any external device you like.

Imagine setting up your full stereo system to work as a clock
radio. The air conditioning can automatically be turned on a half
hour before you come home. Outdoor lighting can operate under
computer control, so you don't have to remember to turn on (or
off) the porch light. The possibilities are truly limitless.

AC CONTROLLER

Many of the devices we will want to place under computer control operate on standard house current (120 volts ac). Of course,
the CPU cannot supply or directly gate this voltage. But it can operate an SCR that can turn on the flow of ac power.

The CPU only needs to turn the SCR on with a brief pulse.
The SCR will then latch on indefinitely, while the CPU turns its
attention elsewhere. This allows the CPU to turn on any ac-powered
device at any time. But, we also want the CPU to automatically
cut off power. Removing the on pulse won't help, because the SCR

181

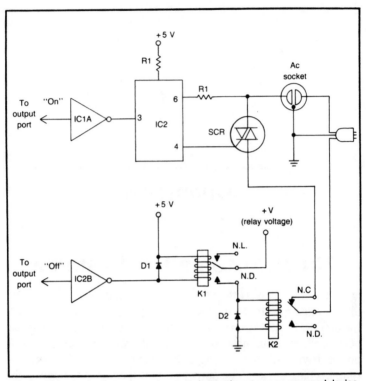

Fig. 8-1. This circuit allows computer control over almost any ac-powered device.

is a latching device. A second control pulse won't do anything. To turn off an SCR, the current flow from cathode to anode must be momentarily interrupted.

Figure 8-1 shows a computer-controlled SCR circuit. Notice that there are two digital control inputs—one to turn the SCR on, and the other to turn it back off. For both control inputs, a logic 0 means no change, and a logic 1 initiates the associated action (turn on or turn off). A parts list for this circuit is given in Table 8-1.

Because ac voltages flow through this circuit, you must use careful construction techniques. All wiring must be enclosed. It should be impossible for anyone to ever touch any exposed conductor. If a metal chassis is used, it must be 100% isolated from all of the circuitry. Do not use the chassis for a circuit ground!

Notice that yet another fuse is used. This is partially to protect the SCR and its associated circuitry against output shorts, but, more importantly, it is to protect anyone using the project against potentially fatal electrical shock. Before applying power check

Table 8-1. Parts List for Fig. 8-1.

IC1	75492 Hex Inverter/Buffer
IC2	HEP P5002 Optocoupler
SCR	HEP R1723 SCR (600 watts)
K1	Small relay
K2	Ac relay
D1, D2	1N4004 Diode
R1, R2	330 Ω 1/2-watt Resistor
F	4.5-amp Fuse

everything over very, very carefully. Then check it all again. You can't possibly be too careful when working with ac voltages.

ADDRESSING

Figure 8-2 illustrates how the CPU can address a bank of SCR circuits. Each byte can control up to four of these circuits (two bits each):

bit 0	A on
bit 1	A off
bit 2	B on
bit 3	B off
bit 4	C on
bit 5	C off
bit 6	D on
bit 7	D off

The circuitry shown here uses the address &H1F FF. Changing the inverters on the address lines can change the address. As far as the CPU is concerned, this is a memory location. LOAD commands can be used to activate any control combination. Some combinations, such as &H03 should never be used. This value would

B0	B1	B2	B3	B4	B5	B6	B7
A on	A off	B on	B off	C on	C off	D on	D off

Fig. 8-2. The CPU can easily address a bank of SCR control circuits. (Fig. 8-1.)

try to simultaneously turn device A both on and off. The valid control values are as follows:

&H00	no change
&H01	A on
&H02	A off
&H04	B on
&H05	A on/B on
&H06	A off/B on
&H08	B off
&H09	A on/B off
&H0A	A off/B off
&H10	C on
&H11	A on/C on
&H12	A off/C on
&H14	B on/C on
&H15	A on/B on/C on
&H16	A off/B on/C on
&H18	B off/C on
&H19	A on/B off/C on
&H1A	A off/B off/C on
&H20	C off
&H21	A on/C off
&H22	A off/C off
&H24	B on/C off
&H25	A on/B on/C off
&H26	A off/B on/C off
&H28	B off/C off
&H29	A on/B off/C off
&H2A	A off/B off/C off
&H40	D on
&H41	A on/D on
&H42	A off/D on
&H44	B on/D on
&H45	A on/B on/D on
&H46	A off/B on/D on
&H48	B off/D on
&H49	A on/B off/D on
&H4A	A off/B off/D on
&H50	C on/D on
&H51	A on/C on/D on
&H52	A off/C on/D on

&H54	B on/C on/D on
&H55	A on/B on/C on/D on
&H56	A off/B on/C on/D on
&H58	B off/C on/D on
&H59	A on/B off/C on/D on
&H5A	A off/B off/C on/D on
&H60	C off/D on
&H61	A on/C off/D on
&H62	A off/C off/D on
&H64	B on/C off/D on
&H65	A on/B on/C off/D on
&H66	A off/B on/C off/D on
&H68	B off/C off/D on
&H69	A on/B off/C off/D on
&H6A	A off/B off/C off/D on
&H80	D off
&H81	A on/D off
&H82	A off/D off
&H84	B on/D off
&H85	A on/B on/D off
&H86	A off/B on/D off
&H88	B off/D off
&H89	A on/B off/D off
&H8A	A off/B off/D off
&H90	C on/D off
&H91	A on/C on/D off
&H92	A off/C on/D off
&H94	B on/C on/D off
&H95	A on/B on/C on/D off
&H96	A off/B on/C on/D off
&H98	B off/C on/D off
&H99	A on/B off/C on/D off
&H9A	A off/B off/C on/D off
&HA0	C off/D off
&HA1	A on/C off/D off
&HA2	A off/C off/D off
&HA4	B on/C off/D off
&HA5	A on/B on/C off/D off
&HA6	A off/B on/C off/D off
&HA8	B off/C off/D off
&HA9	A on/B off/C off/D off
&HAA	A off/B off/C off/D off

SOFTWARE

The software for this type of project is quite simple. The CPU should be instructed to cycle through a time-wasting/counting loop. Each loop should be set up so it lasts a specific amount of time (X number of clock cycles). We can keep time by counting the loop cycles. For example, if each loop lasts 0.5 second, 120 loops will equal 1 minute.

When the count value (time) equals a preset value, the appropriate control value is LOADed into the pseudomemory location (output port). Then the CPU returns to the loop and continues counting and biding its time until the next scheduled event.

Chapter 9

Security Systems

I N THE LAST CHAPTER, WE SAW HOW WE COULD USE SIMPLE
on/off output ports to set up an automation system. In this chapter we will be using simple on/off input ports to sense various conditions and trigger an alarm (or some other indicator device) at an output port. It is not at all difficult to create a complete multipurpose security system, including burglar and fire alarms.

BURGLAR FOOLER

Many complete security systems include a timer to turn lights on and off at certain times. The idea is to fool a burglar into thinking someone is home when the building is unoccupied. The problem is that a smart burglar might watch a target house several nights before breaking in. A simple timer will switch on and off at about the same time each night. This is clearly a mechanical device, rather than a living human being going about his business. Rather than fooling the potential burglar, the simple light timer can actually be a help for the burglar—it proves quite conclusively that no one's at home.

A CPU-based system can do a much better job. Lights in various parts of the house can be switched on or off at multiple and differing times each night. An element of randomness can even be added to the program. If you want to include a burglar fooler in your security system, simply include some of the timing/automation circuits from the last chapter.

DOOR/WINDOW SWITCHES

The simplest security system devices are nothing more than switches mounted on doors and windows. Often magnetic switches are used. These devices are housed in two units. One unit contains a permanent magnet, while the other contains a reed switch that is sensitive to the magnetic field. When the magnetic unit is held close to the switch unit, the switch is held in one position. Moving the magnet causes the switch to reverse states. The use of such a switch is illustrated in Fig. 9-1. The magnet unit is mounted on the door, and the switch unit is mounted on the door frame. When the door is closed, the two units are close to each other. Opening the door moves the magnet away from the switch unit.

Magnetic switches are available in two types—*normally open* and *normally closed*. A normally-open switch has open contacts when the magnet unit is at a distance. Moving the magnet unit close to the switch unit closes the contacts. A normally-closed switch functions in exactly the opposite manner. To summarize:

Normally Open

Magnet near	contacts closed
Magnet far	contacts open

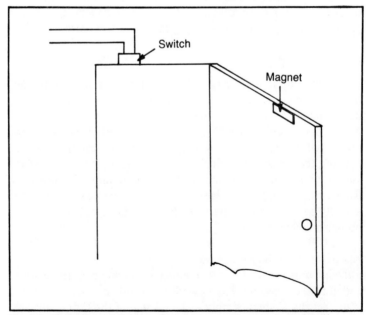

Fig. 9-1. Magnetic switches are frequently used in security systems.

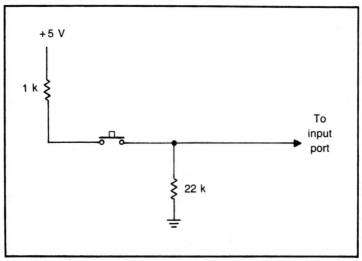

Fig. 9-2. This circuit allows a NO intrusion switch as a one-bit input to the CPU.

Normally Closed

Magnet near	contacts open
Magnet far	contacts closed

Generally, in security systems, normally-closed switches are preferred. This is because if the connecting wires are cut, normally-open switches will be defeated, but in a normally-closed system, a broken wire will trigger the alarm.

On the other hand, a normally-open system tends to involve considerably simpler circuitry. If cut wires are not likely to be a problem, normally-open switches may be a better choice.

In a CPU based security system, there isn't much difference in circuit complexity between NO and NC systems. Figure 9-2 shows an input circuit for one NO switch. This circuit inputs one bit to the CPU. Eight of these circuits can be accommodated on a one-byte input port. A NC circuit is shown in Fig. 9-3. It is basically the same as the NO version, except an inverter is added. Figure 9-4 shows how the input port can be addressed as a read-only-memory location. The circuitry shown here addresses &H1F FD.

Why bother using the computer to monitor simple switches like this? A less complicated analog circuit can be used to trigger an alarm from any of a number of switches. The advantage of the computer is that it can tell which switch has been activated, how long

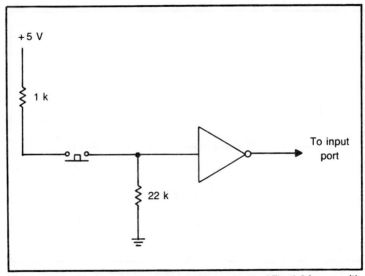

Fig. 9-3. The addition of an inverter converts the circuit of Fig. 9-2 for use with a NC switch.

it is activated, and exactly when it was activated, depending on the programming. Such information can give you a much more powerful security system.

BROKEN BEAM DETECTORS

Many burglar alarm systems include motion detectors in addition to door and window switches. If an intruder gets past the entry alarms, he can still be foiled by a system that can detect his movements in a protected area.

The simplest type of motion detector is the broken-beam detector. A broken beam detector is made of two separate parts—a light source, and a light sensor. The light source emits a beam of light at the light sensor. If anything blocks the beam of light, the light sensor is triggered. A broken-beam detector system is illustrated in Fig. 9-5.

Obviously, the sensor must be shielded from any ambient light in the protected area. Such systems function best in a darkened area. A shield around the light sensor, as illustrated in Fig. 9-6, helps cut down on problems from external light sources.

An infrared light source can be used instead of a visible light source. It might be a little more expensive, but the light beam will be invisible, and therefore harder to avoid.

A light sensor circuit for a computer system is shown in Fig. 9-7. Table 9-1 is the parts list for this circuit. The detector is a photocell. If you use an infrared light source, an infrared sensitive photocell should be used. Such devices are almost as readily available as photocells that are sensitive to visible light. Each such detector circuit is one input bit to the CPU.

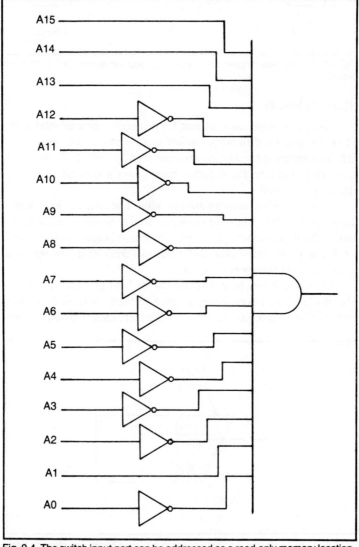

Fig. 9-4. The switch input port can be addressed as a read-only memory location.

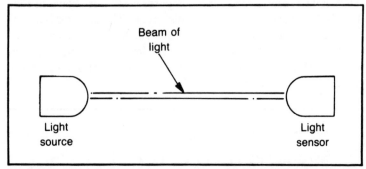

Fig. 9-5. Broken beam detectors are another popular approach for intrusion detection.

HEAT SENSOR

Security systems are not just for protection against intruders. They are also used to warn against unsafe conditions, especially fire. The simplest fire alarms are activated by heat. If the ambient temperature around the detector rises above a specific point, the alarm is triggered.

Switch type heat sensors are available. They usually look something like Fig. 9-8. These devices are used essentially in the same way as the door and window circuits discussed earlier in this chapter. If the temperature exceeds a value (determined by the sensor's manufacturer) the switch closes.

A more sensitive heat detector can be built using a *thermistor*. This is a thermally-sensitive resistance element. In most cases, the resistance decreases as the temperature increases. This is referred

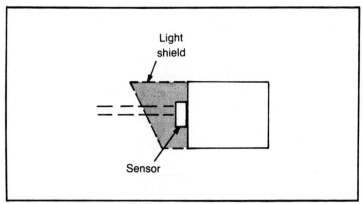

Fig. 9-6. A shield around the light sensor in a broken beam detector can help cut down on false triggering problems from external light sources.

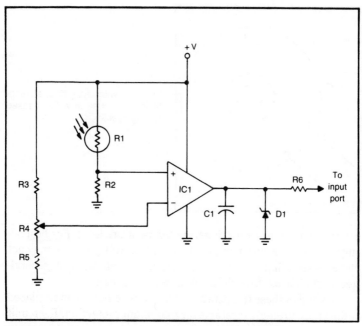

Fig. 9-7. A light sensor circuit for use with the CPU system.

to as a negative temperature coefficient (NTC). Some thermistors operate with a positive temperature coefficient (PTC). That is, the resistance rises with the temperature. PTC thermistors are relatively rare.

The circuit shown in Fig. 9-9 uses a NTC thermistor as a monitoring device, which is triggered when the temperature exceeds a user determined level. Basically, this circuit is a comparator. A logic-1 bit appears at the output when the thermistor (RT) resistance is less than that of the reference resistance (RR). If a potentiometer is used for this reference resistance element, the user

Table 9-1. Parts List for Fig. 9-7.

IC1	Op Amp (1/4 LM324, or similar)
D1	5.1-volt Zener Diode
R1	Photoresistor
R2	68 kΩ Resistor
R3, R5	100 kΩ Resistor
R4	1 MΩ Potentiometer (Sensitivity)
R6	10 kΩ Resistor
C1	0.1 μF Capacitor

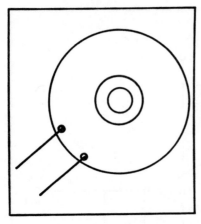

Fig. 9-8. Switch-type heat sensors are ideal for use in a CPU-based security system.

can manually adjust the triggering temperature level. For best accuracy, use a ten-turn trimpot. This high accuracy may or may not be necessary, depending on the individual application. A generalized parts list for this circuit is given in Table 9-2.

Several of these temperature monitoring circuits can be placed at different strategic locations for maximum protection. Each unit

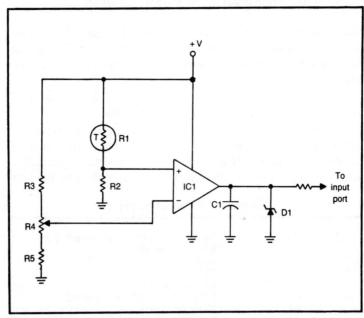

Fig. 9-9. This circuit will trigger the CPU if the temperature exceeds a preset level.

194

Table 9-2. Parts List for Fig. 9-9.

IC1	Op Amp (1/4 LM324, or similar)
D1	5.1-volt Zener Diode
R1	Thermistor
R2	68 kΩ Resistor
R3, R5	100 kΩ Resistor
R4	1 MΩ Potentiometer (Sensitivity)
R6	10 kΩ Resistor
C1	0.1 μF Capacitor

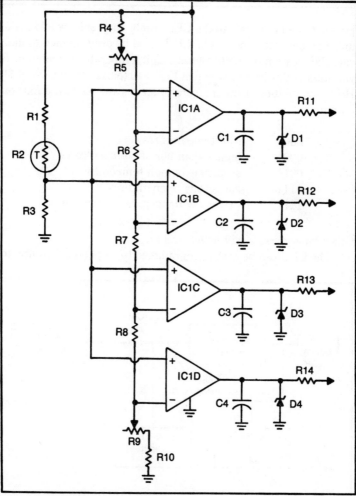

Fig. 9-10. This more advanced thermometer circuit can indicate five different temperature ranges.

Table 9-3. Parts List for Fig. 9-10.

IC1	LM324 Quad Op Amp
D1-D4	5.1-volt Zener Diode
R1, R3, R4, R6, R7, R8, R10	100 kΩ Resistor
R2	Thermistor
R5, R9	500 kΩ Potentiometer (Upper/Lower Range Set)
R11-R14	10 kΩ Resistor
C1-C4	0.1 μF Capacitor

puts out one bit of data to the CPU. Eight such units would make up a one byte input port. The CPU could be programmed to indicate the location of the triggering high temperature condition. A variation of this idea is shown in Fig. 9-10 (parts list in Table 9-3). Here several thermistor comparator stages are used for a four bit output:

0000	safe temperatures
0001	higher than normal temperatures
0011	suspiciously high temperatures
0111	dangerous temperatures
1111	extremely dangerous temperatures

Other binary codes will never occur.

The CPU can be easily programmed to respond differently to

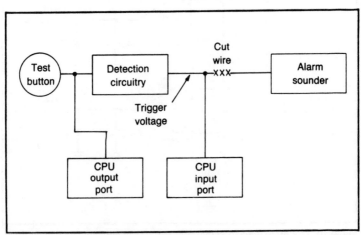

Fig. 9-11. A commercial smoke detector can be adapted for use with a CPU-based security system.

each possible input condition. Two of these 4-bit circuits can be combined to form a one byte input port.

All of these circuits can easily be adapted to respond to lower than normal (rather than higher than normal) temperatures where freezing could be a problem.

SMOKE DETECTORS

Heat sensors are fine and dandy in some applications. Unfor-

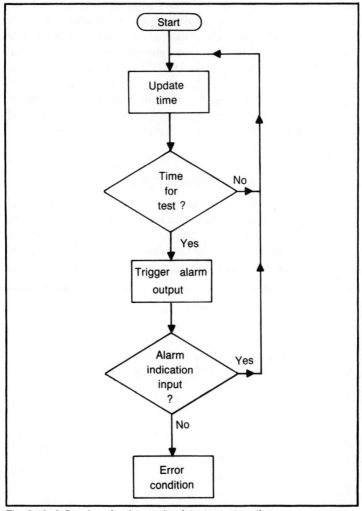

Fig. 9-12. A flowchart for the smoke detector test routine.

197

tunately, most fire related deaths are due to smoke inhalation. Smoke can reach dangerous levels in many fires without excessive heat reaching any of the heat sensors. You may want to include a few smoke detectors to your security system.

The design of a good smoke detector is a little tricky, and the sensors are not very easy to come by. A complete smoke detector can be purchased for under ten bucks, so there isn't much point in going to unnecessary efforts to build our own.

Figure 9-11 shows how a commercial smoke detector may be adapted for inclusion in a CPU-based security system. The internal alarm is bypassed, and the triggering signal is sent to the CPU instead (via bit A). The CPU can distinguish between several smoke detector units in different locations and indicate the danger area.

Bit B is connected to one of the CPU's output ports. This allows the CPU to automatically test the smoke detector at programmed intervals, without disturbing anyone. The alarm will not go off during the test unless the smoke detector does not respond correctly to the test. A flowchart for programming this function is shown in Fig. 9-12.

OUTPUT ALARMS AND INDICATORS

So far we have worked on several methods for letting the CPU know when an alarm condition exists. Now, we need some way to allow the CPU to notify us of the condition. Figure 9-13 shows a simple electronic alarm circuit that can be triggered by a single-bit output pulse from the CPU. Adjusting the potentiometers will

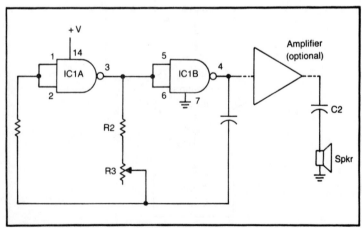

Fig. 9-13. This circuit is a simple but effective alarm signaller.

198

Table 9-4. Parts List for Fig. 9-13.

IC1	CD4011
R1	1 MΩ Resistor
R2	47 kΩ Resistor
R3	100 kΩ Potentiometer (pitch)
C1	0.01 μF Capacitor
C2	0.1 μF Capacitor
Spkr	Small speaker

alter the sound produced. If you prefer, you can replace the potentiometers with fixed resistors. Nothing in this circuit is terribly critical. The parts list is given in Table 9-4. Several of these alarm circuits could be placed at various locations.

Another approach would be for the CPU to trigger a standard 12-volt alarm siren or bell. A circuit for accomplishing this is shown in Fig. 9-14. Different alarm sounding devices could be used to indicate different alarm conditions. For example, a bell could indicate a fire, while a siren could be used for the burglar alarm.

One of the big advantages of using a CPU as a security system control center is that it can distinguish between the various alarm triggering devices. A LED indicator panel could be used for a display of the trouble area, saving time in emergencies.

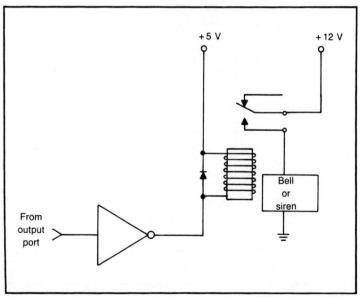

Fig. 9-14. A standard 12-volt alarm or bell can be activated by the CPU.

199

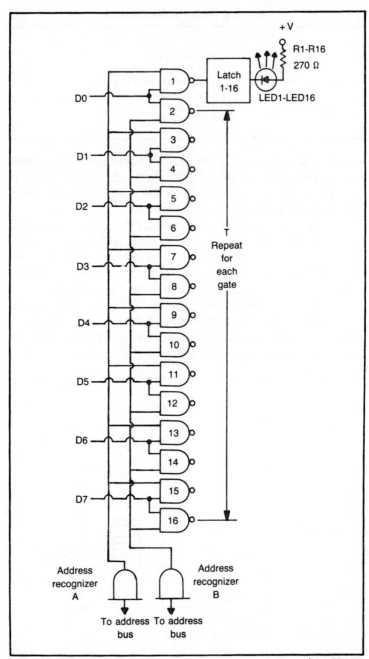

Fig. 9-15. Multiple alarm locations can be pinpointed with this 16-bit LED display panel.

Figure 9-15 shows a display panel circuit for 16 bits (two bytes). Each LED corresponds to one of the input devices. Arranging the LEDs in a convenient pattern (as shown in Fig. 9-16) and labelling them will allow you to find the trouble spot at a glance and take appropriate action. This principle can be expanded for any number of LEDs.

RESET

Any alarm system needs some sort of manual override and/or reset. If the alarm is falsely triggered, you need to be able to shut it off. Also, there are times when you don't want the alarm to function. It would be very obnoxious if the alarm went off everything you opened your front door.

The simple circuit shown in Fig. 9-17 will take care of these problems. Switch S1 is used for override. The program should be set up so that when S1 is closed, the CPU will ignore all intrusion alarms, but not the fire alarms.

Switch S2 is a NO pushbutton. Depressing it momentarily will cause the CPU to cancel out any current alarm condition (turn off

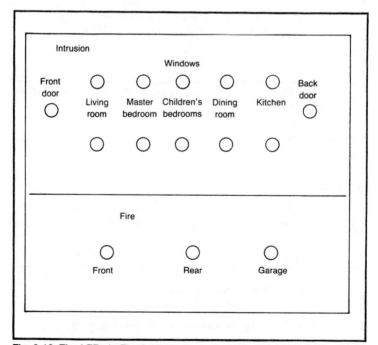

Fig. 9-16. The LEDs in Fig. 9-15 can be arranged in any convenient pattern.

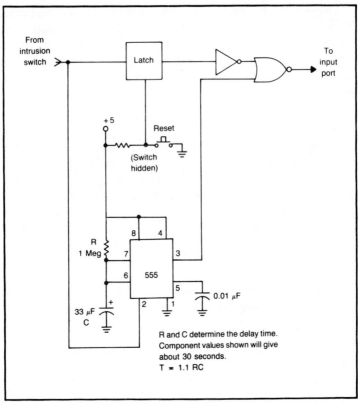

Fig. 9-17. This delay circuit will prevent the security alarm from triggering during legitimate entry.

the alarm sounder, and extinquish the indicator LED). Once again, this must be supported with appropriate software.

SOFTWARE

The programming for the security system project will vary considerably depending on the exact application and the options cho-

Table 9-5. A Typical System Might Include These Components.

2	Door intrusion switches
8	Window intrusion switches
2	Smoke detectors
1	5-range temperature sensor (see Fig. 9-10)

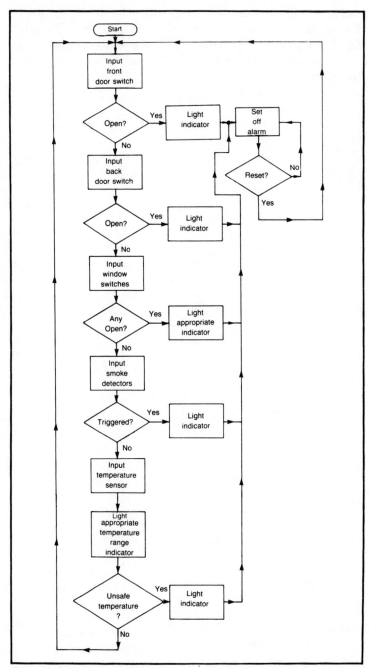

Fig. 9-18. Software for a typical security system is illustrated in this flowchart.

203

sen for the system. Certain features will probably be common to all systems. A typical system is outlined in Table 9-5. This table identifies the input and output devices at each port, or pseudomemory location. The software for this particular system is flowcharted in Fig. 9-18.

Chapter 10

Test Equipment

I F YOU'RE READING THIS BOOK, I THINK IT'S REASONABLE TO assume that you work with electronics, and know the value of test equipment. In this chapter we will be using the CPU as a master control center for various test equipment applications.

D/A AND A/D CONVERTERS

Most of the signals to be measured in electronic circuits are analog rather than digital quantities. The CPU can only deal with digital signals. We need some way to convert between analog and digital values.

D/A Converter

A D/A (digital-to-analog) converter is used as the CPU's output ports. It converts the digital values output from the CPU into a proportional analog voltage. (The basic principles of D/A converters were discussed in Chapter 5.)

A practical D/A converter circuit is shown in Fig. 10-1. The parts list is given in Table 10-1. This circuit will be used in most of the projects described in this chapter.

A/D Converter

An A/D (analog-to-digital) converter works in just the opposite way as a D/A converter. It is used to provide digital input signals

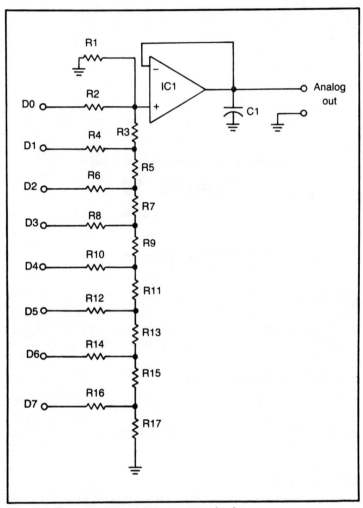

Fig. 10-1. This is a practical D/A converter circuit.

Table 10-1. Parts List for Fig. 10-1.

IC1	Op Amp (1/4 LM324, or equivalent)
R1, R3, R5, R7, R9, R11, R13, R15	9.1 kΩ Resistor
R2, R4, R6, R8, R10, R12, R14, R16, R17	18 kΩ Resistor
C1	0.47 μF Capacitor

to the CPU. An existing analog voltage is converted into a proportional binary (digital) value. (A/D conversion was also discussed in Chapter 5.)

The A/D converter circuit we will be using in the projects in this chapter is shown in Fig. 10-2. Table 10-2 is the parts list for this project. Notice that this A/D circuit is considerably more complex than the D/A converter of Fig. 10-1. A/D converters are, by nature, relatively complicated beasts. So far, no one has devised a way around this. Both D/A converters and A/D converters are available in IC form, but A/D converter chips tend to be more expensive, because of the necessary circuit complexity.

VOLTMETER

The simplest CPU-based test equipment project is a digital voltmeter. The input stage is simply an A/D converter that converts the analog voltage into a binary byte, which is then displayed in BCD format by the CPU.

Why should we bother with the CPU at all? Many inexpensive digital voltmeters are available. There are several useful tricks we can do with a CPU-based voltmeter that would not be possible with a more traditional instrument. I'll just give a few suggestions here.

The CPU can remember past measurements and compare them. Often we only need to know if the voltage is going up, going down, or remaining steady. Figure 10-3 offers a circuit for displaying this information directly on three LEDs. The parts list is given in Table 10-3. As shown here, this circuit would be connected to an output port as pseudomemory (write only) location &HFF A0. Latches are used, so the LEDs will remain lit, even when the CPU is working on other tasks.

Table 10-2. Parts List for Fig. 10-2.

IC1	TL507
IC2	74LS04 Hex Inverter
IC3	74LS02 Quad 2-Input NOR Gate
IC4, IC5	74LS193 Counter
IC6	74LS08 Quad 2-Input AND Gate
IC7	555 Timer
IC8	74LS374 A/D Converter
R1	4.7 kΩ Resistor
R2	220 Ω Resistor
R3	10 kΩ Resistor
C1	500 pF Capacitor

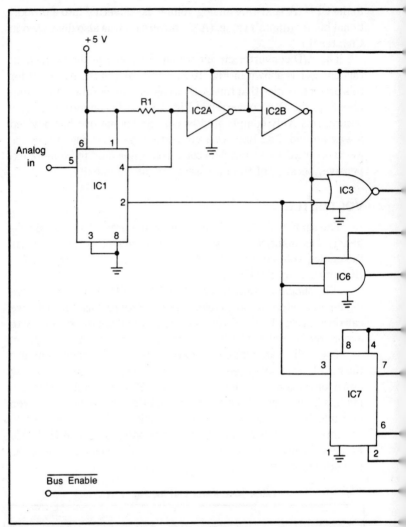

Fig. 10-2. This is a practical A/D converter circuit for use with the projects in this chapter.

Figure 10-4 is a flowchart for a simple program utilizing this circuit. The input voltage is periodically sampled. Each sample is compared to a previously stored value in register B, and an appropriate value is stored in &HFF A0. There are only three possible output values:

☐ 1 SAMPLE > B

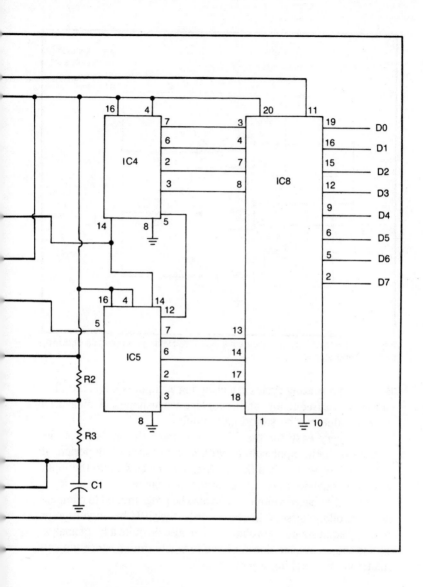

□ 2 SAMPLE = B
□ 3 SAMPLE < B

Once the output procedure is completed, the current sample value replaces the old comparison value in register B, and the cycle repeats. The displayed data is constantly updated.

The CPU can also keep track of how rapidly a voltage changes.

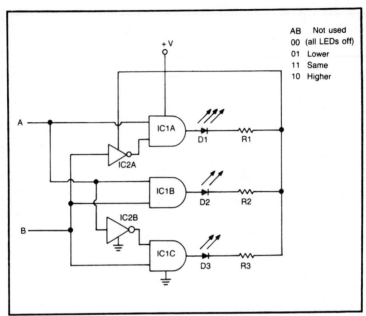

Fig. 10-3. Three LEDs can indicate if a monitored voltage is going up or down, or remaining stable.

By finding repeating cycles in a changing ac input voltage, the CPU can measure frequency, and recognize waveshapes. A measured voltage value can be stored indefinitely.

It is very easy for the CPU to identify the highest (or the lowest—or both) input voltage within any desired time period. It can also determine when (how often, and for how long) the input voltage is outside a specific programmed range.

The CPU-based voltmeter can also be programmed to compensate for voltage offsets. In other words, the CPU-based voltmeter doesn't just measure the voltage. It can also do quite a bit of analyzing, so the technician doesn't have to waste time performing calculations, or watching a meter.

Table 10-3. Parts List for Fig. 10-3.

IC1	Quad 2-Input AND Gate
IC2	Hex Inverter
D1, D2	LED
R1, R2, R3	270 Ω Resistor

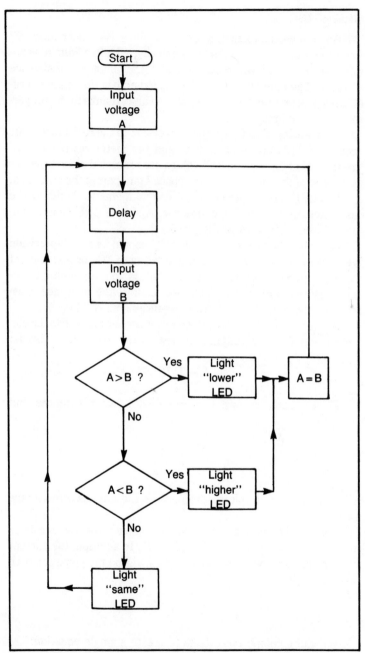

Fig. 10-4. This flowchart illustrates typical software for use with the circuit shown in Fig. 10-3.

OHMMETER

An ohmmeter, which measures resistance, isn't much more difficult to create than a voltmeter. Basically, a known voltage is applied across a known resistance and the unknown resistance element. The amount of voltage dropped across the unknown resistance element reveals the resistance value, thanks to the properties of Ohm's law.

In an analog ohmmeter, the conversion to the resistance scale requires a little special circuitry, and the meter reads out non-linearly. That is, wide-spread values are crammed close together at one end of the meter scale, and spaced far apart at the other end.

In a CPU-based ohmmeter, we can mathematically derive the resistance, using Ohm's law directly. A simple CPU-based ohmmeter circuit is shown in Fig. 10-5.

Note that the reference resistor (R_r) should be a high-precision type. Use a resistor with a tolerance rating of 1%, or less. Do not use a standard 5% or 10% resistor, unless you are willing to accept very rough readings. The more accurate the reference resistance is, the more accurate the measurements can be.

According to Ohm's law, the current across any resistance element is equal to the voltage, divided by the resistance. That is:

$$I = E/R$$

In this case, we are concerned with two resistances and voltages:

$$I_r = E_r/R_r$$
$$I_x = E_x/R_x$$

E_x is the measured voltage drop across the unknown resistance element.

Because the full five volts must be dropped across the two resistors, $E_x + E_r = 5$ volts. Or, $5 - E_x = E_r$. In addition, the current flowing through two resistors in series will be the same for both resistance elements. That is:

$$I_r = I_x$$

We can combine these facts to create a single equation:

$$E_x/R_x = (5 - E_x)/R_r$$

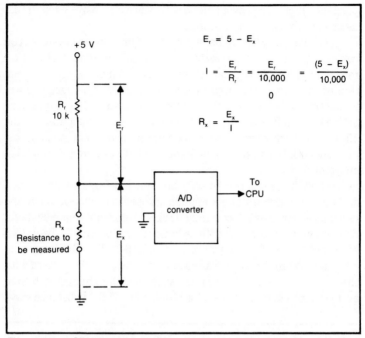

Fig. 10-5. In a CPU-based ohmmeter, we can mathematically derive the resistance using Ohm's law.

Algebraically rearranging this equation to solve for R_x, we get:

$$R_x = (E \times R_r)/(5 - E_x)$$

R_r is a hardware constant, and E_x is the measured input voltage, so the computer can quickly and efficiently perform the calculation, and determine the value of R_r.

The advantages of a CPU-based ohmmeter are essentially the same as those discussed earlier for the voltmeter project.

CAPACITANCE METER

Analog and even dedicated digital voltmeters and ohmmeters are easy enough to come by. It's hard to imagine anyone working with electronics without a VOM (volt/ohm/milliammeter) of some kind. The computer system offers some special advantages and conveniences, but there is nothing new in principle.

Capacitance measurement is another story. Accurately measuring capacitances with analog circuitry is no easy task. Digital ca-

213

pacitance meters are available, but they are expensive enough that most experimenters go without.

Because you already have your CPU breadboard system, you can set up a capacitance meter for just a little more cost and effort. A simple go/no-go capacitance meter can use a simple variation of the ohmmeter circuit discussed earlier. The variant form is illustrated in Fig. 10-6. The difference is an added momentary action switch. Pushing this switch shorts out the capacitor's leads, allowing it to discharge. Hold the button down for a moment, especially with fairly large capacitance units to be sure it is fully discharged.

When the switch is released, the capacitor leads are separated, and the reference voltage is applied across the capacitor. Then the resistance is measured over time. It should start out relatively high, drop down to a low value, then build up exponentially back to a high resistance. This is graphed in Fig. 10-7. The CPU can take several resistance readings a second, and compare the pattern with the correct sequence. If the resistance does not change with time as it is supposed to, the capacitor is defective. If the resistance stays

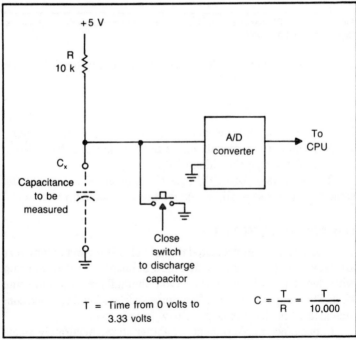

Fig. 10-6. A CPU-based capacitance meter is quite similar to an ohmmeter.

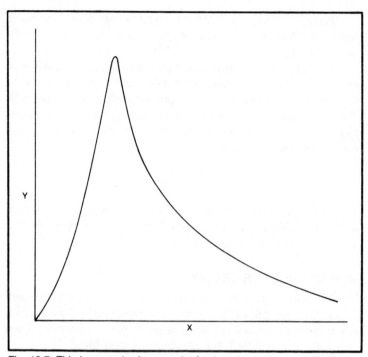

Fig. 10-7. This is a graph of a capacitor's changing resistance with time.

low, the capacitor is shorted. If it stays high, without the initial drop, it is probably open.

This test can be performed on any standard analog ohmmeter, but it is often difficult to guess which range is set the meter on for best visibility of the pointer movement. Very small capacitors may change resistance too fast for the pointer to move very far, or for the eye to see well if it does move. Very large capacitors may move the pointer so slowly it may be difficult to be sure that it really is moving. This type of test isn't at all practical on most digital ohmmeters. The numerical readout will just be a meaningless blur until the final resistance value settles.

A CPU makes this approach a lot more convenient. In addition, with a little additional programming, it can measure the capacitance with reasonable accuracy. This is done by measuring the time constant. The time constant is defined as the time it takes a capacitor to charge up to 67% of its full value (the applied voltage) through a specific resistance. In other words:

$$T = RC$$

The applied voltage is known, and it is easy enough to calculate the 67% level. The resistance element is the reference resistor of the ohmmeter.

You can find the approximate range of an unknown capacitance by timing the pointer's movement on an analog ohmmeter, but it is virtually impossible to be very precise using manual methods. The CPU, on the other hand, can make timing measurements precise to a fraction of a second. Once time T is known, the CPU can easily calculate the value of C:

$$C = T/R$$

The appropriate programming for this project is flowcharted in Fig. 10-8. Most commercial digital capacitance meters use some variation on this basic approach.

SEMICONDUCTOR TESTER

A semiconductor junction theoretically allows current to pass in one direction, but not in the other. In more practical terms, with one polarity of applied voltage, the resistance is very low. When the polarity is reversed, the resistance is very high.

Diode and bipolar transistor junctions can be measured on any standard ohmmeter, but it is awkward at best, especially with a transistor's three leads. Keeping the sequence of lead connections and polarities straight can be tricky. This is a good task to turn over to a computer.

A semiconductor testing circuit is shown in Fig. 10-9. The computer outputs a series of three-bit binary values and measures the resistance for each combination. It then compares the relative results with a stored table to determine if the transistor is good or not.

If a diode is being tested, connect it across E and B. An input from the keypad could be used to tell the CPU what type of device to expect. For example, 1 for diode, or 2 for bipolar transistor.

A simple go/no-go test program is shown in the flowchart of Fig. 10-10. With a little ingenuity, you could extend this program for the CPU to actually calculate the alpha and beta of a transistor and/or to test other semiconductor devices.

DIGITAL CIRCUIT TESTS

The CPU can also be used to test other digital circuits in several

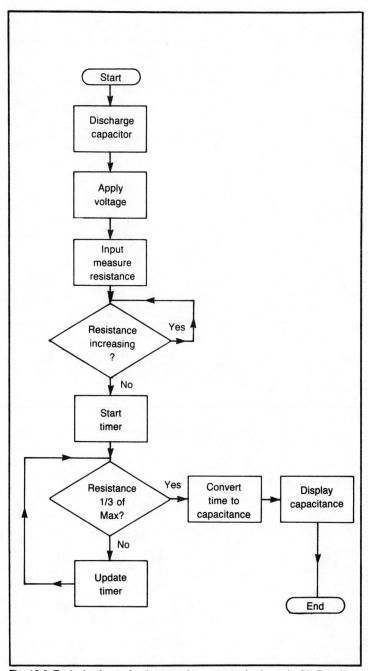

Fig. 10-8. Typical software for the capacitance meter is shown in this flowchart.

217

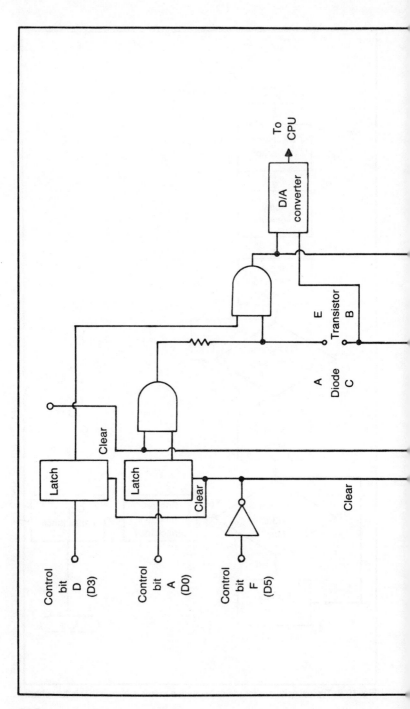

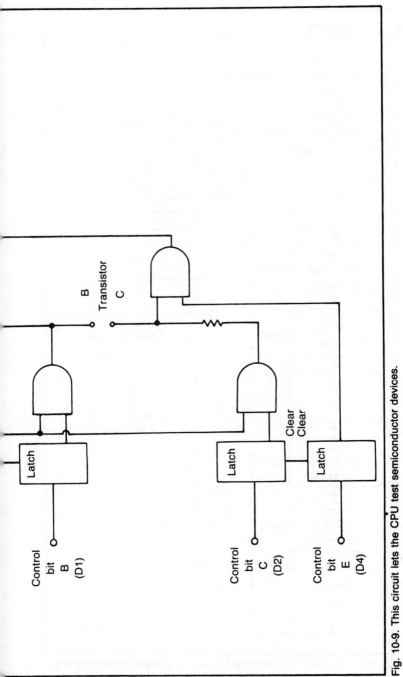

Fig. 10-9. This circuit lets the CPU test semiconductor devices.

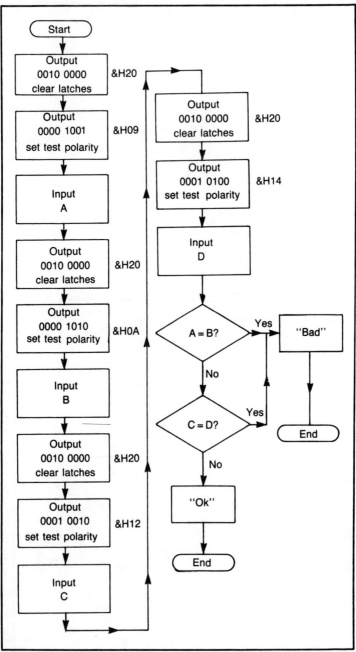

Fig. 10-10. This flowchart shows the software for a simple go/no-go semiconductor test.

220

different ways. A very useful piece of test equipment for digital work is the logic probe. This is simply a one-bit testing device that indicates if the signal at the test point is a logic 1, a logic 0, or a train of pulses (switching back and forth between states). An intelligent CPU-based digital probe, can compare several different test points, determine when the logic state changes, the frequency and duty cycle of a pulse train, and other useful information, depending on the programming used.

A simple four-bit digital probe circuit is shown in Fig. 10-11. It can simultaneously monitor four different test points. The parts list is given in Table 10-4. The ground clip must be connected to the ground of the circuit being tested. The test probes should be

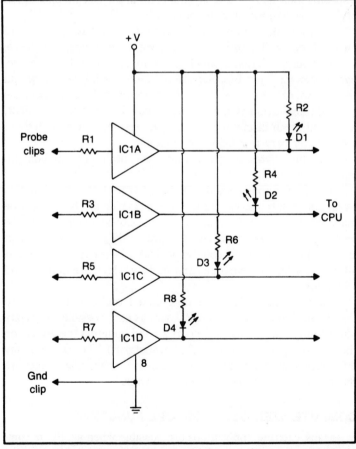

Fig. 10-11. This simple 4 bit digital probe circuit can perform many useful tests.

Table 10-4. Parts List for Fig. 10-11.

IC1	CD4050 Hex Noninverting Buffer
D1-D4	LED
R1, R3, R5, R7	10 kΩ Resistor
R2, R4, R6, R8	470 Ω Resistor

a spring-loaded hook, as illustrated in Fig. 10-12, to free the technician's hands.

The digital probes in Fig. 10-12 are connected to an input port. Similar circuitry could also be connected to an output port to serve as a digital signal injector. The CPU would then be able to insert a specific logic state into a specific point in the circuit, and digital probes can then monitor the effects.

Another application would be to test digital ICs. There are hundreds of possible combinations, so we will be very general here, and limit our discussion to simple gates. Figure 10-13 shows a three-byte tester for 8-pin ICs. Sixteen-pin (and 14-pin) devices would require two of these circuits, and six bytes from the CPU. Because the additional circuitry for larger ICs would simply be redundant, we will limit our discussion to the 8-pin version, even though there are actually very few 8-pin digital ICs.

The three bytes are divided into two output ports and one input port.

The first output port allows the CPU to define specific pins as inputs or outputs. Notice that the power connections must be made manually. This information can usually be obtained from the manufacturer's specification sheet or from a data book. If the pinout is not available, the CPU could conceivably be programmed to test all the possible combinations and deduce which are outputs and which are inputs.

Once the pinout has been determined, and port 1 has set up the proper signal routing, the CPU outputs each possible input combination in sequence (through port 2), and monitors the effects on the chip's outputs through port 3 (the input port). There are so many different possible approaches to this system, a generalized software flowchart would probably be of little value.

COMPUTERIZED OSCILLOSCOPE FUNCTIONS

Many exciting applications are possible when a CPU is combined with an oscilloscope. The most direct marriage of an oscillo-

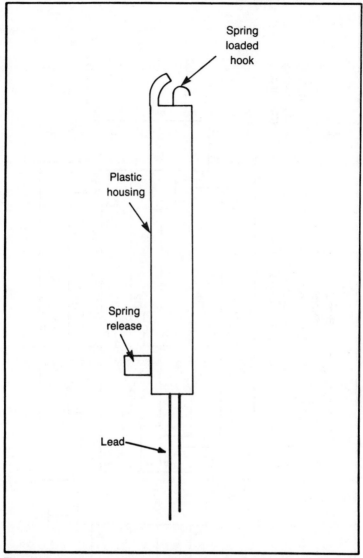

Fig. 10-12. A spring-loaded hook makes a good probe for the circuit shown in Fig. 10-11.

scope and CPU would be for the CPU system to memorize a digitized equivalent of a waveform. It can then be fed back into the oscilloscope to be studied as long as you like. This is very useful for examining brief, nonrecurring signals. A true storage scope would cost well over a thousand dollars. Our CPU breadboard sys-

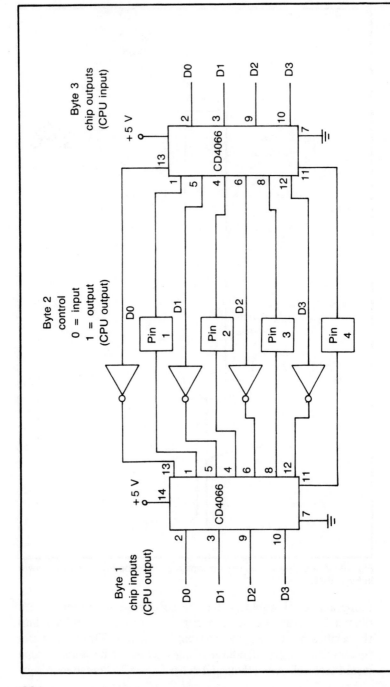

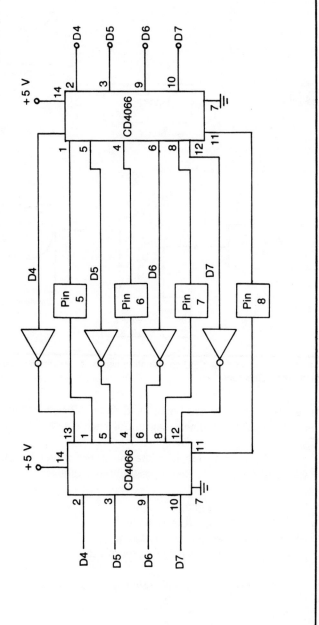

Fig. 10-13. This is a 3-byte test circuit for 8-pin DIP gate ICs.

225

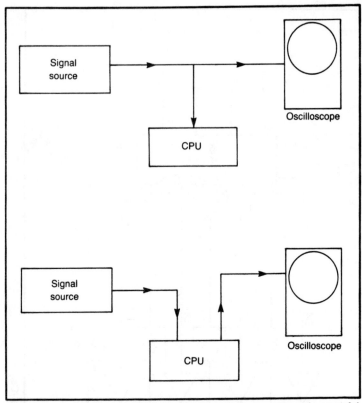

Fig. 10-14. An oscilloscope/CPU combination can be an extremely powerful piece of test equipment.

tem can inexpensively add "quick and dirty" storage capabilities to any oscilloscope. A block diagram of such a system is shown in Fig. 10-14.

The CPU could also manipulate the stored waveform almost any way you might like. Some possibilities include:

☐ Inverting the signal
☐ Running the signal in reverse
☐ Isolating a portion of the signal
☐ Comparing two or more stored signals

I'm sure you can come up with other ideas of your own.

Chapter 11

Robots

MANY ELECTRONICS HOBBYISTS ARE GETTING INVOLVED with robotics. There are at least two regularly published newsletters on the subject. Because virtually all robots (except for a few simple toys) are CPU based, they are a natural for inclusion here.

If you're like most people, however, you may not have had much personal experience with robots. Most people's ideas about robots come from science fiction movies. If you're expecting to build C3PO, you might as well forget about it. Nobody—not even the biggest, best equipped major laboratory—can build that kind of robot, at least not yet. The technology does not yet exist.

One of the first things you'll have to give up is humanoid appearance. It is exceedingly difficult to get the weight balanced properly, and to build a walking robot is probably far beyond the capabilities of any of today's hobbyists. It's best to stick with rolling robots—that is, use wheels instead of legs. In appearance, you can build a robot that looks like R2D2, although it will be considerably less intelligent.

Once again, we will only be giving suggestions for experimentation in this chapter, rather than complete plans for a specific robot. There are so many possible options. I think it is far better for each individual hobbyist to design his own system.

BASIC MOBILITY

For our purposes, a robot is a self-mobile computer. Unless

you want to be stuck with the nuisance of interconnecting wires, you'll probably want to make everything as self-contained as possible. Battery powered operation is almost a must.

Four ni-cad (nickel-cadmium) rechargeable batteries in series add up to five volts. Use several sets of batteries to power various stages of the system to avoid undue current drain. Even so, be prepared to have to recharge your batteries often. A robot is going to use up a lot of power.

To start building a robot, you will need a sturdy base (but not too heavy). If possible, all heavy components (such as motors and batteries) should be mounted directly on the base, with lighter weight circuit boards mounted higher. A top-heavy robot isn't going to be of much use for anything. Watching it topple over everytime it tries to move gets old very fast. For maximum stability, keep the center of balance in your robot as close to the floor as possible.

Wheels should be attached directly to the bottom of the base. A triangular arrangement, such as shown in Fig. 11-1 is very stable. An alternative arrangement is shown in Fig. 11-2. This four wheel arrangement isn't inherently more stable, but the extra wheel offers more control in steering.

The wheels should be turned via a simple dc motor. The motor must be powerful enough to carry the entire weight of the completed system without strain, but you don't have to go overboard. A motor that can handle 100 pounds is pure overkill in a 25 pound robot. The over-sized motor will just add to the cost and the bulk of the unit.

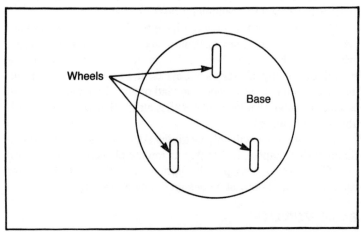

Fig. 11-1. A three-wheeled base gives excellent stability.

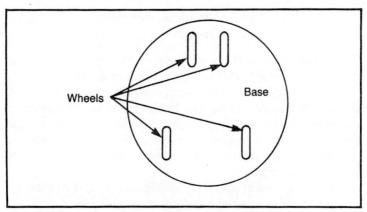

Fig. 11-2. Two front wheels give added control for steering.

By definition, we want the robot's motors to be under direct CPU control. A simple motor control circuit is shown in Fig. 11-3. Two bits are output from the CPU. The meaning of each combination is as follows:

00	motor off
01	Motor on (forward)

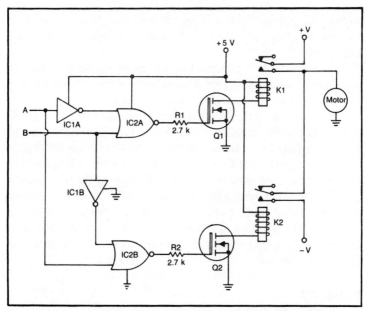

Fig. 11-3. Two output bits can control forward and reverse motion of the motor.

10	motor on (reverse)
11	not used

In the reverse mode, the power supply connections to the motor are simply reversed. This will work for most dc motors.

There are several possible approaches to steering the robot. One is to physically turn the wheels with gears. Such a gearing arrangement can be tricky to get right. A simpler way is to separate the control of the wheels on each side of the machine. Powering the wheels on the right side, for example, will force the robot to turn on its right axis.

Our basic control circuit is modified in Fig. 11-4 to allow for steering. Now the control code runs over three bits:

000	motors off
001	all motors on (forward)
010	all motors on (reverse)
011	not used
100	not used
101	right motor on only
110	left motor on only
111	not used

Notice that several control codes are not used. You may expand the system to take advantage of these unused codes for additional functions.

You should also notice that this system allows the robot to only turn in the forward direction. This is because the robot must stop forward or reverse movement to make a turn.

You can make a turn while moving if you can control the speed of the wheels. For instance, to turn right, the right wheels should be turning faster than the left wheels. The greater the difference in the two speeds, the sharper the turning radius will be (within certain limits, depending on the physical design of the robot itself).

Control of the robot's speed while in motion is also a desirable feature in many applications. A speed control circuit is shown in Fig. 11-5. The parts list is given in Table 11-1. Variations on this circuit may be used either to control the robot's moving speed, or for turning, or both.

SENSORS

Because our robot is going to move around in the real world,

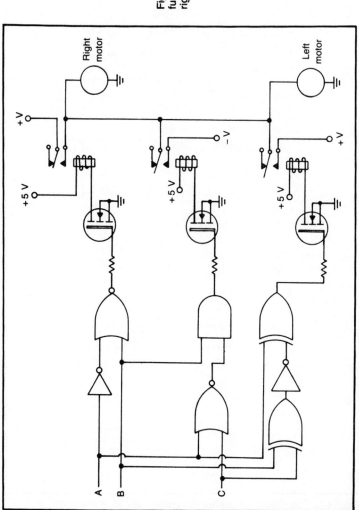

Fig. 11-4. Three control bits can give full control over forward, backward, right, and left movement.

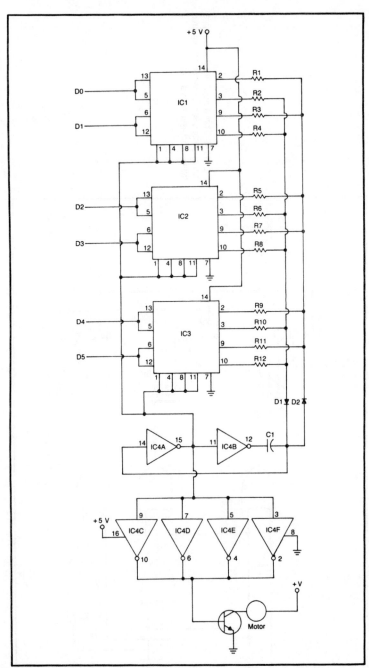

Fig. 11-5. This circuit can control the running speed of the motor.

Table 11-1. Parts List for Fig. 11-5.

IC1, IC2, IC3	CD4066 Quad Bilateral Switch
IC4	CD4049 Hex Inverter
Q1	Almost any npn Power Transistor (2N3055, or similar)
D1, D2	1N4148 Diode
R1, R12	100 kΩ Resistor
R2, R11	910 kΩ Resistor
R3, R10	330 kΩ Resistor
R4, R9	680 kΩ Resistor
R5, R8	470 kΩ Resistor
R6, R7	560 kΩ Resistor
C1	0.022 μF Capacitor

it will need some senses of some kind so it can interact with its environment.

There are many different approaches you can take with robot sensors. In this section we will briefly look at just a few possibilities. In all computer/design work, imagination is an important ingredient, and that is especially true for robotics.

Human beings have five basic senses:

☐ sight
☐ hearing
☐ touch
☐ smell
☐ taste

Our first thoughts on a robots sensors would probably be devices to simulate some of these senses, particularly the first three. Smell and taste aren't likely to be very useful in most robot applications, although a gas detector or smoke detector could be used as a pseudo-nose, if appropriate.

For experimenter purposes, detailed robot sight and even shape detection would be too difficult. Commercial robot manufacturers are just beginning to make some headway. For our purposes, it may be best to limit ourselves to simple light/dark differentiation. This can be accomplished with photocells. A photocell is a light-sensitive component. There are several variations:

☐ photcell or solar battery (voltage source)
☐ photoresistor (resistance element)
☐ photodiode
☐ phototransistor

For the experimenter, photoresistors and phototransistors are the most useful. A lot of recent hobbyist publications seem to be treating the photoresistor as if it was obsolete. It is still a very handy component, and can be used in thousands of circuits. Often the circuitry will be simpler than if the currently more popular phototransistor is used. In other cases, the reverse is true. Sometimes there will be no particular advantage one way or the other. The best rule of thumb is to consider both on a case-by-case basis, and select the most convenient component for the specific application at hand.

With either photoresistor or phototransistor sensors, the robot can be programmed to turn towards, turn away from, move towards, move away from, or move parallel to the brightest light or the darkest area. Large light-colored objects can be distinguished from large dark objects. Small objects probably can not be detected using this method.

Figure 11-6 shows a simple photoresistor light detector circuit. The parts list is given in Table 11-2. Note that this circuit includes a simple built-in flash (parallel) A/D converter. As the resistance of the photocell varies, the voltage drop across this component will change. This voltage is converted to digital form, and fed into the CPU.

A simpler version is shown in Fig. 11-7. This circuit is an on/off detector that serves as one input bit to the CPU. If the light level is above a pre-set level (set via potentiometer R1), a logic 1 is sent. If the light level is below this point, the sensor circuit puts out a logic 0.

Several photosensor circuits can be mounted at various points around the robot's body (or head, if you prefer). You can design a robot that can "see" a full 360° circle, if you like. This would make it easy for it to locate the lightest or darkest direction without wasted movement.

An interesting use of a photosensor is the track follower system. Several photosensors and a small light source are mounted on the bottom of the robot, as illustrated in Fig. 11-8. Light colored tape (such as ordinary masking tape) can then be placed on a dark floor. The robot can then be easily programmed to follow the path laid out by the tape. The light source is needed to compensate for the robot's own shadow. Otherwise, everything under the robot will be dark.

Some photocells are designed to respond to infrared light. You can build a robot that can "see" things people can't. A sound sensor (or robotic "ear") can be a simple carbon microphone element,

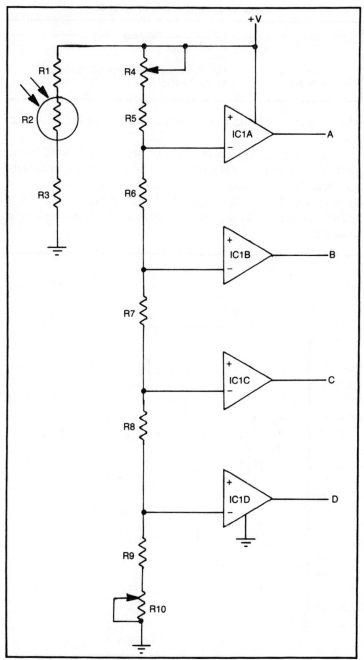

Fig. 11-6. A photoresistor can serve as robotic eyes.

235

IC1	LM324 Quad Op Amp
R1, R3	22 kΩ Resistor
R2	Photoresistor
R4, R10	500 kΩ Potentiometer (range controls)
R5-R9	10 kΩ Resistor

which can usually be purchased from a parts dealer for a dollar or two.

Speech recognition will probably be beyond the capabilities of most experimenters, but it's not hard to devise a circuit for detecting a loud burst of sound, such as a hand-clap, or a loudly spoken word. A typical circuit is shown in Fig. 11-9. The parts list is given in Table 11-3. The potentiometer is used to adjust the microphone's sensitivity.

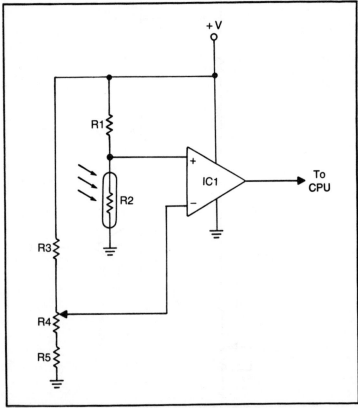

Fig. 11-7. This is a simpler on/off light detector circuit.

236

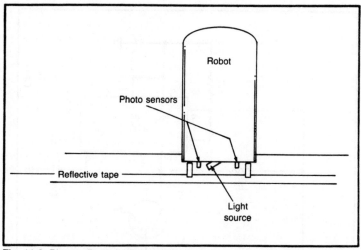

Fig. 11-8. Photocells and a light source mounted on the underside of a robot permit it to follow a path laid out with light colored tape.

It's not hard to work up a simple sequential code. Different numbers of sound pulses in a specific time limit will correspond to different commands. For example:

1 pulse	move forward
2 pulses	turn right
3 pulses	turn left
4 pulses	stop

You might even be able to fool some of your friends into thinking the robot is responding to verbal commands, by controlling your word count. For instance:

"GO"
"TURN RIGHT"
"NOW TURN LEFT"
"ALL RIGHT, STOP NOW"

Once again, the key is to use your imagination.

A somewhat different approach is to include a tone decoder in the sound sensor circuit. The sensor will only respond to sounds of a specific frequency. The robot can now be controlled via a small, self-contained tone generator circuit. Different commands can be activated using a pulse sequence code, as described above, or differ-

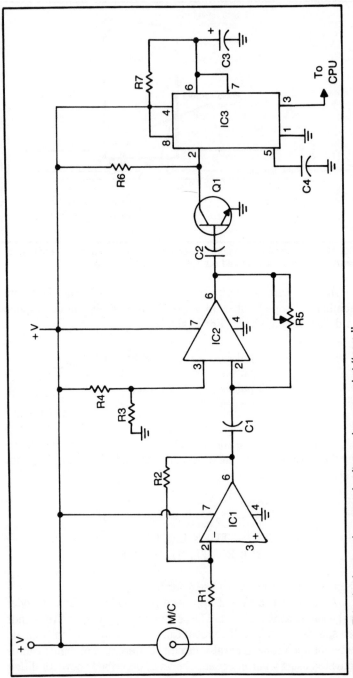

Fig. 11-9. This simple sound sensor circuit can give your robot "ears."

238

Table 11-3. Parts List for Fig. 11-9.

IC1, IC2	Op Amp (741 or similar)
IC3	555 Timer
Q1	Almost any npn transistor (2N2222 or similar)
R1	10 kΩ Resistor
R2	100 kΩ Resistor
R3, R4	3.9 kΩ Resistor
R5	1 MΩ Potentiometer (sensitivity)
R6, R7	1 kΩ Resistor
C1, C2	0.47 μF Capacitor
C3	10 μF Electrolytic Capacitor
C4	0.01 μF Capacitor
MIC	Electret condenser microphone element

ent commands can be controlled by different frequencies. Tone control will tend to be more reliable and controllable than the simple sound detector. In the example described above, if you knock something over with a crash, the robot might think you want it to start moving forward.

Also remember, the robot can conceivably "hear" things we can't. You might consider using ultrasonic tones (frequencies above 20 kHz), or even radio (rf) signals. An antenna can serve as a robotic ear as well as a microphone.

Robotic touch can also be achieved in many different ways. Probably the simplest is the bumper switch system, illustrated in Fig. 11-10. If the robot runs into something, a bumper will be pushed in, closing one of the sensor switches (normally-open momentary push buttons). The switch closure can easily be digitally encoded and fed into the CPU. When the robot runs into some-

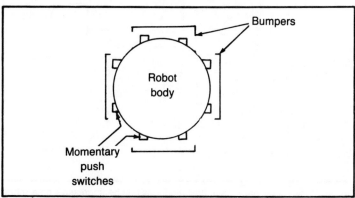

Fig. 11-10. Simple bumper switches let the robot "feel" obstacles in its path.

thing, the programming should tell it to back up a little and change direction.

There are so many sensor possibilities, we couldn't possibly mention more than a tiny fraction of them here. I can only stress once more—use your imagination.

FRILLS

A hobbyist robot can perform many simple practical tasks. But let's admit it, to some extent it's still something of a glorified toy. So why not enjoy it with a few frills just for fun?

Blinking LEDs in strategic locations on the robot's body can be very impressive, even if the light patterns don't really mean anything. The LEDs can be under CPU control, or an independent circuit could handle the decorative flashing lights. The effect is best when the LEDs are flashed at different rates. Figure 11-11 is a block diagram of a typical system. The clocks are just simple astable mul-

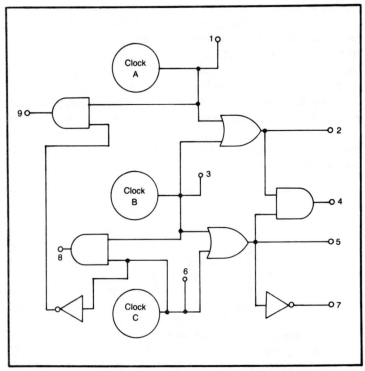

Fig. 11-11. Complex patterns of flashing LEDs can be impressive on a robot, even if they don't really serve any practical purpose.

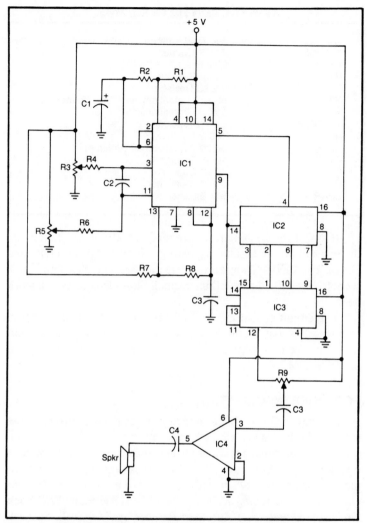

Fig. 11-12. This simple circuit generates pseudorandom "robotic" sounds.

tivibrator circuits, set up for different rates. The gates are optional, but they will increase the number of flash rates. The clock frequencies should not be multiples of each other. This is one possible combination:

0.3 Hz.
0.5 Hz.
1.7 Hz.

Table 11-4. Parts List for Fig. 11-12.

IC1	556 Dual Timer
IC2, IC3	74191 Counter
IC4	LM386 Audio Amplifier
R1	15 kΩ Resistor
R2	2.2 kΩ Resistor
R3	500 kΩ Potentiometer (Tone Change Rate)
R5	500 kΩ Potentiometer (Tone)
R4, R6, R7	4.7 kΩ Resistor
R8	100 Ω Resistor
R9	50 kΩ Potentiometer (Volume)
C1, C4	10 μF Capacitor
C2	15 μF Capacitor
C3	0.1 μF Capacitor
SPKR	8 Ω Speaker

If any of the flashing rates are made greater than about 5 Hz, the eye might not be able to distinguish between the individual blinks. The LED will appear to be continuously lit, although it may seem to be a little dimmer than normal. Slow clock rates will work best.

The circuit shown in Fig. 11-12 is another fun frill. It generates weird "robot sounds" to give your creation more of a traditional science fiction quality. The parts list for this circuit is given in Table 11-4.

FOR MORE INFORMATION

It is impossible to do more than just scratch the surface of the subject of robotics in a single brief chapter like this. If you are interested in this area, a number of fine books in this area have been published in recent years. The TAB Books Inc. catalog contains many books on robotics including; *How to Design and Build Your Own Self-Programming Robot* by David L. Heiserman (TAB book No. 1341) *Handbook of Advanced Robotics* by Edward L. Safford. Jr. (TAB book No. 1421).

Chapter 12

Sound Synthesis

SOUND SYNTHESIS CIRCUITS HAVE ALWAYS BEEN PARTICU-
larly intriguing to me. Many people are not aware that music
is actually based on mathematical relationships. This suggests that
it is an ideal application for a CPU. In this chapter we will examine a few of the many possible approaches to computerized music.

INTERFACING WITH AN ANALOG SYNTHESIZER

With a simple D/A converter at the output port, a CPU system can easily be made to serve as a super controller for an analog
music synthesizer that allows external control of voltage inputs.
Most modern analog synthesizers use voltage control to adjust all
major parameters of the sound. This allows various oscillators
(sound sources) and filters (sound modifiers) to track each other
precisely. Many complicated effects that would not otherwise be
possible are quite simple to achieve in a voltage-controlled system.

It wasn't long after the development of voltage control that
someone came up with the idea of the sequencer. This is a circuit
that produces a series (or sequence) of predetermined control voltages in a repeating pattern. A sequencer basically allows the synthesizer to "play itself."

A CPU-based sequencer can be a very powerful device. Some
of the tricks possible here include:

☐ Transposition to another key

☐ Automated speed changes (even within a single sequence)
☐ Inversion (notes go up instead of down, or vice versa)
☐ Playing the sequence backwards
☐ Pseudorandom variations on the sequence
☐ Extremely long sequences
☐ Mathematically based nonrepeating sequences
☐ Rhythm changes (even within a single sequence)

If output latches are used, several different independent control voltages can be outputted by the CPU to control various devices. The possibilities are limited only by your imagination. If you'd like to know more about synthesizer systems, allow me to refer you to two of my earlier books: *Electronic Music Synthesizers* (TAB book No. 1167) and *Music Synthesizers: A Manual of Design and Construction* (TAB book No. 1565).

DIRECT DIGITAL SYNTHESIS

A CPU can generate sounds directly, just by outputting a repeating pattern of binary numbers into a D/A converter. If the numerical pattern repeats itself within the audio range (20 to 15,000 times a second) an audible tone will be produced. If we look at this signal with an oscilloscope, we will see a periodic waveform of some kind. Theoretically, any conceivable waveform can be generated in this fashion. Some examples are illustrated in Fig. 12-1.

A variation on this idea is to feed an audio signal into the CPU via an A/D converter. The CPU can then manipulate the digitalized signal in any of an almost infinite variety of ways before it is fed back out through the D/A converter. In addition, the digitized signal can be stored indefinitely, and rerecorded as many times as you like without an increase in distortion or noise. Digital synthesis techniques are a complex topic. It would require a complete book to even begin to cover this topic.

PSG

General Instruments makes a powerful sound generator IC that is ideal for our purposes here. It is a complete sound synthesizer on a single chip. It is designed to be operated under computer control. Therefore, it can easily be interfaced with our CPU system.

General Instruments calls this device a PSG, or *Programmable Sound Generator*. It is available in two versions. The AY-3-8910, shown in Fig. 12-2 is a 40-pin IC and has two built-in 8-bit I/O ports.

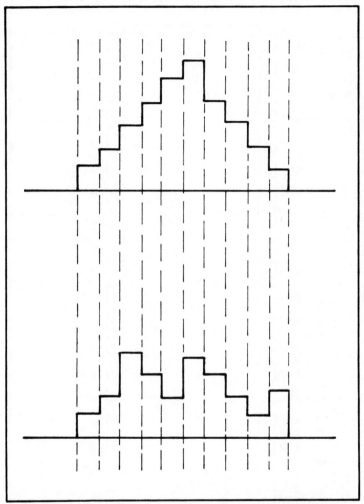

Fig. 12-1. Theoretically, any conceivable waveform can be generated digitally.

The AY-3-8912, shown in Fig. 12-3, is in a 28-pin package and has just a single 8-bit I/O port. There are no other differences between the two versions.

The I/O ports are provided for use with commercial computer systems with a limited number of I/O ports accessible to the user. The PSG will use up one of these ports. The I/O port(s) built into the PSG replace the used up ports.

In our system we can interface directly to the CPU and use memory mapped I/O. There is no particular need to conserve I/O

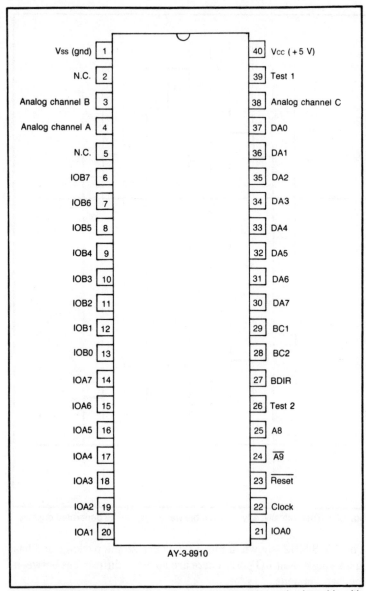

Vss (gnd)	1	40	Vcc (+ 5 V)
N.C.	2	39	Test 1
Analog channel B	3	38	Analog channel C
Analog channel A	4	37	DA0
N.C.	5	36	DA1
IOB7	6	35	DA2
IOB6	7	34	DA3
IOB5	8	33	DA4
IOB4	9	32	DA5
IOB3	10	31	DA6
IOB2	11	30	DA7
IOB1	12	29	BC1
IOB0	13	28	BC2
IOA7	14	27	BDIR
IOA6	15	26	Test 2
IOA5	16	25	A8
IOA4	17	24	$\overline{A9}$
IOA3	18	23	$\overline{Reset}$
IOA2	19	22	Clock
IOA1	20	21	IOA0

AY-3-8910

Fig. 12-2. The Av-3-8910 PSG in a 40 pin-programmable synthesizer chip with two full eight bit I/O ports.

ports. The 28-pin AY-3-8912 version will be adequate for our needs, because we probably won't be using the built-in PSG I/O ports. Of course, if you have a AY-3-8910 available, there is no reason why you can't use it. Just be sure to compensate for the differences in pin numbering. Compare Figs. 12-2 and 12-3.

A block diagram of the PSG's internal circuitry is shown in Fig. 12-4. You can see that it is a complete sound synthesis system on a chip.

The subsections of the PSG are fairly straightforward in concept. There are six primary types of modules:

☐ tone generators
☐ noise generator

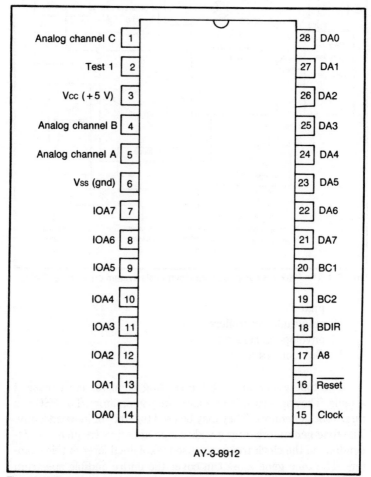

Fig. 12-3. The 28 pin AY-3-8912 is identical to the AY-3-8910, except it has only one I/O port.

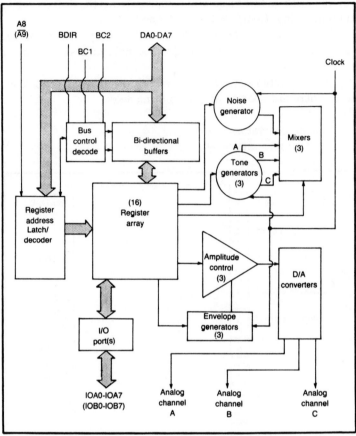

Fig. 12-4. The PSG is a complete sound synthesis system on a single IC chip.

- ☐ mixers
- ☐ amplitude controllers
- ☐ envelope generators
- ☐ D/A converters

The tone generators are the starting point for most musical sounds. They are essentially square wave generators. The PSG has three tone generators. They may be used together or independently. The tone generators offer a wide range of output frequencies, depending on the clock frequency used (explained later in this chapter). The tone generators can cover the entire audible spectrum (20 Hz to 20 kHz), plus considerable subaudible (below 20 Hz) and ultrasonic (above 20 kHz) frequency ranges.

The noise generator is used for percussive type effects. It produces a nonperiodic waveform without a definite frequency. Actually this is a frequency-modulated pseudorandom pulsewidth square-wave signal. It sounds pretty much like random noise, and that's what counts.

The mixers do just what their name implies. They mix together the outputs of the three tone generators and the noise generator, as desired by the user for each output channel. There are three output channels, and one mixer for each channel.

The amplitude controllers are essentially volume controls for the internal D/A converters. A fixed amplitude can be set directly under CPU control, or a variable amplitude pattern can be achieved via the envelope generators.

The envelope generator, produce amplitude envelope patterns for automatically changing volume levels for a signal. This is a form of amplitude modulation. Both the shape and the cycle of the envelopes are user selectable. Finally, each output channel has its own built-in 16-step D/A converter.

On the software level, the PSG is set up much like a slave CPU. It relies heavily on sixteen internal registers, which are similar to the internal registers of the CPU itself. The 16 PSG registers are described as follows:

R0/R1	A tone period
R2/R3	B tone period
R4/R5	C tone period
R6	Noise period
R7	Enable
R10	A amplitude
R11	B amplitude
R12	C amplitude
R13/R14	Envelope period
R15	Envelope shape/cycle
R16	I/O port A data strobe
R17	I/O port B data strobe (8910 only)

Note that the registers are numbered in octal format. The register functions are outlined in more detail in Table 12-1.

The PSG's registers are memory mapped. As far as the CPU is concerned, the look like a 16-byte block out of 1024 possible addresses. The appropriate register is selected via the four low-order data/address bits on the PSG bus (DA0 through DA3). The other

Table 12-1. Summary of The PSG's Internal Registers.

#	Function	B7	B6	B5	B4	B3	B2	B1	B0
R0	Channel A Tone Period	8-Bit Fine Tune							
R1		x	x	x	x	4-Bit Coarse Tune			
R2	Channel B Tone Period	8-Bit Fine Tune							
R3		x	x	x	x	4-Bit Coarse Tune			
R4	Channel C Tone Period	8-Bit Fine Tune							
R5		x	x	x	5-Bit Period Control				
R6	Noise Period	x	x	x	5-Bit Period Control				
R7	Enable	I/O		Noise			Tone		
		IOB	IOA	C	B	A	C	B	A
R10	Channel A Amplitude	x	x	x	M	L3	L2	L1	L0
R11	Channel B Amplitude	x	x	x	M	L3	L2	L1	L0
R12	Channel C Amplitude	x	x	x	M	L3	L2	L1	L0
R13	Envelope Period	8-Bit Fine Tune							
R14		8-Bit Coarse Tune							
R15	Envelope Shape/Cycle	x	x	x	x	CN	AT	AL	H
R16	I/O Port A Data Store 8-Bit Parallel I/O On Port A								
R17	I/O Port B Data Store 8-Bit Parallel I/O On Port B (8910 version only)								

x = Not Used
M = Mode
CN = Continue
AT = Attack
AL = Alternate
H = Hold

four data/address bits must be at logic 0. A9 must also be 0, and A8 must be 1 to address a PSG register.

Once the register has been selected, the eight DA bits are used to carry data for either a write or PSG (load register) or read from PSG operation. The type of operation is determined by the logic states of the BDIR, BC1, and BC2 pins, as follows:

BDIR	BC1	BC2	PSG FUNCTION
0	1	0	inactive (DA0-DA7 in high impedance state)
0	1	1	READ FROM PSG
1	1	0	WRITE TO PSG
1	1	1	LATCH ADDRESS (DA0-DA3 contain register address as described above)

Note that BC1 is a logic 1 for all valid function states.

The timing of a typical PSG command sequence will follow this pattern:

 ☐ Bus Controls set up Inactive State
 ☐ Bus Controls set up Latch Address State (register address placed on data bus)
 ☐ Bus Controls set up Inactive State (data placed on data bus by PSG or CPU)
 ☐ Bus Controls set up Read from PSG or Write to PSG state
 ☐ Bus Controls set up Inactive State

Multiple reads and writes can be performed on a single register without readdressing the register. This can be handy in some programs.

Let's examine how the data from the CPU controls the PSG's functions. For convenience, all values in the equations will be given in decimal form.

The *Tone Period* of each tone generator is defined by two registers, a 4-bit *Coarse-Tune* register (R1, R3, or R5) and an 8-bit *Fine-Tune* register (R0, R2, or R4). We will identify the data values as CT (Coarse-Tune) and FT (Fine-Tune). The Tone Period (TP) is then equal to:

$$TP = 256CT + FT$$

For example, if CT = 5, and FT = 133, the Tone Period would work out to:

$$TP = 256 \times 5 + 133$$
$$= 1280 + 133$$
$$= 1413$$

The Tone Period is then combined with the clock frequency (CL) to find the tone frequency, using this formula:

$$F = CL/16TP$$

If, for instance, the clock frequency (CL) is 2 MHz (2,000,000 Hz), the frequency for our sample Tone Period would work out to:

$$F = 2000000/(16 \times 1413)$$
$$= 2000000/22608$$
$$= 88.5 \text{ Hz}$$

The Noise Period (NP) (register R6) determines the basic frequency of the noise signal. It acts something like the cut-off frequency of a filter. The equation for the Noise Frequency is as follows:

$$F_n = CL/16NP$$

Register 7 is labelled *Enable*. It is used to turn on and off the signals to the channel mixers, and to control the I/O ports. The first three bits control the tone generators:

B0	B1	B2	tone enabled on channel
0	0	0	A B C
0	0	1	A B –
0	1	0	A – C
0	1	1	– – C
1	0	0	– B C
1	0	1	– B –
1	1	0	A – –
1	1	1	– – –

The next three bits (B3, B4, and B5) perform the same function for the noise signal:

B3	B4	B5	noise enabled on channel
0	0	0	A B C
0	0	1	A B –
0	1	0	A – C
0	1	1	– – C
1	0	0	– B C
1	0	1	– B –
1	1	0	A – –
1	1	1	– – –

The last two bits (B6 and B7) control the function of the I/O ports. Bit B6 controls I/O port A, and bit B7 controls I/O port B. For both of these control bits, a logic 0 sets the appropriate port for input, and a logic 1 sets it for output. Since the 8912 version omits the second I/O port, bit B7 is simply ignored in this version. The PSG doesn't care about its value.

The next three registers (R10, R11, and R12) control the amplitude, or volume, of each analog output channel. The three highest bits (B5, B6, and B7) are not used. Bit B4 is a mode-control switch. When this bit is a 0, the amplitude is controlled by the remaining four bits (B0-B3), giving sixteen discrete volume levels. If bit B4 is made a 1, bits B0 through B3 will be ignored, and the amplitude will be controlled by the envelope generator.

Note that an output channel cannot be turned completely off by disabling all of the inputs in register R7. To turn off a channel, set its amplitude to 0000 in the appropriate amplitude control register.

If bit B4 of the amplitude register is set to 1, the amplitude is controlled by the PSG's internal envelope generator. The envelope parameters are set via registers R13, R14, and R15.

Registers R13 and R14 are used to determine the period of one complete envelope period, that is, how long the envelope will last. R14 is the most significant byte (Coarse Tune), and R13 holds the least significant byte (Fine Tune). The total envelope period (EP) can be calculated with this equation:

$$EP = 256CT + FT$$

The envelope frequency is then equal to:

$$F_e = CL/256EP$$

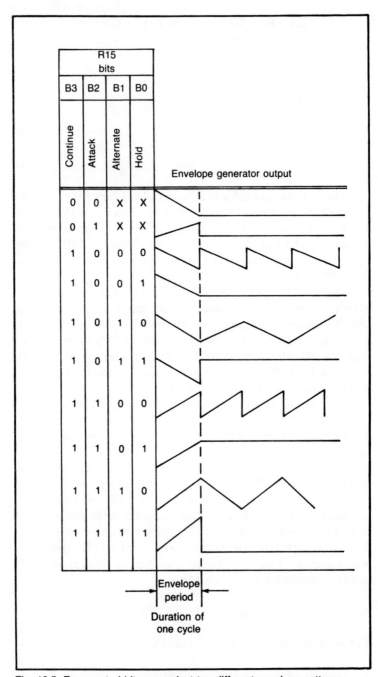

R15 bits				Envelope generator output
B3	B2	B1	B0	
Continue	Attack	Alternate	Hold	
0	0	X	X	
0	1	X	X	
1	0	0	0	
1	0	0	1	
1	0	1	0	
1	0	1	1	
1	1	0	0	
1	1	0	1	
1	1	1	0	
1	1	1	1	

Envelope period

Duration of one cycle

Fig. 12-5. Four control bits can select ten different envelope patterns.

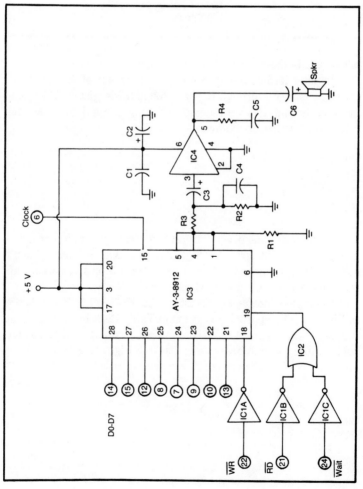

Fig. 12-6. This is a complete circuit for interfacing the PSG with the CPU.

255

Table 12-2. Parts List for Fig. 12-6.

IC1	CD4009 Hex Inverter
IC2	74C32 Quad 2-Input OR Gate
IC3	AY-3-8912 PSG
IC4	LM386 Audio Amplifier
R1	1 kΩ Resistor
R2	470 Ω Resistor
R3	5.1 kΩ Resistor
R4	10 Ω Resistor
C1	0.1 μF Capacitor
C2	10 μF Capacitor
C3	2.2 μF Capacitor
C4	330 pF Capacitor
C5	0.047 μF Capacitor
C6	220 μF Capacitor
SPKR	8 Ω Speaker

where CL is the system Clock frequency.

Register R15 is used to control other aspects of the envelope. Only four bits (B0 through B3) are used in this register. The upper bits (B4 through B7) are ignored. The four active bits in register R15 are identified as follows:

B0 Continue
B1 Attack
B2 Alternate
B3 Hold

These four control bits interact to create ten different envelope patterns, as illustrated in Fig. 12-5. Note that "x" means "don't care." Any bit marked "x" may be either a 0 or a 1, without affecting the envelope pattern in any way.

A complete interfacing circuit for the AY-3-8912 PSG is shown in Fig. 12-6. The parts list is given in Table 12-2. Remember that if you use the 40-pin AY-3-8910 version, you will need to change some of the pin numbers. Refer back to Figs. 12-2 and 12-3.

Chapter 13

Programming

N O CPU BASED PROJECT IS GOING TO BE ANY GOOD AT ALL without software, or programming. A program is simply a set of instructions in sequence, for the CPU to execute. When writing software, it is a good idea to bear two seemingly contradictory facts in mind: *The biggest advantage of computers is that they do exactly what they are told. The biggest disadvantage of computers is that they do exactly what they are told.*

Computers follow instructions precisely. This means that they will come up with predictable and consistent results. Running the same program repeatedly with the same data will give the same results. This is handy for confirming results, or to locate errors in the software (called "bugs").

By the same token, computers are very literal-minded beasts with no trace of common sense. If you make an error—no matter how minor—the computer will make no corrections. If the CPU doesn't recognize a command code, it will reject the instruction (the program will "bomb"). More troublesome is what happens if you type in the wrong (but valid) command code. The CPU will assume you meant it to do precisely what the instruction says, even if it has to go into an endless loop, trying to solve an impossible task. Similarly, the CPU has no way to recognize and question (or reject) nonsensical data, unless a test routine is included in the program.

People talk a lot about computer errors. Actually, computers very rarely make mistakes. Usually if the problem stems from the computer itself, it will just lock up and refuse to do anything. While computers generally don't make mistakes, programmers and computer operators (being human) often do, and the computer gets blamed. If your program doesn't do what you expected, you probably made a mistake somewhere along the line. It is not likely to be the CPU's fault.

Fortunately, except for a few rare heavy robotic projects, an error in the program will do no damage to the equipment. You can try again. Don't be afraid to experiment with your programming to find out what various commands might do under various circumstances. The worst that will happen is that the program won't work. No lasting damage will be done.

You will need to write your own software for all of the projects in this book. Because this book deals with customized projects with many different options, it is impossible for me to include finished programs here. This chapter will briefly cover the basics of programming. Unfortunately, there is not enough space to go into the subject in detail in this volume. Several good books on machine language and assembly language programming are available.

A lot of hobbyists are skeptical about their ability to learn machine and assembly language. Actually, once you get the hang of it, it isn't all that difficult. It *is* tedious detail work, and you have to pay close attention all along the way. It is all too easy for errors to sneak in. It is a good idea to doublecheck all your work regularly.

Your first few programs will probably take you a few hours to get right. It gets easier with practice. Start by programming relatively simple tasks, sticking to the basics. You can add frills and special features later.

Even an experienced programmer rarely gets everything right on the first draft of a program. At least half the effort involved in writing a program goes to debugging (locating and correcting errors). The secret of machine/assembly language programming is to work slowly, take plenty of breaks, doublecheck your work frequently, and be patient.

MACHINE LANGUAGE AND ASSEMBLY LANGUAGE

If you have experience working with personal computers, you probably have at least some familiarity with one of the high-level programming languages, such as BASIC, COBOL, LOGO, or Pascal. English-like words are used for the various commands. For example, in BASIC, if you want to print out some data, you type in the command word, "PRINT."

Unfortunately, a CPU does not understand any high level languages. It can only understand machine language. In a personal computer that is programmed in BASIC, a special translation program is included in ROM. This translator converts the high-level language commands into machine-language commands. Some high-level language commands may translate into several machine-language commands.

It is undeniably easier to program in a high-level language. The meanings of the command statements are clearer. Common tasks may be called up with a single word, even if the CPU requires a dozen or so machine-language instructions to execute the routine. But a high-level language comes at a price. A translation program must be written in machine language, and it must be placed in the computer's memory, preferably in ROM. High-level language programs generally run somewhat slower than comparable machine-language programs. The high-level commands also tend to use up more memory. Because alphanumeric characters are used to spell out the high level commands, a full ASCII keyboard is required.

For our purposes in the projects described in this book, a high-level programming language would probably be more trouble than it's worth. We will only have to write relatively simple, and short programs for these projects, so the inherent awkwardness of machine language won't be too great a burden.

If you have done much work with computers, you probably have at least heard of assembly language. Assembly language is a sort of compromise language. Each machine-language command is given a two, three, or four letter name (or mnemonic), such as ADD, or LD (LoaD). This is easier to read and remember than strings of 1's and 0's. A translation program is required to run an assembly-language program directly on a CPU. Each mnemonic is converted into the appropriate binary number.

To avoid the need for a translation program and an alphanumeric keyboard, I have limited the projects in this book to direct machine-language programming. The commands can be entered as hexadecimal numbers to avoid the confusion caused by large binary numbers. 5C is certainly easier to get right than 01011100.

However, when in the initial stages of writing your programs, it will probably be easier to use the assembly-language mnemonics. When the program looks good on paper, you can manually convert the assembly-language commands into hexadecimal machine-language code. It is admittedly a rather tedious job, but it is not too difficult, at least for short programs. Work slowly, and doublecheck everything. This will minimize the number of errors.

Don't feel bad or frustrated if some errors creep in anyway. I'd be surprised if they didn't. Even an experienced programmer working in a high-level language usually has to do quite a bit of debugging to get a program running right. If you keep good notes, work carefully, and concentrate on one step at a time, your errors should be fairly easy to locate and correct. Some errors can be very subtle and sneaky. This is just part of the nature of computer programming. Expect such problems to crop up now and then, so they won't be too unpleasant a surprise.

Z80 COMMANDS

The types of commands used by the Z80 were introduced in Chapter 3. The entire instruction set of this CPU is listed in Appendix A. Appendix B gives the hexadecimal machine-language equivalent for each available command. Use this appendix for the translation process.

FLOWCHARTS

A very useful tool in writing and debugging computer programs is the flowchart. A flowchart is simply a graphic illustration of the various steps in a program. It allows you to see and easily follow the "flow" of the program. Several flowcharts were presented in some of the earlier chapters. The symbols used in flowcharts are not entirely standardized. You can use any system you like, as long as you are consistent. Usually different shapes are used to indicate different types of functions. The basic shapes I generally use are shown in Fig. 13-1.

A squashed oval indicates a START or END point for a program or routine. A diamond is used to represent a decision or comparison test to be performed by the CPU. For example, is A > B? A test block has two exit paths. If the expression being tested is true, the next step will be indicated on the "YES" line. If the expression being tested is not true (false), the program will proceed along the "NO" line.

A rectangle is used for INPUT and OUTPUT operations. Finally, a square is used for any functions not covered by the other symbols.

In writing a program, the first step is to determine what results are desired, and what data is initially available. Then you have to

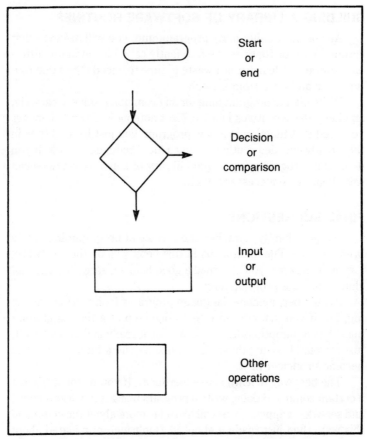

Start

Decision
comparison

Input

Other
operations

Fig. 13-1. Standardized symbols are used in programming flow-charts.

figure out what steps will need to be taken to get from the available data to the desired results.

In complex programs it is often convenient to work with several generations of flowcharts. The first generation outlines steps in broad blocks. For example, one step might be indicated as "Convert Decimal Value to Binary Value." This would take several commands to accomplish, but in the early stages of laying out the flowchart, you may want to lump them together as a single step. Later, you will expand each of the steps into individual routine flowcharts. In each new generation of your flowcharts get more specific. Eventually, each step on the flowchart will represent a single command. From this point it's a simple matter to encode the steps outlined in the final flowchart.

BUILDING A LIBRARY OF SOFTWARE ROUTINES

As you start doing more programming, you will discover that certain tasks, or routines are frequently called for in many different programs. Clearly it is a waste of time to encode the same routine over and over from scratch.

Write out the programming for any common routine separately, and keep these routines in a looseleaf notebook. Then, whenever you need that function in a new program, you just have to type in the already encoded routine, saving a lot of redundant work. If you do a lot of programming, a good library of software routines can save hours of unnecessary work.

FINAL SUGGESTIONS

We have barely scratched the surface of programming in this brief chapter. The main focus in this book was on the hardware. I strongly suggest you also read a good book on assembly and machine language programming.

Remember, machine language programs look terribly imposing, but if you just concentrate on one step at a time, and don't make any assumptions (the CPU won't), it really isn't too difficult, just tedious. Like anything else, it takes quite a bit of practice to become proficient at it.

The best way to learn is to experiment. If you're not sure what a certain command does, write a program using it in various ways, and see what happens. You will learn far more about the command this way, then just reading about it. Don't feel intimidated about such experimentation. Remember, even if you use the command wrong (or make some other mistake), the program will either give unexpected results, or it won't work at all. If a program "bombs," nothing will be hurt, except for the program itself. The commands you enter into RAM might be affected when the program "crashes." At worst, you'll have to waste a little time, typing the program back in from scratch.

The CPU, and other computer circuitry is completely unaffected by software errors. The CPU will try to execute all commands it can recognize. If it can't recognize a command, or if a command is impossible to execute, the CPU will simply stop running the program and wait until you give it proper instructions.

Appendix A

The Z80 Instruction Set

				Flags		
Mnemonic	Format	Description	S	Z	P/V	C
ADC HL, SS	11101101/01ss1010	HL+ss+CY to HL	X	X	X	X
ADC A, r	10001r	A+r+CY to A	X	X	X	X
ADC A, n	11001110/n	A+n+CY to A	X	X	X	X
ADC A, (HL)	10001110	A+(HL)+CY to A	X	X	X	X
ADC A, (IX+d)	11011101/10001110/d	A+(IX+d)+CY to A	X	X	X	X
ADC A, (IY+d)	11111101/10001110/d	A+(IY+d)+CY to A	X	X	X	X
ADD A, n	11000110/n	A+n to A	X	X	X	X
ADD A, r	10000r	A+r to A	X	X	X	X
ADD A, (HL)	10000110	A+(HL) to A	X	X	X	X
ADD A, (IX+d)	11011101/10000110/d	A+(IX+d) to A	X	X	X	X
ADD A, (IY+d)	11111101/10000110/d	A+(IY+d) to A	X	X	X	X
ADD HL, ss	00ss1001	HL+ss to HL	–	–	–	X
ADD IX, pp	11011101/00pp1001	IX+pp to IX	–	–	–	X
ADD IY, qq	11111101/00qq1001	IY+rr to IY	–	–	–	X
AND r	10100r	A AND r to A	X	X	X	0
AND n	11100110/n	A AND n to A	X	X	X	0
AND (HL)	10100110	A AND (HL) to A	X	X	X	0
AND (IX+d)	11011101/10100110/d	A AND (IX+d) to A	X	X	X	0
AND (IY+d)	11111101/10100110/d	A AND (IY+d) to A	X	X	X	0
BIT b, r	11001011/01br	Test bit b of r	X	X	–	–

Mnemonic	Machine Code	Operation	S	Z	H	P/V	N	C
BIT b, (HL)	1001011/01b110	Test bit b of (HL)	X	X	X	X	X	–
BIT b, (IX+d)	1101101/1001011/d/01b110	Test bit b of (IX+d)	X	X	X	X	X	–
BIT b, (IY+d)	1111101/1001011/d/01b110	Test bit b of (IY+d)	X	X	X	X	X	–
CALL cc, nm	11c100/n/n	CALL subroutine at nn if cc	–	–	–	–	–	–
CALL nm	11001101/n/n	Unconditionally CALL nn	–	–	–	–	–	–
CCF	00111111	Complement Carry Flag	–	–	X	–	X	X
CP r	1011r	Compare A:r	X	X	X	X	X	X
CP n	11111110/n	Compare A:n	X	X	X	X	X	X
CP (HL)	10111110	Compare A:(HL)	X	X	X	X	X	X
CP (IX+d)	11011101/10111110/d	Compare A:(IX+d)	X	X	X	X	X	X
CP (IY+d)	11111101/10111110/d	Compare A:(IY+d)	X	X	X	X	X	X
CPD	11101101/10101001	Block compare, no repeat	X	X	X	X	X	–
CPDR	11101101/10111001	Block compare, repeat	X	X	X	X	X	–
CPI	11101101/10100001	Block compare, no repeat	X	X	X	X	X	–
CPIR	11101101/10110001	Block compare, repeat	X	X	X	X	X	–
CPL	00101111	Complement A (1s complement)	–	–	X	–	X	–
DAA	00100111	Decimal adjust A	X	X	X	X	–	X
DEC r	00r101	Decrement r by 1	X	X	X	X	X	–

				Flags		
Mnemonic	**Format**	**Description**	**S**	**Z**	**P/V**	**C**
DEC (HL)	00110101	Decrement (HL) by one	X	X	X	–
DEC (IX+d)	11011101/0110101/d	Decrement (IX+d) by one	X	X	X	–
DEC (IY+d)	11111110/0110101/d	Decrement (IY+d) by one	X	X	X	–
DEC IX	11011101/00101011	Decrement IX by 1	–	–	–	–
DEC IY	11111101/00101011	Decrement IY by 1	–	–	–	–
DEC ss	00ss1011	Decrement register pair	–	–	–	–
DI	11110011	Disable interrupts	–	–	–	–
DJNZ e	00010000/e−2	Decrement B and JR if B <> 0	–	–	–	–
EI	11111011	Enable interrupts	–	–	–	–
EX (SP), HL	11100011	Exchange (SP) and HL	–	–	–	–
EX (SP), IX	11011101/11100011	Exchange (SP) and IX	–	–	–	–
EX (SP), IY	11111101/11100011	Exchange (SP) and IY	–	–	–	–
EX AF, AF'	00001000	Set prime AF active	–	–	–	–
EX DE, HL	11101011	Exchange DE and HL	–	–	–	–
EXX	11011001	Set prime B−L active	–	–	–	–
HALT	01110110	Halt	–	–	–	–
IM 0	11101101/01000110	Set interrupt mode 0	–	–	–	–
IM 1	11101101/01010110	Set interrupt mode 1	–	–	–	–
IM 2	11101101/01011110	Set interrupt mode 2	–	–	–	–
IN A, (n)	1101011/n	Load A with input from n	–	–	–	–

Instruction	Description	Encoding						
IN r, (C)	Load r with input from (C)	11101101/01r000	X	X	X	X	–	–
INC r	Increment r by 1	00r100	X	X	X	X	–	–
INC (HL)	Increment (HL) by one	00110100	X	X	X	X	–	–
INC (IX + d)	Increment (IX + d) by one	11011101/00110100/d	X	X	X	X	–	–
INC (IY + d)	Increment (IY + d) by one	11111101/00110100/d	X	X	X	X	–	–
INC IX	Increment IX by 1	11011101/00100011	–	–	–	–	–	–
INC IY	Increment IY by 1	11111101/00100011	–	–	–	–	–	–
INC ss	Increment register pair	00ss0011	–	–	–	–	–	–
IND	Block I/O input from (C)	11101101/10101010	X	X	X	X	–	–
INDR	Block I/O input, repeat	11101101/10111010	X	X	X	X	–	–
INI	Block I/O input from (C)	11101101/10100010	X	X	X	X	–	–
INIR	Block I/O input, repeat	11101101/10110010	X	X	X	X	–	–
JP (HL)	Unconditional jump to (HL)	11101001	X	–	–	–	–	–
JP (IX)	Unconditional jump to (IX)	11011101/11101001	–	–	–	–	–	–
JP (IY)	Unconditional jump to (IY)	11111101/11101001	–	–	–	–	–	–
JP cc, nn	Jump to nn if cc	11c010/n/n	–	–	–	–	–	–
JP nn	Unconditional jump to nn	11000011/n/n	–	–	–	–	–	–
JR C, e	Jump relative if carry	00111000/e – 2	–	–	–	–	–	–
JR e	Unconditional jump relative	00011000/e – 2	–	–	–	–	–	–
JR NC, e	Jump relative if no carry	00110000/e – 2	–	–	–	–	–	–
JR NZ, e	Jump relative if non-zero	00100000/e – 2	–	–	–	–	–	–

| | | | | | Flags | |
Mnemonic	Format	Description	S	Z	P/V	C
JR Z, e	0010000/e − 2	Jump relative if zero	–	–	–	–
LD A, (BC)	00001010	Load A with (BC)	–	–	–	–
LD A, (DE)	00011010	Load A with (DE)	–	–	–	–
LD A, I	11101101/01010111	Load A with I	X	X	X	–
LD A, (nn)	00111010/n/n	Load A with location nn	–	–	–	–
LD A, R	11101101/01011111	Load A with R	X	X	X	–
LD (BC), A	00000010	Store A to (BC)	–	–	–	–
LD (DE), A	00010010	Store A to (DE)	–	–	–	–
LD (HL), n	00110110/n	Store n to (HL)	–	–	–	–
LD dd, nn	00dd0001/n/n	Load register pair with nn	–	–	–	–
LD dd, (nn)	11101101/01dd1011/n/n	Load register pair with location nn	–	–	–	–
LD HL, (nn)	00101010/n/n	Load HL with location nn	–	–	–	–
LD (HL), r	01110r	Store r to (HL)	–	–	–	–
LD I, A	11101011/01000111	Load I with A	–	–	–	–
LD IX, (nn)	11011101/00101010/n/n	Load IX with location nn	–	–	–	–
LD IX, nn	11011101/00100001/n/n	Load IX with nn	–	–	–	–
LD (IX+d), n	11011101/00110110/d/n	Store n to (IX+d)	–	–	–	–
LD (IX+d), r	11011101/01110r/d	Store r to (IX+d)	–	–	–	–
LD IY, nn	11111101/00100001/n/n	Load IY with nn	–	–	–	–
LD IY, (nn)	11111101/00101010/n/n	Load IY with location nn	–	–	–	–

Mnemonic	Opcode	Description						
LD (IY+d), n	11111101/00110110/d/n	Store n to (IY+d)	—	—	—	—	—	—
LD (IY+d), r	11111101/01110r/d	Store r to (IY+d)	—	—	—	—	—	—
LD (nn), A	00110010/n/n	Store A to location nn	—	—	—	—	—	—
LD (nn), dd	11101101/01dd0011/n/n	Store register pair to location nn	—	—	—	—	—	—
LD (nn), HL	00100010/n/n	Store HL to location nn	—	—	—	—	—	—
LD (nn), IX	11011101/00100010/n/n	Store IX to location nn	—	—	—	—	—	—
LD (nn), IY	11111101/00100010/n/n	Store IY to location nn	—	—	—	—	—	—
LD R, A	11101101/01001111	Load R with A	—	—	—	—	—	—
LD r, r'	01rr'	Load r with r'	—	—	—	—	—	—
LD r, n	00r110/n	Load r with n	—	—	—	—	—	—
LD r, (HL)	01r110	Load r with (HL)	—	—	—	—	—	—
LD r, (IX+d)	11011101/01r110/d	Load r with (IX+d)	—	—	—	—	—	—
LD r, (IY+d)	11111101/01r1109/d	Load r with (IY+d)	—	—	—	—	—	—
LD SP, HL	11111001	Load SP with HL	—	—	—	—	—	—
LD SP, IX	11011101/11111001	Load SP with IX	—	—	—	—	—	—
LD SP, IY	11111101/11111001	Load SP with IY	—	—	—	—	—	—
LDD	11101101/10101000	Block load, forward, no repeat	—	—	X	—	—	—
LDDR	11101101/10111000	Block load, forward, repeat	—	—	0	—	—	—
LDI	11101101/10100000	Block load, backward, no repeat	—	—	X	—	—	—

			Flags			
Mnemonic	Format	Description	S	Z	P/V	C
LDIR	11101101/10110000	Block load, backward, repeat	–	–	0	–
NEG	11101101/01000100	Negate A (two's complement)	X	X	X	X
NOP	00000000	No operation	–	–	–	–
OR r	10110r	A OR r to A	X	X	X	0
OR n	11110110/n	A OR n to A	X	X	X	0
OR (HL)	10110110	A OR (HL) to A	X	X	X	0
OR (IX+d)	11011101/10110110/d	A OR (IX+d) to A	X	X	X	0
OR (IY+d)	11111101/10110110/d	A OR (IY+d) to A	X	X	X	0
OTDR	11101101/10111011	Block output, backward, repeat	X	X	X	–
OTIR	11101101/10110011	Block output, forward, repeat	X	X	X	–
OUT (C), r	11101101/01r001	Output r to (C)	–	–	–	–
OUT (n), A	11010011/n	Output A to port n	–	–	–	–
OUTD	11101101/10101011	Block output, backward, no repeat	X	X	X	–
OUTI	11101101/10100011	Block output, forward, no repeat	X	X	X	–
POP IX	11011101/11100001	Pop IX from stack	–	–	–	–

Mnemonic	Code	Operation				
POP IY	1111101/11100001	Pop IY from stack	—	—	—	—
POP qq	11qq0001	Pop qq from stack	—	—	—	—
PUSH IX	1011101/11100101	Push IX onto stack	—	—	—	—
PUSH IY	1111101/11100101	Push IY onto stack	—	—	—	—
PUSH qq	11qq0101	Push qq onto stack	—	—	—	—
RES b, r	1001011/10br	Reset bit b of r	—	—	—	—
RES b, (HL)	1001011/0b110	Reset bit b of (HL)	—	—	—	—
RES b, (IX+d)	1011101/1001011/d/10b110	Reset bit b of (IX+d)	—	—	—	—
RES b, (IY+d)	1111101/1001011/d/10b110	Reset bit b of (IY+d)	—	—	—	—
RET	11001001	Return from subroutine	—	—	—	—
RET cc	11c000	Return from subroutine if cc	—	—	—	—
RETI	1101101/01001101	Return from interrupt	—	—	—	—
RETN	1101101/01000101	Return from nonmaskable interrupt	—	—	—	—
RL, r	11001011/00010r	Rotate left through carry r	X	X	X	X
RL (HL)	1001011/00010110	Rotate left through carry (HL)	X	X	X	X
RL (IX+d)	1011101/1001011/d/00010110	Rotate left through carry (IX+d)	X	X	X	X
RL (IY+d)	1101101/1001011/d/00000110	Rotate left through carry (IY+d)	X	X	X	X
RLA	00010111	Rotate A left through carry	X	—	X	X
RLC r	1001011/00000r	Rotate left circular r	X	X	X	X

Flags

Mnemonic	Format	Description	S	Z	P/V	C
RLC (HL)	11001011/00000110	Rotate left circular (HL)	X	X	X	X
RLC (IX+d)	10111101/11001011/d/00000110	Rotate left circular (IX+d)	X	X	X	X
RLC (IY+d)	11111101/11001011/d/00000110	Rotate left circular (IY+d)	X	X	X	X
RLCA	00000111	Rotate left circular A	–	–	–	X
RLD	11101101/01101111	Rotate BCD digit left (HL)	X	X	X	–
RR r	11001011/00011r	Rotate right through carry r	X	X	X	X
RR (HL)	11001011/00011110	Rotate right through carry (HL)	X	X	X	X
RR (IX+d)	11011101/11001011/d/00011110	Rotate right through carry (IX+d)	X	X	X	X
RR (IY+d)	00011110/11001011/d/00011110	Rotate right through carry (IY+d)	X	X	X	X
RRA	00011111	Rotate A right through carry	–	–	–	X
RRC r	11001011/00001r	Rotate r right circular	X	X	X	X
RRC (HL)	11001011/00001110	Rotate (HL) right circular	X	X	X	X
RRC (IX+d)	10111101/11001011/d/00001110	Rotate (IX+d) right circular	X	X	X	X
RRC (IY+d)	11111101/11001011/d/00001110	Rotate (IY+d) right circular	X	X	X	X
RRCA	00001111	Rotate A right circular	–	–	–	X
RRD	11101101/01100111	Rotate BCD digit right (HL)	X	X	X	–
RST p	11p110	Restart to location p	–	–	–	–
SBC A, r	1001r	A – r – CY to A	X	X	X	X

Mnemonic	Code	Operation					
SBC A, n	11011110/n	A – n – CY to A	X	X	X	X	X
SBC A, (HL)	10011110	A – (HL) – CY to A	X	X	X	X	X
SBC A, (IX+d)	11011101/10011110/d	A – (IX+d) – CY to A	X	X	X	X	X
SBC A, (IY+d)	11111101/10011110/d	A – (IY+d) – CY to A	X	X	X	X	X
SBC HL, ss	11101101/01ss0010	HL – ss – CY to HL	X	X	X	X	1
SCF	00110111	Set carry flag	–	–	–	–	1
SET b, (HL)	11001011/11b110	Set bit b of (HL)	–	–	–	–	–
SET b, (IX+d)	11011101/11001011/d/11b110	Set bit b of (IX+d)	–	–	–	–	–
SET b, (IY+d)	11111101/11001011/d/11b110	Set bit b of (IY+d)	–	–	–	–	–
SET b, r	11001011/11br	Set bit b of r	–	–	–	–	–
SLA r	11001011/00100r	Shift r left arithmetic	X	X	X	X	X
SLA (HL)	11001011/00100110	Shift (HL) left arithmetic	X	X	X	X	X
SLA (IX+d)	11011101/11001011/d/00100110	Shift (IX+d) left arithmetic	X	X	X	X	X
SLA (IY+d)	11111101/11001011/d/00100110	Shift (IY+d) left arithmetic	X	X	X	X	X
SRA r	11001011/00101r	Shift r right arithmetic	X	X	X	X	X
SRA (HL)	11001011/00101110	Shift (HL) right arithmetic	X	X	X	X	X
SRA (IX+d)	11011101/11001011/d/00101110	Shift (IX+d) right arithmetic	X	X	X	X	X
SRA (IY+d)	11111101/11001011/d/00101110	Shift (IY+d) right arithmetic	X	X	X	X	X
SRL r	11001011/00111r	Shift r right logical	X	X	X	X	X
SRL (HL)	11001011/001111110	Shift (HL) right logical	X	X	X	X	X
SRL (IX+d)	11011101/11001011/d/00111110	Shift (IX+d) right logical	X	X	X	X	X
SRL (IY+d)	11111101/11001011/d/00111110	Shift (IY+d) right logical	X	X	X	X	X
SUB r	10010r	A – r to A	X	X	X	X	X

Flags			

Mnemonic	Format	Description	S	Z	P/V	C
SUB n	1010110/n	A – n to A	X	X	X	X
SUB (HL)	10010110	A – (HL) to A	X	X	X	X
SUB (IX+d)	11011101/10010110/d	A – (IX+d) to A	X	X	X	X
SUB (IY+d)	11111101/10010110/d	A – (IY+d) to A	X	X	X	X
XOR r	10101r	A EXCLUSIVE-OR r to A	X	X	X	0
XOR n	11101110/n	A EXCLUSIVE-OR n to A	X	X	X	0
XOR (HL)	10101110	A EXCLUSIVE-OR (HL) to A	X	X	X	0
XOR (IX+d)	11011101/10101110/d	A EXCLUSIVE-OR (IX+d) to A	X	X	X	0
XOR (IY+d)	11111101/10101110/d	A EXCLUSIVE-OR (IY+d) to A	X	X	X	0

Flag Condition Codes

X   affected
–   unaffected
1   set
0   reset

274

Additional Key Codes

b	bit field (0-7)			
c	condition field	0 = NZ	1 = Z	2 = NC	3 = C
		4 = PO	5 = PE	6 = P	7 = M
d	indexing displacement (− 128 to + 127)				
dd	register pair	0 = BC	1 = DE	2 = HL	3 = SP
e	relative jump displacement (− 128 to + 127)				
n	immediate or address value				
pp	register pair	0 = BC	1 = DE	2 = IX	3 = SP
qq	register pair	0 = BC	1 = DE	2 = IY	3 = SP
r	register	0 = B	1 = C	2 = D	3 = E
		4 = H	5 = L	7 = A	
r'	primed register	(same as r)			
ss	register pair	0 = BC	1 = DE	2 = HL	3 = SP
t	RST field				
Location = t × 8					

275

Instruction Classifications

A REGISTER OPERATIONS

Complement	CPL
Decimal	DAA
Negate	NEG

ADDING/SUBTRACTING TWO 8-BIT NUMBERS
A and Another Register

ADC A, r
ADD A, r
SBC A, r
SUB A, r

A and Immediate Operand

ADC A, n
ADD A, n
SBC A, n
SUB A, n

A and Memory Operand

ADC A, (HL)
ADC A, (IX + d)
ADC A, (IY + d)
ADD A, (HL)
ADD A, (IX + d)
ADD A, (IY + d)
SBC (HL)
SBC (IX + d)
SBC (IY + d)
SUB (HL)
SUB (IX + d)
SUB (IY + d)

ADDING/SUBTRACTING TWO 16-BIT NUMBERS
HL and Another Register Pair

ADC HL, ss
ADD HL, ss
SBC HL, ss

IX and Another Register Pair

ADD IX, pp
ADD IY, rr

BIT INSTRUCTIONS
Test Bit

	Register	BIT b, r
	Memory	BIT b, (HL)
		BIT b, (IX + d)
		BIT b, (IY + d)
Reset Bit		
	Register	RES b, r
	Memory	RES b, (HL)
		RES b, (IX + d)
		RES b, (IY + d)
Set Bit		
	Register	SET b, r
	Memory	SET b, (HL)
		SET b, (IX + d)
		SET b, (IY + d)

CARRY FLAG

| | Complement | CCF |
| | Set | SCF |

COMPARE TWO 8-BIT OPERANDS
A and Another Register

CP r

A and Immediate Operand

CP n

A and Memory Operand

CP (HL)
CP (IX + d)
CP (IY + d)

Block Compare

CPD
CPDR
CPI
CPIR

DECREMENTS/INCREMENTS
Single Register

DEC r
INC r

Register Pair

DEC ss
INC ss
DEC IX

	INC IX
	DEC IY
	INC IY
Memory	
	DEC (HL)
	INC (HL)
	DEC (IX + d)
	INC (IX + d)
	DEC (IY + d)
	INC (IY + d)

EXCHANGES
  DE and HL   EX DE, HL
  Top Of Stack
                   EX (SP), HL
                   EX (SP), IX
                   EX (SP), IY

INPUT/OUTPUT
  I/O To/From A and Port
                   IN A, (n)
                   OUT (n), A
  I/O To/From Register and Port
                   IN r, (C)
                   OUT (C), r
  Block
                   IND
                   INDR
                   INR
                   INIR
                   OTDR
                   OTIR
                   OUTD
                   OUTI

INTERRUPTS
  Disable   DI
  Enable   EI
  Interrupt Mode
                             IM 0
                             IM 1
                             IM 2

Return From Interrupt

                        RETI
                        RETN

JUMPS
  Unconditional

                        JP (HL)
                        JP (IX)
                        JP (IY)
                        JP (nn)
                        JR e
  Conditional

                        JP cc, nn
                        JR C, e
                        JR NZ, e
                        JR Z, e
  Special Conditional

                        DJNZ e

LOADS
  A Load Memory Operand

                        LD A, (BC)
                        LD A, (DE)
                        LD A, (nn)
  A and Other Registers

                        LD A, I
                        LD A, R
                        LD I, A
                        LD R, A
  Between Registers, 8-Bit

                        LD r, r'
  Immediate 8-Bit

                        LD r, n
  Immediate 16-Bit

                        LD dd, nn
                        LD IX, nn
                        LD IY, nn
  Register Pairs From Other Register Pairs

                        LD SP, HL
                        LD SP, IX
                        LD SP, IY
  From Memory, 8-Bits

LD r, (HL)
LD r, (IX + d)
LD r, (IY + d)

From Memory, 16-Bits

LD HL, (nn)
LD IX, (nn)
LD IY, (nn)
LD dd, (nn)

Block

LDD
LDDR
LDI
LDIR

LOGICAL OPERATIONS 8 BITS WITH A
A and Another Register

AND r
OR r
XOR r

A and Immediate Operand

AND n
OR n
XOR n

A and Memory Operand

AND (HL)
OR (HL)
XOR (HL)
AND (IX + d)
OR (IX + d)
XOR (IX + d)
AND (IY + d)
OR (IY + d)
XOR (IY + d)

PRIME/NON-PRIME
  Switch AF   EX AF, AF'
  Switch Others   EXX

SHIFTS
              Circular (Rotate)

  A Only   RLA

	RLCA
	RRA
	RRCA
All Registers	
	RL r
	RLC r
	RR r
	RRC r
Memory	

RL (HL)
RLC (HL)
RR (HL)
RRC (HL)
RL (IX + d)
RLC (IX + d)
RR (IX + d)
RRC (IX + d)
RL (IY + d)
RLC (IY + d)
RR (IY + d)
RRC (IY + d)

Registers

Logical

Memory

SRL r
SRL (HL)
SRL (IX + d)
SRL (IY + d)

Registers

Arithmetic

SLA r
SRA r

Memory

SLA (HL)
SRA (HL)
SLA (IX + d)
SRA (IX + d)
SLA (IY + d)
SRA (IY + d)

STACK OPERATORS

PUSH IX
PUSH IY
PUSH qq
POP IX

POP IY
POP qq

STORES
Of A Only

LD (BC), A
LD (DE), A
LD (HL), A
LD (nn), A

All Registers

LD (HL), r
LD (IX + d), r
LD (IY + d), r

Immediate Data

LD (HL), n
LD (IX + d), n
LD (IY + d), n

16-Bit Registers

LD (nn), dd
LD (nn), IX
LD (nn), IY

SUBROUTINE ACTIONS
Conditional Call   CALL cc, nn
Unconditional Call   CALL nn
Conditional Return   RET cc
Unconditional Return   RET
Special Call   RSTP

MISCELLANEOUS
Halt   HALT
No Operation   NOP

Appendix B

Hexadecimal Instruction Codes for the Z80

Hexadecimal	Instruction	Hexadecimal	Instruction
00	NOP	16 nn	LD D,nn
01 nn nn	LD BC,nn	17	RLA
02	LD (BC),A	18 e – 2	JR e
03	INC BC	19	ADD HL,DE
04	INC B	1A	LD A,(DE)
05	DEC B	1B	DEC DE
06 nn	LD B,nn	1C	INC E
07	RLCA	1D	DEC E
08	EX AF,AF'	1E nn	LD E,nn
09	ADD HL,BC	1E CB d 1E	RR (IY + d)
0A	LD A, (BC)	1F	RRA
0B	DEC BC	20 e – 2	JR NZ,e
0C	INC C	21 nn nn	LD HL,nn
0D	DEC C	22 nn nn	LD (nn),HL
0E nn	LD C,nn	23	INC HL
0F	RRCA	24	INC H
10 e – 2	DJNZ e	25	DEC H
11 nn nn	LD DE,nn	26 nn	LD H,nn
12	LD (DE),A	27	DAA
13	INC DE	28 e – 2	JR Z,e
14	INC D	29	ADD HL,HL
15	DEC D	2A nn nn	LD HL,(nn)

Hexadecimal	Instruction	Hexadecimal	Instruction
2B	DEC HL	55	LD D,L'
2C	INC L	56	LD D,(HL)
2D	DEC L	57	LD D,A'
2E nn	LD L,nn	58	LD E,B'
2F	CPL	59	LD E,C'
30 e – 2	JR NC,e	5A	LD E,D'
31 nn nn	LD SP,nn	5B	LD E,E'
33	INC SP	5C	LD E,H'
34	INC (HL)	5D	LD E,L'
35	DEC (HL)	5E	LD E,(HL)
36 nn	LD (HL),nn	5F	LD E,A'
37	SCF	60	LD H,B'
38 e – 2	JR C,e	61	LD H,C'
39	ADD HL,SP	62	LD H,D'
3A nn nn	LD A,(nn)	63	LD H,E'
3B	DEC SP	64	LD H,H'
3C	INC A	65	LD H,L'
3D	DEC A	66	LD H,(HL)
3E nn	LD A,nn	67	LD H,A'
3F	CCF	68	LD L,B'
40	LD B,B'	69	LD L,C'
41	LD B,C'	6A	LD L,D'
42	LD B,D'	6B	LD L,E'
43	LD B,E'	6C	LD L,H'
44	LD B,H'	6D	LD L,L'
45	LD B,L'	6E	LD L,(HL)
46	LD B,(HL)	6F	LD L,A'
47	LD B,A'	70	LD (HL),B
48	LD C,B'	71	LD (HL),C
49	LD C,C'	72	LD (HL),D
4A	LD C,D'	73	LD (HL),E
4B	LD C,E'	74	LD (HL),H
4C	LD C,H'	75	LD (HL),L
4D	LD C,L'	76	HALT
4E	LD C,(HL)	77	LD (HL),A
4F	LD,C,A'	78	LD A,B'
50	LD D,B'	79	LD A,C'
51	LD D,C'	7A	LD A,D'
52	LD D,D'	7B	LD A,E'
53	LD D,E'	7C	LD A,H'
54	LD D,H'	7D	LD A,L'

Hexadecimal	Instruction	Hexadecimal	Instruction
7E	LD A,(HL)	A6	AND (HL)
7F	LD A,A'	A8	XOR B
80	ADD A,B	A9	XOR C
81	ADD A,C	AA	XOR D
82	ADD A,D	AB	XOR E
83	ADD A,E	AC	XOR H
84	ADD A,H	AD	XOR L
85	ADD A,L	AE	XOR (HL)
86	ADD A,(HL)	AE nn	XOR nn
87	ADD A,A	B0	OR B
88	ADC A,B	B1	OR C
89	ADC A,C	B2	OR D
8A	ADC A,D	B3	OR E
8B	ADC A,E	B4	OR H
8C	ADC A,H	B5	OR L
8D	ADC A,L	B6	OR (HL)
8E	ADC A,(HL)	B7	OR A
8F	ADC A,A	B8	CP B
90	SUB B	B9	CP C
91	SUB C	BA	CP D
92	SUB D	BB	CP E
93	SUB E	BB E3	EX (SP),IX
94	SUB H	BC	CP H
95	SUB L	BD	CP L
96	SUB (HL)	BE nn	CP (HL)
96 nn	SUB nn	BF	CP A
97	SUB A	C0	RET NZ
98	SBC A,B	C1	POP BC
99	SBC A,C	C2 nn nn	JP NZ,nn
9A	SBC A,D	C3 nn nn	JP nn
9B	SBC A,E	C4 nn nn	CALL NZ,nn
9C	SBC A,H	C5	PUSH BC
9D	SBC A,L	C6 nn	ADD A,nn
9E	SBC A,(HL)	C8	RET Z
9E nn	SBC A,nn	C9	RET
A0	AND B	CA nn nn	JP Z,nn
A1	AND C	CB xa	RES b,r
A2	AND D	CB xb	RES b,(HL)
A3	AND E	CB xc	SET b,(HL)
A4	AND H	CB xd	SET b,r
A5	AND L	CB xx	BIT b,r

Hexadecimal	Instruction	Hexadecimal	Instruction
CB xy	BIT b,(HL)	CB 28	SRA B
CB 00	RLC B	CB 29	SRA C
CB 01	RLC C	CB 2A	SRA D
CB 02	RLC D	CB 2B	SRA E
CB 03	RLC E	CB 2C	SRA H
CB 04	RLC H	CB 2D	SRA L
CB 05	RLC L	CB 2E	SRA (HL)
CB 06	RLC (HL)	CB 2F	SRA A
CB 07	RLC A	CB 38	SRL B
CB 08	RRC B	CB 39	SRL C
CB 09	RRC C	CB 3A	SRL D
CB 0A	RRC D	CB 3B	SRL E
CB 0B	RRC E	CB 3C	SRL H
CB 0C	RRC H	CB 3D	SRL L
CB 0D	RRC L	CB 3E	SRL (HL)
CB 0E	RRC (HL)	CB 3F	SRL A
CB 0F	RRC A	CC nn nn	CALL Z,nn
CB 10	RL,B	CD nn nn	CALL nn
CB 11	RL,C	CE nn	ADC A,nn
CB 12	RL,D	D0	RET NC
CB 13	RL,E	D1	POP DE
CB 14	RL,H	D2 nn nn	JP NC,nn
CB 15	RL,L	D3 nn	OUT (nn),A
CB 16	RL,(HL)	D4 nn nn	CALL NC,nn
CB 17	RL,A	D5	PUSH DE
CB 18	RR B	D5 CB d 06	RL (IY + d)
CB 19	RR C	D8	RET C
CB 1A	RR D	D9	EXX
CB 1B	RR E	DA nn nn	JP C,nn
CB 1C	RR H	DB n	IN A,(n)
CB 1D	RR L	DC nn nn	CALL C,nn
CB 1E	RR (HL)	DD 09	ADD IX,BC
CB 1F	RR A	DD 9E d	SBC A,(IX + d)
CB 20	SLA B	DD 19	ADD IX,DE
CB 21	SLA C	DD 21 nn nn	LD IX,nn
CB 22	SLA D	DD 22 nn nn	LD (nn),IX
CB 23	SLA E	DD 23	INC IX
CB 24	SLA H	DD 29	ADD IX,IX
CB 25	SLA L	DD 2A nn nn	LD IC,(nn)
CB 26	SLA (HL)	DD 2B	DEC IX
CB 27	SLA A	DD 34 d	INC (IX + d)

Hexadecimal	Instruction	Hexadecimal	Instruction
DD 35 d	DEC (IX + d)	E3	EX (SP),HL
DD 36 d nn	LD (IX + d),nn	E4 nn nn	CALL PO,nn
DD 39	ADD IX,SP	E5	PUSH IY
DD 46 d	LD B,(IX + d)	E6 nn	AND nn
DD 4E d	LD C,(IX + d)	E8	RET PE
DD 56 d	LD D,(IX + d)	E9	JP (HL)
DD 5E d	LD E,(IX + d)	EA nn nn	JP PE,nn
DD 66 d	LD H,(IX + d)	EB	EX DE,HL
DD 6E d	LD L,(IX + d),	EB 47	LD I,A
DD 70 d	LD (IX + d),B	EC nn nn	CALL PE,nn
DD 71 d	LD (IX + d),C	ED 40	IN B,(C)
DD 72 d	LD (IX + d),D	ED 41	OUT (C),B
DD 73 d	LD (IX + d),E	ED 42	SBC HL,BC
DD 74 d	LD (IX + d),H	ED 43 nn	LD (nn),BC
DD 75 d	LD (IX + d),L	ED 44	NEG
DD 77 d	LD (IX + d),A	ED 45	RETN
DD 7E d	LD A,(IX + d)	ED 46	IM 0
DD 86 d	ADD A,(IX + D)	ED 48	IN C,(C)
DD 8E d	ADC A,(IX + d)	ED 49	OUT (C),C
DD 96 d	SUB (IX + d)	ED 4A	ADC HL,BC
DD A6 d	AND (IX + d)	ED 4B nn nn	LD BC,(nn)
DD AE d	XOR (IX + d)	ED 4D	RETI
DD B6 d	OR (IX + d)	ED 4F	LD R,A
DD BE d	CP (IX + d)	ED 50	IN D,(C)
DD CB d xb	RES b,(IX + d)	ED 51	OUT (C),D
DD CB d xc	SET b,(IX + d)	ED 52	SBC HL,DE
DD CB d xy	BIT b b,(IX + d)	ED 53 nn	LD (nn),DE
DD CB d 06	RLC (IX + d)	ED 56	IM 1
DD CB d 0E	RRC (IX + d)	ED 57	LD A,1
DD CB d 16	RL (IX + d)	ED 58	IN E,(C)
DD CB d 1E	RR (IX + d)	ED 59	OUT (C),E
DD CB d 2E	SRA (IX + d)	ED 5A	ADC, HL,DE
DD CB d 3E	SRL (IX + d)	ED 5B nn nn	LD DE,(nn)
DD E1	POP IX	ED 5E	IM 2
DD E5	PUSH IX	ED 5F	LD A,R
DD E9	JP (IX)	ED 60	IN H,(C)
DD EB d 26	SLA (IX + d)	ED 61	OUT (C),H
DD F9	LD SP,IX	ED 63 nn	LD (nn),HL
E0	RET PO	ED 67	RRD
E1	POP IY	ED 68	IN L,(C)
E2 nn nn	JP PO,nn	ED 69	OUT (C),L

Hexadecimal	Instruction	Hexadecimal	Instruction
ED 6A	ADC HL,HL	FD 22 nn nn	LD (nn),IY
ED 6B nn nn	LD HL,(nn)	FD 23	INC IY
ED 6F	RLD	FD 29	ADD IY,IY
ED 72	SBC HL,SP	FD 2A nn nn	LD IY,(nn)
ED 73 nn	LD (nn),SP	FD 2B	DEC IY
ED 78	IN A,(C)	FD 34 d	INC (IY + d)
ED 79	OUT (C),A	FD 35 d	DEC (IY + d)
ED 7A	ADC HL,SP	FD 36 d nn	LD (IY + d),nn
ED 7B nn nn	LD SP,(nn)	FD 39	ADD IY,SP
ED A0	LDI	FD 46 d	LD B,(IY + d)
ED A1	CPI	FD 4E d	LD C,(IY + d)
ED A2	INI	FD 56 d	LD D,(IY + d)
ED AB	LDD	FD 5E d	LD E,(IY + d)
ED A9	CPD	FD 66 d	LD H,(IY + d)
ED AA	IND	FD 6E d	LD L,(IY + d)
ED A3	OUT1	FD 70 d	LD (IY + d),B
ED AB	OUTD	FD 71 d	LD (IY + d),C
ED B0	LDIR	FD 72 d	LD (IY + d),D
ED B1	CPIR	FD 73 d	LD (IY + d),E
ED B2	INIR	FD 74 d	LD (IY + d),H
ED B3	OTIR	FD 75 d	LD (IY + d),L
ED B8	LDDR	FD 77 d	LD (IY + d),A
ED B9	CPDR	FD 7E d	LD A,(IY + d)
ED BA	INDR	FD 86 d	ADD A,(IX + d)
ED BB	OTDR	FD 8E d	ADC A,(IY + d)
F0	RET P	FD 96 d	SUB (IY + d)
F1	POP SP	FD 9E d	SBC A,(IY + d)
F2 nn nn	JP P,nn	FD A6 d	AND (IY + d)
F3	DI	FD AE d	XOR (IY + d)
F4 nn nn	CALL P,nn	FD B6 d	OR (IY + d)
F5	PUSH SP	FD BE d	CP (IY + d)
F6 nn	OR nn	FD CB d xb	RES b,(IY + d)
F8	RET M	FD CB d xc	SET b,(IY + d)
F9	LD SP,HL	FD CB d xy	BIT b,(IY + d)
FA nn nn	JP M,nn	FD CB d 06	RLC(IY + d)
FB	E1	FD CB d 0E	RRC (IY + d)
FB E3	EX (SP),IY	FD CB d 2E	SRA (IY + d)
FC nn nn	CALL M,nn	FD CB d 3E	SRL (IY + d)
FD 09	ADD IY,BC	FD E9	JP (IY)
FD 19	ADD IY,DE	FD EB d 26	SLA (IY + d)
FD 21 nn nn	LD IY,nn	FD EF	PUSH IY

Hexadecimal	Instruction	Hexadecimal	Instruction
FD F9	LD SP,IY	FE nn	CP nn

xx = 01br where b = bit field (000 -111) and r = register

$$000 = B$$
$$001 = C$$
$$010 = D$$
$$011 = E$$
$$100 = H$$
$$101 = L$$
$$111 = A$$

$$xy = 01b110$$
$$xa = 10br$$
$$xb = 10b110$$
$$xc = 11b110$$
$$xd = 11br$$

Appendix C

Sample Computer Programs

T HE SAMPLE PROGRAMS ARE INTENDED JUST TO GET YOU
started. They can be changed to suit your individual applications (see Table C-1). The sample programs are listed in standard
assembly language form. There are six columns:

Column 1	Memory location
Column 2	Machine-language command
Column 3	Line number (for convenient reference)
Column 4	Labels (optional)
Column 5	Assembly-language command
Column 6	Comments

HOW TO ENTER THE PROGRAMS

To enter the program, use the memory stepper to set to the
beginning of the memory (&H0001). Enter the first two digit
hexadecimal number in column 2 on the keypad. Advance the memory stepper, then enter the next two digits. Continue with this procedure until all the numbers in column 2 have been entered. The other
columns are given to make the functioning of the program easier
to follow.

DIRECTIONS FOR USING THE EPROM PROGRAMMER

This device is easier to use than it might appear.

1. Load the program into RAM in the normal manner.
2. Set the memory stepper to 0000.
3. Carefully insert EPROM chip.
4. Hit LOAD button.
5. Advance memory stepper.
6. Repeat steps 4 and 5 until you have stepped through the entire program.

PROGRAM 1
SAMPLE SOFTWARE FOR PROJECT 9
AC CONTROLLER (FIG. 7-1)

```
0001    01 02 00    0100    LD BC,0200    ; LOAD BC WITH 1024
0004    0B 2B       0110    DEC BC        ; DECREMENT
0006    00          0120    NOP           ; WASTE TIME
0007    00          0130    NOP           ; WASTE TIME
0008    CA 00 0E    0140    JR Z,000E     ; JUMP IF ZERO
000B    C3 00 04    0150    JP 0004       ; JUMP BACK
000E    3D 01       0160    LD A,01       ; SET UP SWITCHING
                                              VALUE
0010    32 1F FF    0170    LD 1FFF       ; TO PORT
0013    01 02 00    0180    LD BC,0200    ; REPEAT
0016    0B 2B       0190    DEC BC        ; DECREMENT
```

0018	00	0200	NOP	; PROCEDURE
0019	00	0210	NOP	; PROCEDURE
001A	CA 00 20	0220	JR Z,0020	; PROCEDURE
001D	C3 00 16	0230	JP 0016	; PROCEDURE
0020	3D 02	0240	LD A,02	; SET UP SWITCHING VALUE
0022	32 1F FF	0250	LD 1FFF	; TO PORT
0025	C3 00 01	0260	JP 0001	; START OVER
0028	76	0270	HALT	; END PROGRAM

This program will turn device A on and off repeatedly, with brief delays between actions.

PROGRAM 2
SAMPLE SOFTWARE FOR PROJECT 10
INTRUSION DETECTOR (FIG. 9-2)

0001	3A 1F FD	0100	LD A,1FFD	; CHECK PORT VALUE
0004	FE 05	0110	CP 05	; COMPARE SWITCH PATTERN
0006	CA 00 0C	0120	JP Z,000C	; JUMP IF EQUAL
0009	C3 00 01	0130	JP 0001	; JUMP BACK
000C	3D 01	0140	LD A,01	; LOAD ALARM VALUE
000E	32 1F FF	0150	LD 1FFF	; OUT TO ALARM PORT
0021	C3 00 0E	0160	JP 000E	; LOOP
0024	76	0170	HALT	; END PROGRAM

PROGRAM 3
SAMPLE SOFTWARE FOR PROJECT 14
MULTILEVEL TEMPERATURE DETECTOR (FIG. 9-10)

0001	3A 1F FA	0100	LD A,(1FFA)	; CHECK INPUT PORT
0004	FE 03	0110	CP 03	; HIGH TEMPERATURE?
0006	CA 00 16	0120	JP Z,0016	; JUMP IF ZERO
0009	FE 07	0130	CP 07	; DANGEROUS TEMPERATURE?
000B	CA 00 1C	0140	JP Z, 0001C	; JUMP IF ZERO
000E	FE 0F	0150	CP 0F	; VERY DANGEROUS TEMPERATURE?
0010	CA 00 20	0160	JP Z, 0020	; JUMP IF ZERO
0013	C3 00 01	0170	JP 0001	; JUMP BACK
0016	3E 01	0180	LD A,01	; SET ALARM VALUE
0018	C3 00 22	0190	JP 0022	; JUMP TO ALARM
001C	3E 02	0200	LD A, 02	; SET ALARM VALUE

001E	C3 00 22	0210	JP 0022	; JUMP TO ALARM
0020	3E 04	0220	LD A, 04	; SET ALARM VALUE
0022	32 1F EA	0230	LD 1FEA	; OUTPUT TO ALARM PORT
0025	C3 00 22	0240	JP 0022	; LOOP
0028	76	0250	HALT	; END PROGRAM

PROGRAM 4
SAMPLE SOFTWARE FOR PROJECT 19
OHMMETER (FIG. 10-5)

0001	ED 8B 1F F0	0100	LD BC, (1FF0)	; INPUT VOLTAGE
0005	DD 2A 27 10	0110	LD IX,2710	; LOAD Rr VALUE
0009	21 00 00	0120	LD HL,0000	; CLEAR HL
000C	ED 4A	0130	ADC HL, BC	; ADD
000E	DD 2B	0140	DEC IX	; DECREMENT COUNTER
0010	CA 00 16	0150	JP Z,0016	; JUMP IF ZERO
0013	C3 00 0C	0160	JP 000C	; JUMP BACK
0016	3E 05	0170	LD A, 005	; CALCULATE
0018	91	0180	SUB C	; DENOMINATOR
0019	32 00 40	0190	LD (0040),A	; STORE
001C	ED 4B 00 40	0200	LD BC,(0040)	; LOAD BC
0020	3E 00	0210	LD A,00	; CLEAR A
0022	96	0220	SUB (HL)	; – HL TO A
0023	81	0230	ADD A,C	; ADD
0024	F2 00 2C	0240	JP V,002C	; JUMP IF OVERFLOW
0027	DD 23	0250	INC IX	; INCREMENT COUNTER
0029	C3 00 23	0260	JP 0023	; LOOP BACK
002C	DD 22 1F EF	0270	LD 1FEF,IX	; STORE RESISTANCE TO OUTPUT PORT
0030	76	0280	HALT	; END PROGRAM

PROGRAM 5
SAMPLE SOFTWARE FOR THE
IC TESTER CIRCUIT (FIG. 10-13)

I/O PORTS

&H1FA1	PIN I/O SELECT	CPU OUTPUT
&H1FA2	PIN INPUTS	CPU OUTPUT
&H1FA3	PIN OUTPUTS	CPU INPUT

Pin patterns are stored beginning at location &H0040.

| 0001 | 3E 36 | 0100 | LDA,36 | ; SET UP INPUT OUTPUT |

0003	32 1F A1	0110	LD(1FA1),A	; PATTERN
0006	16 00	0120	LD D,00	; SET UP MEMORY
0008	1E 40	0130	LD E,40	; COUNTER
000A	06 00	0140	LD B,00	; CLEAR B
000C	47	0150	LD A,B	; A = B
000D	32 1F A2	0160	LD(1FA2),A	; A TO PORT
0010	3A 1F A3	0170	LD A,(1FA3)	; GET IC OUTPUT DATA
0013	12	0180	LD(DE),A	; STORE DATA
0014	13	0190	INC DE	; INCREMENT MEMORY COUNTER
0015	04	0200	INC B	; INCREMENT TEST PATTERN
0016	DA 00 1C	0210	JP V,001C	; JUMP IF OVERFLOW
0019	C3 00 0C	0220	JP 000C	; LOOP BACK
001C	76	0230	HALT	; END PROGRAM

PROGRAM 6
SAMPLE SOFTWARE FOR THE
MOTOR CONTROL CIRCUIT (FIG. 11-3)

0001	3E 00	0100	LD A,00	; MOTOR OFF
0003	32 **IF** FB	0110	LD(1FFB),A	; TO PORT
0006	3E FF	0120	LD A, FF	; SET UP COUNTER
0008	D6 01	0130	SUB 1	; DECREMENT
000A	CA 00 10	01400	JP Z,0010	; JUMP IF ZERO
000D	C3 00 08	0150	JP 0008	; LOOP BACK
0010	3E 01	0160	LD A,01	; MOTOR FORWARD
0012	32 1F FB	0170	LD(1FFB),A	; TO PORT
0015	3E FF	0180	LD A, FF	; SET UP COUNTER
0017	D6 01	0190	SUB 1	; DECREMENT
0019	CA 00 0E	0200	JP Z,000E	; JUMP IF ZERO
001B	C3 00 17	0210	JP 001B	; LOOP BACK
001E	3E 00	0220	LD A,00	; MOTOR OFF
0020	32 1F FB	0230	LD(1FFB),A	; TO PORT
0023	3E FF	0240	LD A, FF	; SET UP COUNTER
0025	D6 01	0250	SUB 1	; DECREMENT
0027	CA 00 2D	0260	JP Z,002D	; JUMP IF ZERO
002A	63 00 25	0270	JP 0025	; LOOP BACK
002D	3E 02	0280	LD A, 02	; MOTOR REVERSE
002F	32 1F FB	0290	LD(1FFB),A	; TO PORT
0032	3E FF	0300	LD A,FF	; SET UP COUNTER
0034	D6 01	0310	SUB 1	; DECREMENT
0036	CA 00 01	0320	JP Z,0001	; JUMP IF ZERO
0039	C3 00 34	0330	JP 0034	; LOOP BACK
003C	76	0340	HALT	; END PROGRAM

This program will turn a motor at output port &H1FFB on and off in opposite directions for quick pulses.

PROGRAM 7
SAMPLE SOFTWARE FOR THE
SOUND DETECTOR CIRCUIT (FIG. 11-9)

0001	06 01	0100	LD B,01	; SET TEST VALUE
0003	3A 1F F0	0110	LD A,(1FF0)	; CHECK PORT
0005	B8	0120	CP B	; A = B?
0006	CA 00 0C	0130	JP Z,000C	; JUMP IF ZERO
0009	C3 00 03	0140	JP 0003	; JUMP BACK
000C	16 00	0150	LD D,00	; CLEAR D
000E	3A 1F F0	0160	LD A,(1FF0)	; CHECK PORT
0011	B8	0170	CP B	; A = B?
0012	CA 00 1C	0180	JP Z,001C	; JUMP IF ZERO
0015	14	0190	INC D	; INCREMENT D
0016	F2 00 3C	0200	JP V,003C	; JUMP IF OVERFLOW
0019	CA 00 0E	0210	JP 000E	; JUMP BACK
001C	16 00	0220	LD D,00	; CLEAR D
001E	3A 1F F0	0230	LD A,(1FF0)	; CHECK PORT
0021	B8	0240	CP B	; A = B?
0022	CA 00 2C	0250	JP Z,002C	; JUMP IF ZERO
0025	14	0260	INC D	; INCREMENT D
0026	F2 00 50	0270	JP V,0050	; JUMP IF OVERFLOW
0029	CA 00 1E	0280	JP 001E	; JUMP BACK
002C	16 00	0290	LD D,00	; CLEAR D
002E	3A 1F F0	0300	LD A,(1FF0)	; CHECK PORT
0031	B8	0310	CP B	; A = B?
0032	CA 00 70	0320	JP Z,0070	; JUMP IF ZERO
0035	14	0330	INC D	; INCREMENT D
0036	F2 00 60	0340	JP V,0060	; JUMP IF OVERFLOW
0039	CA 00 2E	0350	JP 002E	; JUMP BACK
003C	00	0360	NOP	; 1 PULSE
003D	00	0370	NOP	; ROUTINE
003E	C3 00 01	0380	JP 0001	; JUMP BACK
0050	00	0390	NOP	; 2 PULSE
0051	00	0400	NOP	; ROUTINE
0252	C3 00 01	0410	JP 0001	; JUMP BACK
0060	00	0420	NOP	; 3 PULSE
0061	00	0430	NOP	; ROUTINE
0062	C3 00 01	0440	JP 0001	; JUMP BACK
0070	00	0450	NOP	; 4 PULSE
0071	00	0460	NOP	; ROUTINE
0072	C3 00 01	0470	JP 0001	; JUMP BACK
0075	76	0480	HALT	; END PROGRAM

PROGRAM 8
SAMPLE SOFTWARE FOR THE
PROGRAMMABLE SOUND GENERATOR (FIG. 12-6)

0001	3E 38	0100	LD A,38	; SET ENABLE VALUE

0003	D3 07	0110	OUT (7),A	; OUT TO ENABLE
				PORT
0005	3E 54	0120	LD A,54	; LOAD AMPLITUDE
				VALUE
0007	D3 08	0130	OUT(8),A	; OUT TO EACH
0009	D3 09	0140	OUT(9),A	; AMPLITUDE
000B	D3 0A	0150	OUT(A),A	; PORT
000D	3E 00	0160	LD A,0	; CLEAR A
000F	D3 01	0170	OUT(1),A	; OUT TO EACH
0011	D3 03	0180	OUT(3),A	; COARSE-TUNE
0013	D3 05	0190	OUT(5),A	; PORT
0015	06 00	0200	LD B,00	; CLEAR B
0017	00	0210	NOP	; WASTE TIME
0018	00	0220	NOP	; WASTE TIME
0019	04	0230	INC B	; INCREMENT B
001A	F2 00 21	0240	JP V,0021	; JUMP IF OVERFLOW
001D	C3 00 17	0250	JP 0017	; JUMP BACK
0021	C6 01	0260	ADD A,01	; INCREMENT A
0023	C3 00 0F	0270	JP 000F	; REPEAT
0026	76	0280	HALT	; END PROGRAM

This program will generate a continuously changing tone.

Index

300

Edited by Roland S. Phelps